MW00834389

Creating Human Nature

Human genetic enhancement, examined from the standpoint of the new field of political bioethics, displaces the age-old question of truth: What is human nature? This book displaces that question with another: What kind of human nature should humans want to create for themselves? To answer that question, this book answers two others: What constraints should limit the applications of rapidly developing biotechnologies? What could possibly form the basis for corresponding public policy in a democratic society? Benjamin Gregg focuses on the distinctly political dimensions of human nature, where politics refers to competition among competing values on which to base public policy, legislation, and political culture. This book offers citizens of democratic communities a broad perspective on how they together might best approach urgent questions of how to deal with the socially and morally challenging potential for human genetic engineering.

BENJAMIN GREGG is Professor of Social and Political Theory at the University of Texas at Austin.

Creating Human Nature

The Political Challenges of Genetic Engineering

BENJAMIN GREGG
University of Texas, Austin

CAMBRIDGE
UNIVERSITY PRESS

CAMBRIDGE
UNIVERSITY PRESS

Shaftesbury Road, Cambridge CB2 8EA, United Kingdom

One Liberty Plaza, 20th Floor, New York, NY 10006, USA

477 Williamstown Road, Port Melbourne, VIC 3207, Australia

314–321, 3rd Floor, Plot 3, Splendor Forum, Jasola District Centre, New Delhi – 110025, India

103 Penang Road, #05–06/07, Visioncrest Commercial, Singapore 238467

Cambridge University Press is part of Cambridge University Press & Assessment, a department of the University of Cambridge.

We share the University's mission to contribute to society through the pursuit of education, learning and research at the highest international levels of excellence.

www.cambridge.org
Information on this title: www.cambridge.org/9781108841160

DOI: 10.1017/9781108893138

First published 2022

A catalogue record for this publication is available from the British Library.

Library of Congress Cataloging-in-Publication Data
NAMES: Gregg, Benjamin Greenwood, 1954– author.
TITLE: Creating human nature : the political challenges of genetic engineering / Benjamin Gregg.
DESCRIPTION: Cambridge ; New York, NY : Cambridge University Press, 2022. | Includes bibliographical references and index.
IDENTIFIERS: LCCN 2022020683 (print) | LCCN 2022020684 (ebook) | ISBN 9781108841160 (hardback) | ISBN 9781108789714 (paperback) | ISBN 9781108893138 (epub)
SUBJECTS: LCSH: Medical genetics–Moral and ethical aspects. | Medical genetics–Law and legislation. | Genetic engineering–Government policy. | Genetic engineering–Moral and ethical aspects. | Bioethics–Political aspects. | BISAC: POLITICAL SCIENCE / History & Theory
CLASSIFICATION: LCC RB155 .G765 2022 (print) | LCC RB155 (ebook) | DDC 616/.042–dc23/eng/20220613
LC record available at https://lccn.loc.gov/2022020683
LC ebook record available at https://lccn.loc.gov/2022020684

ISBN 978-1-108-84116-0 Hardback
ISBN 978-1-108-78971-4 Paperback

To

the Oxford Uehiro Centre for Practical Ethics

and

the Ethox Centre, Nuffield Department of Population Health,

both at the University of Oxford

where, as their guest, I worked

a hunch into an insight:

political theory with bioethical ambition

Contents

Acknowledgments

Albrecht Dürer (1471–1528) was one of the great artists of the German Renaissance. He traveled throughout his life, picking up inspiration abroad (as well as a few clients). His second major trip took him across the Alps to Venice. There he studied the sculptural nudes of Andrea Mantegna and the Madonnas of Giovanni Bellini. While there, he wrote home to Nürnberg, in southern Germany. In one of his letters, dated October 13, 1506, we find the following sentence: "hÿ pin jch ein her, doheim ein schmarotzer" (here [in a foreign land], I'm treated like a lord, whereas at home: like a parasite). In writing this book, I was myself often enough a foreigner, not only in terms of my passport but also as someone learning bioethics from generous colleagues with whom I share a preoccupation with the oldest philosophical question of all: What are we, as humans? Three institutions in particular were my "Venice" where I was treated intellectually like a lord in the generosity with which colleagues shared their knowledge with me. I thank the Ethox Centre, Nuffield Department of Population Health, University of Oxford, and its director, Michael Parker; the Uehiro Centre for Practical Ethics at the University of Oxford, and its former director, Julian Savulescu and its current director, Roger Crisp; and the Hastings Center, and its director, Eric Parens.

I am grateful as well for thoughtful critiques I received from audiences at invited lectures at the Centre for Biomedical Ethics, Yong Loo Lin School of Medicine, National University of Singapore; the Institut für Biomedizinische Ethik und Medizingeschichte, Universität Zürich, Switzerland; the Instituto de Filosofia da Universidade Nova de Lisboa, Portugal; the Department of Political Science and Public Administration, Istanbul Medipol University, Turkey; the Faculty of Law, Saints Cyril and Methodius University, Skopje, North Macedonia; the Technische Universität Wien, Institut für Information Systems Engineering, Austria; the Centre for Research Ethics and Bioethics, Uppsala University, Sweden; the Department of Philosophy, Stockholm

University; the Stockholm Centre for Health Care Ethics, Sweden; the Department of Philosophy, University of Gothenburg, Sweden; the Fulbright Distinguished Chair Inaugural Address, School of Law, Lund University, Sweden; the Centre de Recherches Interdisciplinaires, Université Paris 5 René Descartes, France; the Information Technology University of Copenhagen, Denmark; the Institut für Geschichte und Ethik der Medizin, Martin-Luther-Universität Halle–Wittenberg, Germany; the St. Cross Lecture in Ethics, Department of Philosophy, University of Oxford; the Katholische Hochschule für Sozialwesen, Berlin, Germany; the School of Psychology, National University of Ireland, Galway; the Norwegian Centre for Human Rights, University of Oslo, Norway; the Institut für Staatsrecht und Politische Wissenschaften, Johannes-Kepler-Universität Linz, Austria; the Erik Castrén Institute of International Law and Human Rights, Helsinki, Finland; DeCode Genetics, Reykjavík, Iceland; the Raul Wallenberg Institute, Lund University, Sweden; the University of the West of Scotland, Paisely, UK; and the Société suisse de Sociologie, Bern, Switzerland.

I also benefited from critical comments offered by audiences at my presentations at conferences: the 24th World Congress of Philosophy, Department of Philosophy, Beijing University, China; the International Society for the History, Philosophy, and Social Study of Biology, Institute of Biosciences, University of São Paulo, Brazil; the 5. Internationale Hartheim Konferenz, Alkoven, Austria; the Annual Meeting of the Association for Politics and the Life Sciences, Madison, Wisconsin; the European Consortium for Political Research General Conference, Standing Group on Political Theory, Université de Montréal, Canada; the International Society for the History, Philosophy, and Social Study of Biology, Université du Québec à Montréal, Canada; and the Political Studies Association, London.

For individualized feedback, I thank David Emory, Ross Zucker, and Marcel van Ackern for their critical commentary on early drafts. And I thank the anonymous reviewers for Cambridge University Press for useful feedback on the earliest draft of all. And I thank Nicholas Gregg for the Michelangelesque cover-image.

For permission to use revised portions of material that first appeared, in somewhat different form, elsewhere, I thank the following:

The Introduction draws on "Genetic Enhancement: A New Dialectic of Enlightenment?," in Dietmar Wetzel, ed., *Perspektiven der Aufklärung: Zwischen Mythos und Realität* (Paderborn: Verlag Wilhelm Fink): 133–146, © 2012 by Fink Verlag. Used by cordial permission of Fink Verlag.

The Introduction also draws on "How to Read for Current Developments in Human Genetics Relevant to Justice," *Politics and the Life Sciences* 37(2): 262–277, © 2018 by *Politics and the Life Sciences*. Used by friendly permission of Cambridge University Press.

Chapter 1 draws on "Proceduralism Reconceived: Political Conflict Resolution under Conditions of Moral Pluralism," *Theory and Society* 31(6):

741–776, © 2002 by *Theory and Society*. Used by kind permission of Springer Nature.

Chapter 1 also draws on "Political Bioethics," *The Journal of Medicine and Philosophy* 47(4): 1–22, © 2022 by *The Journal of Medicine and Philosophy*. Used with cordial permission of Oxford University Press.

Chapter 3 draws on "Against Essentialism in Conceptions of Human Rights and Human Nature," *Human Rights Quarterly* 43: 313–328, © 2021 by *Human Rights Quarterly*. Used by generous permission of Johns Hopkins University Press.

Chapter 4 draws on "Regulating Genetic Engineering Guided by Human Dignity, Not Genetic Essentialism," *Politics and the Life Sciences* 40(2), published online first, 1–16. doi:10.1017/pls.2021.29, © 2021 by *Politics and the Life Sciences*. Used by gracious permission of Cambridge University Press.

Chapter 7 draws on "The Coming Political Challenges of Artificial Intelligence," in Ramón Reichert, Mathias Fuchs, Pablo Abend, and Annika Richterich, eds., *Digital Culture & Society* 4(1): 157–180, © 2018 by Transcript Verlag. Used with cordial permission of Transcript Verlag.

Introduction

Human genetic engineering is one way in which humans can relate to nature. Nature includes the natural environments in which our species lives. It includes our species as it has evolved through natural selection. Our is a species with a capacity for creating artifacts, culture, and understandings of ourselves as moral beings. The borders between our genes and their environments are porous with our cultures. These borders are so porous that the distinction between nature and culture often collapses. For the position I develop in this book, namely bioethics as political theory, or political bioethics, they are profoundly intertwined. They are intertwined as genetic science and biotechnology, both cutting-edge expressions of the seventeenth- and eighteenth-century discourse of the European Enlightenment. Already in those centuries, two understandings of the term *nature* emerge that continue to define core aspects of possible human genetic engineering in the twenty-first century: nature as the basis for *social equality* among persons, and nature as the basis of *human identity*. In the unfinished project of modernity, prospects for engineering in a just society must improve upon the Enlightenment legacy of contemporary genetic science and biotechnology by reconceptualizing nature and its relationship to culture, above all with respect to equality and inequality among persons. This book gives itself that task.

0.1 EQUALITY AMONG MEMBERS OF THE SPECIES

In the name of *natural equality*, various Enlightenment thinkers reject feudal hierarchies that distribute social standing on the basis of birth. But those same thinkers promptly legitimize observable inequalities among human populations – predictably to the disadvantage of the non-white populations of Africa, Asia, and the Americas. Voltaire (1694–1778) promotes a certain *égalité*: all men are equal who by their nature possess the skills relevant to their role in human community. Yet he immediately deploys phenotypical differences between dark- and light-skinned humans to situate each "race" within a discriminatory hierarchy of humankind. (Phenotypical features are the visible characteristics of an organism that follow from the combined effects of genes and environment.) He subordinates sub-Saharan Africans to Europeans: "one could say that, if their intelligence is from no species other than our own, then it is a very inferior intelligence indeed" (Voltaire 1878 12:357).[1] He subordinates Jews with the same gesture: "One may regard them the very way we regard black people: as a species of inferior humans" (11:223).[2]

From an *ethical* viewpoint, Kant (1724–1804) implies that all persons are free by virtue of their species membership alone: "Because the begotten is a person, and because it is impossible to conceptually grasp the begetting – by merely *physical* means – of a being endowed with *freedom*, so from a practical standpoint we can only regard the following idea as thoroughly correct and even necessary: to regard the act of [physical] procreation as an act by which we have placed a [moral] *person* in the world" (Kant 1968: 280–281).[3] Yet from an *anthropological* standpoint, Kant declares various human groups (defined in terms of "race") unequal to each other: "In the white race, humankind finds its highest perfection. By comparison, the yellow Indians are much less able. Black people are much less able still, and some of the indigenous peoples of the Americas have the least ability of all" (Kant 1923: 316).[4]

In his *Supplément au voyage de Bougainville*, Diderot (1713–84) champions diversity among individuals and among cultures. He champions his own version of the idea of a "great chain of being"[5] to legitimize social inequalities among different human communities. He sanctions them as inequalities that follow from differences in motivation, productivity, and social utility. According to his *Encyclopédie* article titled "Animal," "Some men have a very strong faculty of thinking, acting, and feeling whereas others have a faculty less strong, and this faculty becomes ever weaker the lower on the continuum we descend, and apparently at some distant point it disappears"

1 "[O]n peut dire que si leur intelligence n'est pas d'une autre espèce que notre entendement, elle est fort inférieure." All translations by the author (some of them interpretive beyond strict literalness).

2 "On les regardait du même oeil que nous voyons les Nègres, comme une espèce d'hommes inférieure."

3 "Da das Erzeugte eine Person ist und es unmöglich ist, sich von der Erzeugung eines mit Freiheit begabten Wesens durch eine physische Operation einen Begriff zu machen, so ist es eine in praktischer Hinsicht ganz richtige und auch notwendige Idee, den Akt der Zeugung als einen solchen anzusehen, wodurch wir eine Person in die Welt gesetzt haben."

4 "Die Menschheit ist in ihrer größten Vollkommenheit in der Race der Weißen. Die gelben Indianer haben schon ein geringeres Talent. Die Neger sind weit tiefer, und am tiefsten steht ein Theil der amerikanischen Völkerschaften."

5 *Scala naturae, échelle des êtres, Seinskette*: a metaphysical conception of the universe, found in Plato and Aristotle and revived by the Enlightenment authors Descartes, Spinoza, and Leibniz, among others.

(Diderot 1966 12:642).[6] His article on "Humaine Espèce," or the human species, concludes that "originally there was but one sole race of men" but now one can see that some of the non-European peoples constitute "a degenerate race of men," "rude, superstitious and stupid," with all the "traits of a primitive race."[7] They possess "neither morals nor religion."[8] And, he adds, "in general black people are weak-minded" (Diderot 1966 18:348, 344, 345, 347).

For Rousseau (1712–78), nature not human society offers the way of life most appropriate to humankind. His conception of the natural condition of our species betrays neither racism nor anti-Semitism. Yet his notion of the "noble savage,"[9] which serves as the very fulcrum of his civilizational critique in his *Discours sur l'origine es les fondements de l'inégalité parmi les hommes*, too easily resembles the domesticated slave of European colonialism.

In these foremost contributors to a world-historical movement that changed the world in profound ways and remains an ongoing project for many persons and communities today, the Enlightenment is Janus-faced. One face regards nature as yielding to culture: culture as human will and imagination in its limitless plasticity, as the capacity to shape and endlessly reshape ideas, artifacts, and institutions. The opposite face regards nature as a limit to human belief and behavior: the "natural" as a standard by which to reject the "unnatural."

Today this same Janus-face gazes out from the debate over human genetic engineering. Enlightenment ambivalence toward nature disallows the age-old belief that there is some kind of "human nature" – a natural or metaphysical or theological something that provides a fixed, unchallengeable and unchanging normative foundation for human belief and practice.

One abiding topic of human belief and practice concerns questions of equality and inequality among individuals. The debate over human genetic manipulation poses the old Enlightenment question anew, and in a new form: Do the observed social inequalities among persons somehow follow from "nature" – or instead from culture, as social constructs? Where communities come to view inequality as a matter entirely of social construction, rather than

6 "[L]'état de cette faculté de penser, d'agir, de sentir, réside dans quelques hommes dans un degré éminent, dans un degré moins eminent en d'autres hommes, va en s'affaiblissant à mesure qu'on suit la chaîne des etres en descendant, & s'éteint apparemment dans quelque point de la chaîne très éloigné."

7 "[I]l n'y a donc eu originairement qu'une seule race d'hommes"; "une race d'hommes dégénérée"; "grossiers, superstitieux & stupides"; "les traits de la race primitive."

8 "[I]ls n'ont ni moeurs ni religion"; "en général les nègres aient peu d'esprit."

9 In Gregg (2013) I argue that Rousseau's notion of *l'homme Sauvage* has cosmopolitan potential yet contains distinctly anti-cosmopolitan elements: a moral ambivalence that characterizes the other great Enlightenment thinkers as well. The term *noble savage* is not Rousseau's but comes from John Dryden (1672).

as a result of anything natural, there human nature more and more becomes human culture.[10]

If humans are morally responsible for the cultures they create, then they are responsible for the social inequalities within communities and across communities. Those Enlightenment thinkers who accept such responsibility are in favor of revising and improving human culture. Humankind, too, has always been an Enlightenment project of optimization – and now, in our age of biotechnology, all the more so. In this respect, contemporary biotechnology perpetuates elements of the original Enlightenment project. And it perpetuates these elements not only with respect to individuals, in somatic engineering, but also with regard to the species, in germline engineering. In his role as chief editor of the *Encyclopédie ou Dictionnaire raisonné des sciences, des arts et des métiers*, published in 28 volumes between 1751 and 1772, Diderot (1966 5:642) exemplifies this optimizing project: the Enlightenment seeks nothing less than to "change the common way of thinking".[11] In nearly 72,000 articles, the *Encyclopédie* shows how: it would optimize all of human culture by unleashing the potential of rational progress, not only at the level of individuals but in the species entire.

0.2 THE IDENTITY OF THE HUMAN SPECIES

Yet just as the original Enlightenment is, in part, morally ambivalent, so too is the contemporary Enlightenment project of human optimization through genetic engineering. It approaches the human embryo as an object of human technology and medical intervention. It views the embryo as a sliver of nature that (within significant limits) may be made to yield to culture, even to the point of humankind taking control (within significant limits) over some aspects of its own genome and, one day perhaps, over some aspects of its own evolution, by engineering the human germline.

Here the human body appears to bioengineers principally as a phenomenon of the natural environment, one capable of being "improved" according to human design and preference. For example, current average life expectancies might be viewed as defective and inadequate, perhaps even as a disease to be cured. The ambivalent Enlightenment perspective thus transforms at least some anthropological constants into technical options. What we humans are by

[10] I defend a social constructionist approach to social and political analysis and apply it to various spheres of life, including bioethics and the question of a human nature; see Chapters 3 and 4 as well as Gregg (2012a). Even constructionist epistemology has antecedents in Enlightenment thought. Vico (1668–1744), for example, asserts that truth (*verum*, il vero) is something that humans do (*factum*, il fatto): they construct it, just as they make their own history: "*verum* e *factum* sono ... sinonimi o ... si convertono l'uno con l'altro"; "il vero ed il fatto sono la stessa cosa"; and that in the diverse spheres of life, humans can only know that which they themselves have made: "norma del vero è l'averlo fatto" (Vico 2008: 195).

[11] "[C]hanger la façon commune de penser."

nature becomes dependent, to an extent, on decisions we make as creators and carriers of culture.

As nature gradually becomes an Enlightenment undertaking of humankind, human nature gradually becomes in part a contingent expression of human will and cultural imagination. The skeptical face of Janus asks, Does intervention violate individual autonomy as well as species-identity? The other, optimistic face inquires, Is intervention in the human genome a matter of technological freedom and perfectionism? The optimistic answer: As a project for increasing human freedom through technology, genetic manipulation promises *freedom from* diverse forms of misery, such as bodily and mental disease and disability, and *freedom to* greater self-determination of our physical and psychological selves (quite beyond current reproductive technologies, organ transplantations, or medically assisted suicide).

Indeed, bio-optimism regards genetic enhancement as a moral imperative.[12] If, with Kant, one finds the meaning and purpose of nature in the existence of moral beings, and in their moral behavior, then genetic manipulation – to the extent that it "improves" human nature – constitutes the "perfecting" of what Kant calls "die Schöpfung," creation. A Kantian (1963: 148) argument for reproductive cloning and germline gene therapy[13] would advocate, *as an ethical duty*, the "perfection" of man's natural being.[14] If rational nature exists "as an end in itself,"[15] then an enhanced human being might well be regarded as more "rational" than one not enhanced (because human reason commands human improvement) and, if so, enhancement becomes a moral imperative.

By contrast, the skeptical Janus-face sees human genetic engineering as a self-destructive "dialectic of Enlightenment" in which humankind, in its relation to nature, reverts from a species of domination to one of servitude. By engineering its genome, humankind violates species-identity as well as individual autonomy. Max Horkheimer and Theodor Adorno (1981: 193) describe a "dialectical entanglement of enlightenment and domination, a dualistic quality within a kind of 'progress' that leads at once to both cruelty and emancipation" – such that "freedom within political community cannot be separated from Enlightenment thought" because the "social institutions in which it inheres already contain the germ of regression."[16]

Although the authors – refugees from Nazi Germany, writing in exile, Los Angeles, 1944 – were not writing about genetic engineering, their thesis is

12 Compare Persson and Savulescu (2012) for a recent formulation of such an imperative.

13 Such therapy introduces functional genes into sperm or eggs; once integrated into the genomes of the sperm or eggs, the functional genes are heritable.

14 To be sure, what the term *perfection* might mean is far from clear and inevitably controversial.

15 "[D]ie vernüftige Natur als Zweck an sich selbst existiert."

16 "[D]ie dialektische Verschlingung von Aufklärung und Herrschaft, das Doppelverhaltnis des Fortschritts zu Grausamkeit und Befreiung"; "die Freiheit in der Gesellschaft [ist] vom aufklärenden Denken unabtrennbar"; "die Institutionen der Gesellschaft, in die es verflochten ist, schon den Keim zu … Rückschritt enthalten."

plausibly extended to it. Their term *freedom within political community* captures today's increasingly powerful biotechnological capacity and its rapid development. The same could be said of their other term: *the germ of regression*.

Creating Human Nature charts a path within the European Enlightenment, between its two faces. As it does so, it is inevitably speculative inasmuch as the relevant phenomena – beginning with the sheer complexity of polygenic organisms, let alone the nature of human intelligence or the epigenetic effects of social environments – are not well understood, in part or in whole, and they will continue to challenge human insight for a long time to come. In the meantime, speculation about future genetic engineering faces the often daunting task of distinguishing between realistic and unrealistic extrapolations of current scientific understanding and technological capacity.

In the face of such discouragements, *Creating Human Nature* identifies some of the ways that genetic manipulation need not spell a fateful dialectic of Enlightenment. The case is more easily made for therapeutic intervention, which, in the clearest of cases (and many cases are less than clear), aims at prophylaxis, for example to control for birth defects, or a congenital predisposition to cancer, or Parkinson's and Alzheimer's. The case is less easily made with respect to the biotechnological "enhancement" of the eight-cell human embryo's genetic composition (rendering a healthy person "more than well"). To be sure, and as I show, the distinction between therapeutic and enhancing deployments often and easily collapses. More generally, even a cautious embrace of Enlightenment meliorism raises difficult moral and political questions.

Creating Human Nature focuses on the peculiarly *political* dimensions of human genetic engineering. I call this approach *political bioethics* (quite beyond bioethics as an abstract moral project or as a practical set of administrative principles to regulate clinical medical practice).[17] Chapter 1 develops this notion at length. It argues that bioethics belongs to the political sphere insofar as bioethics involves intractable moral questions (involving difficult issues regarding regulatory choices) that cannot have "correct" answers. At least in a liberal democratic society, such decisions can at most be procedurally legitimate. The idea of procedural legitimacy is one way to address the questions, Can politics ever be ethical? Can ethics ever be nonpolitical? Perhaps if ethical entrepreneurs can bring their principled analysis and conclusions to bear in public policy, politics can be ethical. Alternatively, if politics – in pursuit of power, influence, and effect – inevitably colonizes ethical thinking, distorting its normative potential by subverting its moral integrity,

[17] The term *bioethics* first appeared in 1927. In the late 1960s the field itself emerged out of medical ethics for research and clinical practice. Today much of the field examines – often from a utilitarian stance, which Chapters 4 and 8 also entertain – normative issues generated by technical possibilities flowing from rapid developments in biology, medicine, and biotechnology.

then ethics can never be nonpolitical. The ways in which policymakers systematically co-opt professional ethicists discourage the possibility of ethical policymaking. Annabelle Littoz-Monnet (2020) provides empirical evidence that ethics cannot be nonpolitical in the face of bureaucratic, regulatory capture guided not by truth but the effort to achieve predetermined goals, where ethical expertise provides neither guidance nor oversight but simply facilitates the nonethical or unethical imperatives of policymakers. If the integrity of ethical examination requires the integration of nonexperts, indeed of a cross-section of the community, then democratic debate about regulating scientific and technological innovation might indeed generate bioethical expertise independently of political interests. It might insulate ethical examination from the imperatives of policymaking so that bureaucrats cannot preemptively depoliticize issues and close down needed debate. It might, in other words, prevent the colonization of the ethical by the political.[18] But by what organizational means can a public – much of which is disinterested, or not scientifically literate, or simply misinformed – participate helpfully? There is no consensus in modern Western societies about the kind of normative framework that might guide public deliberation and decision. *Creating Human Nature* is my response to this quandary.[19]

By way of anticipating the political nature of all the chapters quite beyond the first, I now show more generally how the technological manipulation of the human genome – in individual bodies as well as in the germline of our species – has profoundly political dimensions. I do so with regard to (a) how the boundaries between the natural phenomenon of human genes and the cultural phenomenon of human-built environments are porous, (b) how human identity must be related to genetic information, (c) how questions about human nature are always also questions about human genetics, and (d) how some of the social values and political visions entailed by the prospect of human genetic engineering implicate justice in multiple senses.

[18] For an analogous proposal to prevent the colonization of the ethical by the economic, see Gregg (2020b) and Gregg (2021b) on the possibility of future corporations that would replace the contemporary human rights due-diligence carrot-and-stick model with a model in which the corporation would produce not only goods and services but human-rights consciousness and practice within itself and in its human, social, economic, and natural environments.

[19] I do not propose genetic engineering as an alternative to the conventional project for realizing justice through politics but as a supplement to it: in cases where conventional means are inadequate or fail. Hence I do not imagine the regulation of genetic engineering as top-down government policy but rather as a form of citizen-oriented political engagement in which as many members of the community as possible are involved, citizens who, despite their many moral and political differences, might sometimes be capable of forging a broadly shared sense of justice when it comes to addressing relevant issues. I preview this idea in Gregg (2020a) with regard to the bioethics of human genetic manipulation.

0.2.1 The Porous Boundaries between Genes and Their Environments

Even as natural organisms, humans are immediately entwined with the myriad cultural constructions of their communities, including the cultural abstractions of regulatory norms, political understandings, and legal systems. Communities perpetually socialize members into these abstractions and frequently struggle to gain for them their widest possible embrace. The question for political bioethics is, In regulating human genetic engineering, which political visions, what sorts of moral principles, what kinds of legislation and socialization, might guide liberal democratic communities, and guide them well? Plausible answers to these questions presuppose the answer to other questions: From a normative standpoint, what kinds of political communities should we want, and for what reasons? Contained within the question, What should humans want?, is another: What exactly are we humans that we might persuade ourselves that we should want to be particular kinds of beings in particular kinds of political communities? And to the extent that we humans can engineer our own biology, the question now becomes, What kind of human nature should we aspire to, and for what reasons? Political bioethics might best respond by addressing both the complexity of the gene–environment relationship and the profound indeterminacy of human identity.

To regard humans as the result of both nature and nurture says nothing about the relative contributions of each. How one regards the relative division of labor between biology (here in the form of genes, G) and culture (here in the form of environment, E) is, according to political bioethics, a matter of taking into account a person's normative preferences and political identity.

Consider an equation that is biological – but also, from this perspective, political: $G \times E$ (the symbol "$\times$" indicates that the relationship between G and E is more complex than a merely additive one). The equation states a proposition about what humans are (but only with respect to genes and their environments) and how they came to be that way. Some scientists would expand the equation to $G \times E \times HE$, where HE refers to heritable epigenetic factors (the topic of Chapter 9). They would expand the equation to include some of the biological consequences, for human bodies, of some aspects of the communities in which people live and reproduce those lives. They would render it political bioethical in the attempt to understand how environment, lifestyle, biography, and even parents' and grandparents' experiences may interact with an individual's genome (in the fetal stage) to produce changes experienced throughout his or her life (and sometimes even passed on to the next generation). They would render it political bioethical also in the attempt to analyze how prenatal and early postnatal environmental factors may influence the adult risk of developing various chronic diseases and behavioral disorders (Jirtle and Skinner 2007). Political bioethics seeks to explain why children born during the Dutch famine of 1944–45 had increased rates of coronary heart disease and obesity in light of maternal exposure to famine during early pregnancy (compared with persons not so exposed) (Painter et al. 2005).

The gene–environment entwinement also has dimensions of a political bioethical quality. Its multidimensionality marks a complexity in both nature and culture. Complexity is both dangerous to human life and necessary for human life. The manipulation of that complex entwinement poses political questions about the acceptability of dangerous risk-taking. Let me explain.

The gene–environment entwinement is multidimensional, beginning with the sheer complexity of the instructions for human life. Evidently "most mutations to functional genes are thought to be harmful" (even as beneficial mutations drive natural evolution); as "many as 75 percent of mutations that swap one DNA base for another within genes cause some sort of reduction in survival or reproductive output" (Solomon 2016: 17). And instead of a "single important genetic variant (or allele), there are often hundreds or thousands that contribute to variation in a given outcome," that is, not one "gene for X" but rather "many variants with small effects" (Conley and Fletcher 2017: 5). Perhaps "93 percent of genes in the human genome are in some way connected," such that "if you tweak a gene in one corner of the network, it may have unanticipated consequences in the actions of other genes" (ibid., 50). As a form of tweaking, human genetic engineering raises very great risks of unintended consequences – in part because the relevant phenomena are so extraordinarily complex.

Complexity in nature parallels complexity in the human culture that manipulates nature. They parallel one another at the level of risks. Consider the unintended consequences around the year 1600 of European colonialism in the Americas, including a small pox pandemic and massive deforestation but also the global trade that followed. Or the unintended consequences of the European Industrial Revolution in the late eighteenth century "when data retrieved from glacial ice cores show the beginning of a growth in the atmospheric concentrations of several 'greenhouse gases,' in particular CO_2 and CH_4" (Crutzen and Stoermer 2000: 17–18). Or when "analyses of air trapped in polar ice showed the beginning of growing global concentrations of carbon dioxide and methane" (Crutzen 2002: 23). Or when, in 1784, James Watt invented the steam engine. Consider the human impact on the planet's ecosystems and geology, on the lithosphere, the atmosphere, and the ecosphere – a risk now so significant that our planet will bear a destructive human signature for millennia, and perhaps for millions of years (the topic of Chapter 10).

Yet even though complexity is part of the danger to the very human life that complexity makes possible, complexity in the shape of genetic diversity is necessary to life. The complexity of genetic diversity constitutes the raw material for evolution by natural selection: the more diverse a population is, the more it can respond to the forces of natural selection. Species diversity increases the odds of species survival; less diverse species are at greater risk of extinction.

Correspondingly, manipulation of the very complex human genome will always involve significant risk, with consequences for human society and the natural environment, consequences some of which cannot be anticipated. The political bioethical question is, Are the risks of genetic engineering unacceptable given the sheer causal complexity of the human organism, in addition to various causal interdependencies (as they inform evolutionary theory, for example)? Another political bioethical question: Is risk taking necessary for the survival of the species? And another: To the "extent that genetic interventions can be used to enhance strengths and compensate for weaknesses in creative ways that expand opportunity without 'normalizing' their recipients," might genetic interventions one day shape a "social force in improving tolerance for human diversity" (Juengst 2009: 57)?

0.2.2 Human Identity and Genetic Information

As a form of information, genetic identity has political dimensions. Consider two that may endanger a person's legal and social status within political community: the control and handling of an individual's genetic identity, and the possible moralization of a shared human identity.

From a standpoint of justice, any form of genetic information is vulnerable to abuse. For example: Can genetic information be owned and, if so, by whom? "Newborns cannot give consent to have their genome sequenced, but they must live with the consequences of this decision for the rest of their lives. Should information about adult-onset conditions such as depression or high blood pressure be disclosed to parents, effectively taking away a child's right not to know (in the future)" (Conley and Fletcher 2017: 175)? Genetic information, when controlled and handled by others, is political where it affects the individual's life and welfare. Political are the questions, What rules should govern the influence others may wield over an individual's genetic information? Should the individual have a right not to know? Should employers and insurance companies have access? Any particular answer to these questions likely presupposes some conception of the person's moral worth.

Further, genetic screening will sometimes lead to false positives. Someone so diagnosed may never suffer the diagnosis, yet she and her family will needlessly suffer the anxious yet pointless anticipation that she may still become ill in line with the diagnosis. Or the information may be inaccurate or mistaken yet nonetheless affect how the individual is seen and treated in political community (consider, for example, an insurance company's or an employer's interest in a client's or employee's genome map). The question poses itself: To what extent should individuals not only control their genetic information but be empowered to challenge and change information held by private and public institutions, especially when the person regards the information as mistaken?

Finally, genetic information may allow medical professionals to predict the person's receptivity to different treatments. To make an individual's access to health care or quality education (among so many other social resources) dependent on whether she can afford it is not so different from providing or withholding resources such as medical treatment dependent on the person's genetic code. (A just community might condemn both as morally reprehensible.) In other words, private genetic information may become a standard part of governmental calculations about the best distribution of such precious social goods such as health and education.

Genetic information may also pose a political risk to *collective* human identity. For example, "scientific belief in nativism, inborn factors, and innateness" may serve "as a proxy for hard-hereditarianism especially of the right-wing kind" (Meloni 2016: 186). On this view, "human beings are born with pre-existing cognitive structures and age-specific capabilities for learning that lead them naturally into society" (Fukuyama 2000: 155). According to Meloni (ibid.), this view in recent decades has become a "political tool of the promotion of a defense of a particular conception of Western democracy." A view more popular on the political left than on the right claims that if human nature is a blank slate, "with no innate structure of mind and no intrinsic needs of a cultural or social character" (Chomsky 1987: 154), then it is defenseless against "the 'shaping of behavior' by the state authority, the corporate manager, the technocrat, or the central committee" (ibid., 254).[20]

Regardless of the merits of their respective analyses, the authors show how human identity is easily politicized in a moralistic way. Dubious as such is the claim that our species, understood genetically, possesses some kind of given, objective standard by which to recognize, criticize, and resist authoritarian political community. But when human genetic engineering is thought to implicate human identity in the sense of altering collective political dispositions and preferences, it may well risk a person's legal and social status within community.

0.2.3 Human Genetics and Human Nature

Additional political bioethical claims: human genetics implies nothing about human nature as a standard by which to guide human behavior in ways just and moral. Genetic knowledge does not provide humankind with any kind of model of human genetic "normality." Claims about "normality" are more likely to be social evaluations than scientific descriptions. So if "natural selection does not homogenize the individuals of a species," then the "search for a normal … nature and body type is futile. And so it goes for the equally futile quest to identify 'human nature'" (Smail 2008: 124–125).

The question of whether some types of genetic engineering might change the very nature of human beings is a matter solely of cultural preferences. If it ever became possible to endow a person with particular traits, or an organ, or an

[20] Evolutionary psychologists are also divided on this issue. Pinker (2002) argues that scientists deny what he takes to be a universal human nature for the reasons Chomsky states. Buller (2005) argues that human biology provides no evidence for a human nature and in this way effectively decouples the question of human nature from the particular political preferences of the discussants.

addition to the brain, traits or organs or additions that no human previously possessed, the organism will certainly have changed in terms of how it can be described scientifically. But whether its human nature thereby is also changed would remain a matter of cultural framing and particular value commitments. It would remain a question of political bioethics.

Genetic science also provides no guidance for such questions as: Is human nature damaged by re-engineering it according to human design? Is a fertilized human egg cell capable of "possessing" dignity and rights? If not, then at what point along the developmental continuum might it be thought to acquire such dignity – and how? Does pre-personal life (such as the eight-celled embryo) partake in some form of morality? Should it be assigned legal rights? Would the genetic manipulation of an embryo violate the embryo in some moral sense?

Even though genetic science entails nothing about morality, all cultures regularly tie human biology and human culture to one another. We do so when we wonder if, as human biology becomes in some part an undertaking of human culture, human nature increasingly becomes a contingent expression of human will and imagination (Sagoff 2005: 72). And we do so in such analyses as this: "Our DNA is a powerful influence on our anatomies and physiologies. In particular, it makes possible the complex brain that characterizes human beings. But having made that brain possible, the genes have made possible human nature, a social nature whose limitations and possible shapes we do not know except insofar as we know what human consciousness has already made possible"; a human being is the "being whose essence is in not having an essence" (Lewontin 1992: 123).

0.2.4 Justice and Human Genetic Engineering

Choices among different forms of organization and regulation involve questions of justice. Philosophers often distinguish two senses of justice. They speak in a narrow sense of moral duties the individual is owed, duties he or she can claim, sometimes as legal rights. Philosophers speak in a broader sense of the individual's moral duties toward others, especially but not only in the public sphere. Some of the social values and political visions entailed by the prospect of human genetic engineering implicate justice in both senses. Consider three examples.

First, the prospect of human genetic engineering poses questions about how best to categorize a life form at different stages of development. Political community must decide, for example, whether pre-personal life (an eight-cell embryo, say) can bear rights, either as such or because it lies on a continuum that leads to an unmistakable human recognizable in community as capable of bearing rights. Community must determine what members owe – morally – not only to fellow humans but to pre-personal life as well.

Second, human bodies and human psyches are fragile and enduringly vulnerable to suffering. The prospect of human genetic engineering might transform the way we humans think about our suffering. Would we still find moral ennoblement in persons confronting their limitations in ways that render them humbler and more modest than they might otherwise be? Might a political community be morally obligated *not* to genetically manipulate anyone for the purpose of overcoming his or her relevant limitations? What if a community rejected as hubris any effort of genetic engineering to extend "normal" life spans beyond what is possible through purely cultural measures (such as the progressive health insurance and public health programs of the modern welfare state)? Would it then be morally obligated *not* to genetically engineer anyone? Or should any political community feel morally obligated to support those forms of genetic engineering that might reduce all genetically based forms of suffering?

Third, some of the ways that humans are embedded within complex social networks with other humans might be powerfully impacted by genetic engineering. Consider athletics, in most cases a group activity organized around various understandings of how to evaluate individual and group performance. If a political community feared that biomedical enhancements of athletes confounded "naturally" occurring differences in athleticism and so destroyed the very object of competition, would athletes be morally obligated not to seek enhancements – and would political community be morally obliged not to offer them?

Questions about justice return us to where I began this introduction: by arguing that human genetic engineering is an extension of the rationalizing project of the European Enlightenment, one that impacts issues of equality and inequality among persons, among groups, and even among global regions. *Creating Human Nature* engages that project as it practices political bioethics. I now show how with a chapter-by-chapter overview.

0.3 OVERVIEW

The book is divided into three parts. Part I develops the political bioethics of regulation along four dimensions: method (proceduralism), standards of validity (more than local, less than universal), notion of human nature (socially constructed), and conception of human dignity (autonomy).

Chapter 1 asks: How might a liberal democratic community best decide whether parents should be allowed to genetically modify their offspring and, if so, within what limits? It proposes a procedural form of decision-making, combining expert bioethics committees and deliberative democracy. From the standpoint of political liberalism, bioethics so understood goes beyond bioethics as an abstract moral project, or as a set of clinical principles that regulate medicine. It aspires to become a democratic project of majoritarian proceduralism that involves ordinary citizens as far as reasonably possible in discussing and even deciding some bioethical issues toward regulation, legislation, and public policy.

Chapter 2 shows that efforts to regulate biotechnological manipulation of humans through fixed, universal standards remain unpersuasive. As an alternative standard for the regulation of human genetic engineering, it proposes a non-universalistic notion of human nature. It constructs human nature as the product of contingent and particular social learning processes. Human nature so understood can provide normative standards that emerge in learning processes, toward agreement locally (but not universally), as a source of regulatory norms for national political organizations but not for global citizen assemblies. These standards are possible because they practice interpretive pluralism, ambiguity, and political compromise.

Chapter 3 observes that complex modern societies confront abiding competition among different normative understandings and commitments that render agreement difficult on urgent issues of bioethics and biotechnologies. It shows how disagreement follows in part from essentialist understandings of human nature as well as from essentialist understandings of human rights. It argues against essentialism in conceptions of human rights and human nature and seeks broad agreement on how to regulate human genetic engineering by means of a naturalistic understanding of both human nature and human rights. It construes human nature politically as oriented on human rights. The respective notions of human rights and human nature are linked in answer to the question, Might we humans construct the human *nature* we have reason to prefer precisely by constructing the human *rights* we have reason to want? The linkage offers a normative standard that – if adopted as a presupposition by participants in the debate on the legal regulation of human genetic engineering – could contribute to a wide embrace of any answer then produced.

Chapter 4 shows that debates on how a liberal democratic community might best regulate human genetic engineering invariably deploy the usually undefined term *human dignity*. Its indeterminacy in meaning and use renders it useless as a guiding principle. This chapter rejects the viewpoint of "genetic essentialism": that the human genome is inherently invested with a moral status. Correspondingly, human rights (which might offer regulatory guidance) are not well understood in terms of genetic essentialism. The chapter develops an alternative understanding of both human nature and human rights: dignity as the decisional autonomy of future persons, held in trust by the current generation. A future person could be expected to have an interest in decisional autonomy. Popular deliberation, combined with expert medical and bioethical opinion, can generate principled agreement on how the decisional autonomy of future persons might be configured at the point of genetic engineering from which that future person will develop.

Part II focuses on human intelligence as perhaps the single most challenging target of possible future genetic editing. It is challenging along three dimensions: toward including citizens as robust participants who would otherwise be excluded because of severe cognitive disability; aiding politics by artificial intelligence but always preserving the uniquely human capacity for mutual responsibility-taking; and identifying the uniquely political quality of debates on whether primary education would be improved by personalized curricula tailored to the individual pupil's genome.

Chapter 5 argues for the cognitive engineering of future persons who, at the stage of development, indicate severe cognitive disability, toward providing the future citizen with a capacity for autonomous participation in the political life of her liberal democratic community. Because various cognitive capacities are relevant to civic participation, cognitive disability can be a political disability. If aspects of participation are equally desirable for the good of the individual and for the collective good, then some forms of cognitive engineering are warranted in a just community, which should then regard, as a political imperative, the provision of the relevant cognitive engineering to the extent possible.

Chapter 6 compares the genetic enhancement of human intelligence with artificial intelligence (where the term *intelligence* is no less indeterminate). It identifies the political capacity of human cognition as the capacity for a mutual attribution of responsibility, in terms of which members of a community understand themselves in civic relation to each other. Whereas genetically engineered human intelligence does not threaten this capacity, future forms of AI might. Yet for reasons of convenience and efficiency, and in hopes of diminishing the frequent failures of conventional politics, AI may tempt citizens one day to outsource forms of social integration that otherwise require a politics of mutual attribution of responsibility. The outsourcing of a unique capacity of human intelligence to AI would undermine democratic political community.

Chapter 7 analyzes not human genetic manipulation but rather the idea of genetically informed personalized primary education. Education so understood involves the use of individual genotypes to tailor curricula to children by deploying individual-level genetic characteristics, in this way to improve child learning by configuring the educational environments guided by predictions about a child's genetic potential. This idea confronts the entwinement of nature and nurture in three ways. It confronts the interrelationship between the pupil's genes and her social environment; the possibility of unintentionally exacerbating social inequalities in providing personalized primary education; and the challenge that conventional approaches to primary education pose to this proposal for a genetically informed approach. Along these dimensions, political bioethics identifies fundamental ambiguities in evaluating the potential benefits, as well as the potential harms, of deploying genetic information in the classroom.

Part III considers several of the ways in which human genetic engineering confronts different kinds of questions about social inequalities: as a possible means to free some persons from the political disadvantages of some genetic disabilities; as a possible means to identify sources of adverse epigenetic effects in the local population for which the community, as one corporate body among others, might be held responsible; and as a meliorist tool of the Anthropocene that will not necessarily perpetuate anthropocenic depredations.

Chapter 8 suggests that, if individual autonomy is a feature of individual well-being, then physical or mental disability can be seen to reduce the disabled person's well-being. Prospective parents might exercise procreative autonomy to screen their embryos for genetic disabilities toward selecting a disability-free embryo. In so doing, the parents seek to facilitate the expectable possible autonomy of a future person, their child. These two forms of autonomy – the autonomy of a future person and the parents' procreative autonomy – are challenged by a third: the autonomy of a disabled person whose genetic characteristics were not screened for disability at the embryonal stage of life, hence a person not "chosen" for her disability-free genetic constitution. The chapter argues against a human right that would prohibit all forms of genetic selection, and for a human right to freedom from genetic disability.

Chapter 9 explores the possibility that epigenetic research may offer an additional means to identify cross-generational transmissions of social inequalities. If some epigenetic effects on a fetus can adversely affect an individual's life-long health, then the mother's (and perhaps the father's and the grandparents') life-experiences effectively disadvantage that individual. If those effects were beyond the control of the forebears when they occurred, then the effects may be the moral if not legal responsibility of the community or sectors within in. In a polity that practices some form of corporate responsibility, epigenetics could be deployed toward the social justice of identifying the source of negative epigenetic consequences for health and of then assigning communal responsibility.

Chapter 10 analyzes human genetic engineering as a technology of the Anthropocene. To name this particular geological epoch the "Age of Humankind" is to mark the profound and enduring ways humankind has affected our planet. It has done so largely through the unintended and unwanted consequences of technological development – and the cultural orientations that foster them. The peculiarly political dangers of the anthropocenic technology of genetic engineering follow from the difference between technical and political cognitive styles. A technical style is guided by instrumental imperatives, seeking the optimal deployment of practical means to achieve preset goals that it does not place into question. By contrast, a political style (in the form of linguistic, symbolically mediated interaction) can be guided by valid social norms. The anthropocenic dangers of genetic engineering will only be avoided if a political community practices socially responsible genetic technology toward realizing the promise of human genetic engineering: to modify some inherited traits into something somewhat responsive to some human preferences and aspirations, thereby reducing human misery and improving possibilities for human flourishing.

From the preceding chapters the Coda distills the core intuition of political bioethics: bioethics as a matter ultimately of political deliberation. Guided by a "soft" naturalism that rejects a scientism that would reduce cultural and normative thinking to natural science, political bioethics is based on an epistemic dualism that bears within itself a certain tension. The objectifying attitude of a naturalist approach to genetic phenomena stands in charged and complicated, causal and conceptual relation with the intersubjective need for moral, legal, and above all political guidelines by which political community might regulate genetic manipulation. As political theory, bioethics attempts a plausible, practical relationship between science and morality. It does so by engaging a notion of political integrity that combines analytic description (of genetic phenomena) with normative evaluation (toward regulating engineering). It combines the cognitive bases of natural science with the prescriptive, critical knowledge contained in normative claims.

PART I

THE POLITICAL BIOETHICS OF REGULATING GENETIC ENGINEERING

1

Regulation Guided by Proceduralism

If bioethical questions cannot be resolved in a manner widely acceptable, by rational argument, but only on the basis of political decision-making, then bioethics belongs to the political sphere. The particular kind of politics practiced in any given society matters greatly: it will determine the kind of bioethical regulation, legislation, and public policy generated there. I approach bioethical questions politically: in terms of decisions that cannot be "correct" but that can be "procedurally legitimate." Two procedures in particular can deliver legitimate bioethical decisions, once combined: expert bioethics committees and deliberative democracy. Bioethics so understood can exceed bioethics as a moral project or as a set of administrative principles to regulate medical practice. It can now aspire to a democratic project that involves ordinary citizens as far as reasonably possible.[1]

I advance this argument in five steps. (§1.1) I show that bioethics is a kind of politics. (§1.2) I then propose a general understanding of proceduralism, (§1.3) combine two types of proceduralism, and (§1.4) offer a defense of majoritarian proceduralism. (§1.5) I conclude by showing that the kind of politics practiced will determine the kind of bioethical regulation generated. I develop my argument in terms of one example: germline gene editing.

[1] A commitment to democracy is a particular value commitment, as is a commitment to social justice, as is a commitment to the scientific establishment of fact. None of these commitments is moral. Here I pursue political bioethics in a democratic register; elsewhere (Gregg 2012b, 2018a, 2018b) I pursue it with respect to social justice.

1.1 THE CLAIM THAT BIOETHICS IS POLITICS

I argue that *bioethics is politics* not in the agreeable sense of a triumphal march toward an ever better society[2] providing ever greater justice but in the disquieting sense of competition: among value commitments and without end. By *politics*, I mean disagreement in the public sphere about issues that require decision for regulation, legislation, or public policy.[3]

Likely no answer to a bioethical question can claim universal validity inasmuch as bioethical questions are matters of normative preference. And these are socially constructed and historically contingent. Normative preferences differ within communities and among them. Competing viewpoints rarely converge. The existence of stable disagreements does not necessarily show that there are no bioethical truths. Rather, stable disagreements show that, even if there is truth in this sphere, we have not been able to recognize it. In natural science, by contrast, we assume that (ideally and ultimately) questions have one correct answer, that every correct answer is correct for all persons at all times in all places, and that all debates eventually will converge on a single answer. To be sure, scientific inquiry does not end in enduring stability: any answer is challengeable and new data or models may qualify or reject what was thought to be a correct answer. Scientific research is a fundamentally inconclusive project; so it politics.

To explore the political quality of bioethical claims, I examine several genetic technologies able to make heritable changes to the human germline by altering the DNA sequences of embryos. Such technologies may have unintended consequences, given the complexity of "gene–environment interactions" as well as of the "pathways of disease (including the interplay between one disease and other conditions or diseases in the same patient)," and given "limits to our knowledge of human genetics" (Baltimore et al. 2015: 37).

I draw first on Christopher Gyngell and colleagues' (2017: 499) observation that "roughly 6% of all babies born have a serious birth defect of genetic or partly genetic origin." The authors advocate germline engineering to "prevent genetic disease" – with the qualification, "if proven acceptably safe." Engineering seeks to prevent disease in future people. Toward that goal,

2 I use the terms *society* and *political community* interchangeably because my focus on societies is specifically and narrowly political. Community so understood does not imply homogeneity of population, consensually held belief, or identity along any dimension other than membership in the same polity.

3 To be sure, the term *politics* can be understood in many ways quite beyond my definition, which is narrow for analytic purposes. To develop a notion of political bioethics, I distinguish it (partially) from ethics. (a) Some political questions are not (deeply) ethical, e.g., Is the nation-state's power best divided among an executive, a legislature, and a judiciary? (b) Some ethical questions are not (necessarily) political, e.g., Is vivisection an ethically acceptable research method? (c) Some issues are at once both ethical and political, e.g., the Catholic Church regards abortion as immoral, while the US Supreme Court case *Roe* v. *Wade* (410 U.S. 113 (1973)) frames abortion politically as a matter of a woman's Fourteenth Amendment right to privacy.

germline gene editing may offer a "novel treatment for single gene disorders" *and* contribute to overcoming polygenic disease (2017: 503).

The technique offers some couples the "only way to avoid passing on single gene disorders" (2017: 500) in cases where neither in vitro fertilization (IVF) nor preimplantation genetic diagnosis (PGD) is possible. PGD is used prior to implantation to help identify genetic defects within embryos so as to prevent certain genetic diseases from being passed on to the child. The embryos used in PGD are usually created during the process of IVF.[4]

Whereas PGD and IVF are "not powerful enough to select against polygenic diseases," germline gene editing "allows multiple changes to be made to a single embryo" and thus may "target many different genes simultaneously" (Gyngell et al. 2017: 501). Multiple targeting is important because the majority of common diseases result not from single-gene mutations but from a "polygenic disposition together with environmental influences." Diabetes involves at least 44 genes, for example, and common cancers, more than 300 (2017: 501).

In this context, we observe a political dimension where Gyngell and colleagues do not take seriously the possibility that applying a technology designed to prevent genetic disease unintentionally might generate "new forms of inequality, discrimination and societal conflict" (2017: 509). Consider unequal access to technology – unequal because not everyone can afford it. Those who can will likely be better off along several interrelated dimensions, from socioeconomic status to level of educational achievement. Unequal access reinforces the social position of better-situated persons and discriminates against weakly situated ones. In these circumstances, not the technology itself but unequal access to technology reveals a political dimension as inherent in some bioethical questions.

We see another political dimension in the fact that many technologies designed for *therapy* (i.e., treatment of an illness or disease) can equally be applied toward *enhancement* (i.e., improvement on a condition not in any way pathological). Such technologies include Lasik eye surgery, PGD, and plastic surgery. This dimension is political because the therapy–enhancement distinction here is inherently ambivalent, that is, difficult to determine in ways that are unambiguous and likely to be widely embraced. Hence it cannot be correct to say that such technologies are necessarily therapeutic or, alternatively, necessarily enhancing. The term *political* then refers to the competition among different perspectives, each seeking to distinguish acceptable therapy from unacceptable enhancement. That competition cannot be settled by an appeal to truth even as, on a continuum from clearly acceptable to clearly unacceptable, cases at either end are less perspectival than cases in the middle. Correspondingly, this competition reveals the perspectival quality of

[4] For example, the UK Human Fertilisation and Embryology Authority (2011) reported that 18.7 percent of women undergoing IVF produced only one embryo viable enough for elective single-embryo transfer.

determining whether applying such technologies is morally desirable or morally objectionable. Thus someone opposed to using technology to *enhance* individuals who are not ill or diseased, yet who advocates its use toward *therapeutic* ends, confronts this political dimension as well.[5]

A political dimension emerges in another claim: that it is "doubtful that the embryo is the type of entity that can be harmed, or at least, harmed in a morally significant way. The embryo does not have experiences or desires, and on some accounts of wellbeing, entities that lack experiences and desires have no wellbeing and thus cannot be harmed" (Gyngell et al. 2017: 504). The political element here has to do with the fact that morally significant harm can be configured in many different ways. The Catholic Church, to take a prominent example, has a view very different from that of Gyngell and colleagues. It regards the embryo as morally vulnerable to almost any intervention. Given the impossibility of deciding rationally between or among such competing views, the task for society here is again political: any public policy decision must choose among incompatible alternatives – and it must do so as a matter of normative preference rather than empirically verifiable truth. A bioethics that regards itself as operating on a plane above politics – a moralized bioethics, for example – cannot address this task.[6] But a liberal democratic community (unlike, say, an authoritarian political community) aspires to a significant degree of freedom of individual conscience (hence tolerates freedoms of conscience, expression, and religious belief and practice). Correspondingly, a liberal democratic community aspires to some degree of decisional autonomy for adult patients. A moralized bioethics would impose particular value commitments. In so doing, it would violate this liberal democratic notion of political community.[7]

After all, normative preferences are political when they reflect competition that matters in the formation of regulation or public policy. And in setting public policy, the competition with the greatest influence often is among elites. The doctrine-makers of a world religion constitute one kind of elite. In modern societies, religious faiths function as private not public organizations and are subject to laws that separate church and state (hence the state may neither favor nor disfavor any particular faith, and legislators violate the constitution if they base legislation or public policy on their religious beliefs).

[5] See, for example, Lanphier et al. (2015).

[6] Human history has witnessed many different kinds of moral thinking. In many cases, from deontology to consequentialism, for example, moral thought claims to show that one answer is clearly preferable to another for nontrivial, nonidiosyncratic reasons. The strongest form of such claims is a claim to truth.

[7] Broad agreement with regard to the legal regulation of biotechnological interventions into the human genome could be facilitated by a political and naturalistic understanding of both human nature and human rights, as an alternative to an essentializing moralized bioethics, as I show in Chapter 3.

The European Parliament is a different kind of elite. It has the authority to pronounce policy on behalf of all EU citizens. In doing so, it projects various particular value commitments onto a very heterogenous population. It can do so even if its pronouncements are intellectually dubious. A 1997 resolution, for example, states that the cloning of human beings constitutes a "serious violation of fundamental human rights and is contrary to the principle of equality of human beings, as it permits a eugenic ... selection of the human race" and "offends against human dignity." The Parliament further declared that "each individual has a right to his or her own genetic identity."[8] These statements are deeply problematic. First, the notion of a human right not to be cloned is incoherent: the donor and the cloned would never be identical (given unavoidable environmental and experiential factors that distinguish each organism from every other). Second, cloning entails nothing about the social or legal equality or inequality of donor and the cloned. Third, the authors of the resolution appear to use the term *eugenic* to appeal to readers' emotions (of fright and disgust) through the suggestive power of words. Yet the term is used in many different ways and only some of them have negative connotations (Bashford and Levine 2010). Fourth, the question of whether the term *human dignity* refers to anything more than respect for individual autonomy is hotly contested. Cloning cannot threaten individual autonomy. Finally, one in every 270 births is an identical twin and a twin is a kind of natural clone (Harris 2016: 8). If one argues that "natural" clones do *not* violate every set of twins' putative equal right to an individual's "unique" genetic identity, then one cannot easily argue that artificial clones *do* violate some such right. In short, the Parliament's declaration misconstrues the scientific understanding of genetic identity and practices a poor form of politics: poor because it is a normative opinion based on misunderstanding if not ignorance of scientific fact.

A scientific elite differs from both religious and political elites, with whom scientific fact does not necessarily carry weight in all cases, as the following examples show. To be sure, individual scientists have normative commitments and worldviews of their own that may be in tension with their disciplines.[9] And all scientists are exposed to, and some are influenced by, at least some corporations, advocacy, and nongovernmental organizations, as well as governmental agencies that may have some interests that conflict with the imperatives of scientific truth. Recent examples include such areas as climate change,[10]

[8] The European Parliament, *Resolution on Cloning*, 1997 O.J. (C 115) 14.4/92 (March 12, 1997), paragraph B and clause 1, respectively.

[9] Tensions are not limited to a scientific commitment to facts. Scientists differ among themselves with regard to their values quite beyond science, including political orientation and moral preference. Such differences can affect scientists' understanding and evaluation of scientifically generated data. See, for example, Segerstrale (2001) for a historical account of an ongoing, politically inflected debate on whether "human nature" is fundamentally biological or fundamentally social (or simply does not exist).

[10] See, for example, Taylor (2014).

agricultural biotechnology, endangered species and biodiversity, and nuclear waste disposal, among others.

In 1998, another political elite, the Council of Europe, declared a prohibition on human cloning.[11] But the Council nowhere explained how or why its prohibition can be based on what the Council referred to as "human rights," "human dignity," or "genetic identity." Because they are indeterminate in meaning, these terms are problematic for regulatory purposes until they are specified as to meaning and application.[12] That specification is possible only in terms of complex theories based on particular value commitments unlikely to be shared by all or even most members of a complex modern society. If specification is unlikely ever to be consensual, then practical applications of these terms within any particular society are likely to be coercive, divisive, and politically destabilizing.

Another example: in 1997, UNESCO's Bioethics Committee proclaimed that the human genome must be preserved as the "common heritage of humanity."[13] But as a product of evolutionary change – a natural phenomenon that exists only within the ongoing historical phenomenon of evolution – the human genome cannot be "frozen" at any particular state of evolutionary development. "Unlike the sea," the genome of any organism "has no top, bottom, or shores: it cannot be 'preserved'" (Juengst 2009: 58). Consider, for example, the spread of lactose tolerance among different human populations. In human infants, the lactase gene is expressed. Once the baby is weaned, this gene shuts down. The introduction of milk into the ordinary diet of some human populations, through the domestication of milk-producing animals, favored those adults who carry the lactase enzyme, for now they had a new food source. Over time, 80 percent of the European population became lactose tolerant. If, therefore, the UNESCO committee intends more narrowly to preserve the "common heritage of humanity" from *human* intervention but not from *natural* evolutionary change, its reasoning succumbs to paradox. For it then falls into the antinomy of distinguishing between humans who are naturally evolved (apparently thereby constituting a "common heritage") and human artifacts (such as genetic manipulations) that evidently violate that common heritage

[11] European Treaty Series, no. 168, *Additional Protocol to the Convention for the Protection of Human Rights and Dignity of the Human Being with Regard to the Application of Biology and Medicine, on the Prohibition of Cloning Human Beings of the Council of Europe*, Paris, 12. I.1998.

[12] I reject the notion of the human genome as somehow invested with a moral status and, in Chapter 4, as an alternative propose dignity as the decisional autonomy of future persons, held in trust by the current generation at the point of genetic engineering.

[13] UN Educational, Scientific and Cultural Organization (UNESCO), 1997, *Universal Declaration on the Human Genome and Human Rights.*

even though human artifacts are expressions of a natural organism and may therefore also be regarded as natural.[14]

Consider another example of a political dimension within a bioethical issue: the claim (for example by Savulescu and Kahane (2009)) that parents are morally obligated to create the biologically best child possible. Bracket the not unproblematic issue of moral obligation and focus on the notion of the "best possible" child. *Best* as defined by what standard? *Political* is the choice of a particular understanding of nature, and so are the particular perspectives from which one evaluates the merits and demerits of evolved human biology and the choice of criteria that would define any given concept of the *best possible child*. After all, nature functions as a *positive* standard when humans value their evolved biology – and then interpret some variations as abnormalities or illnesses, that is, as unwelcome deviations from a standard they themselves construct. Nature functions as a *negative* standard whenever humans would engineer their species in ways that seek improvements to our evolved biology. The choice of criteria that would define any given concept of *improvement* is no less political.

1.2 COPING WITH POLITICS BY MEANS OF PROCEDURALISM

Proceduralism offers one way of coping with some of these bioethical challenges. It can secure agreement under conditions that otherwise discourage agreement. General agreement on political and social norms is unlikely where norms calling for deep moral commitment are not widely shared within a society. But if normative differences preclude agreement on many issues, they need not preclude agreement on procedural rules for coping with difference.[15] *Proceduralism* is the notion that no rule is acceptable apart from a formal, agreed-upon method[16] and that an acceptable method yields an acceptable rule.

[14] The very concept of nature becomes an issue of political bioethics when employed as a normative standard for making decisions. As a standard, it may well be useless, as the following thought experiment shows. If sexual reproduction were in fact not natural but somehow a human artifact, it would fail to satisfy today's regulatory bodies that monitor medical procedures, given the incidence of "sexually transmitted disease," the "high abnormality rate in the resulting children," and the "gross inefficiency in terms of the death and destruction of embryos (estimated to be one in three to one in five deaths per live birth)" (Harris 2016: 8).

[15] See Gregg (2003a).

[16] I refer to agreement among members of a political community, either directly (by voting, for example) or indirectly (by being born into the community and freely remaining within it). Proceduralism can realize fair participation in the public sphere if constructed in ways normatively "neutral" in a sense I develop elsewhere (Gregg 2002). As a general idea, proceduralism encompasses any sort of procedural device for making a decision or resolving a dispute. It takes many different forms. For example, as procedures to settle conflicts, Barry (1970: 85–91) distinguishes among combat, bargaining, discussion on the merits, voting, chance, contest, and authoritative determination. In democratic polities, procedures can specify everything from the forms of participation and adjudication to the forms of implementation. Consider three

The rule in this context would be the answer to a particular bioethical issue or question.

In a liberal democratic order, tolerant of value pluralism, proceduralism makes collective action possible *despite* enduring differences in the value commitments of its various members. It makes agreement possible because it aspires not to *consensus on substance* but to *legitimacy in form*. Even those persons whose preferences did not succeed in the latest procedural decision may regard the outcome as legitimate. Those who disagree with the winning position may continue to argue against it and to marshal support for their preferred alternative. They may even prevail in a future procedural exercise. Then, through majoritarian democratic institutions, a political community can reach binding and authoritative decisions in regulation, legislation, and public policy and thus can move on, in the name of all members, even under conditions of abiding disagreement.[17] I address two features of proceduralism: (a) its normative thinness[18] and (b) some constraints to which it is subject.

1.2.1 Normative Thinness

A procedure is *normatively thin* if it does not affect the content of the procedure. Voting in a democratic election is an example of proceduralism in this sense. The "content" of the procedure, its *normative thickness*, derives from the

prominent examples. Cohen (1994: 610) sees democracy as a "procedure that institutionalizes an idea of citizens as equals." For Rawls (1993: 159), the "only political consensus we can reasonably hope for is confined to democratic political procedures" such as the "right to vote and freedom of political speech and association, and whatever else is required for the electoral and legislative procedures of democracy." Habermas (1996: 296) claims that the "central element of the democratic process resides in the procedure of deliberative politics." Most liberal theories today are proceduralist in arguing for a state that provides a procedural framework dedicated to the substantive norm of democracy but that imposes few other values on citizens. Indeed this framework protects individuals from such impositions, allowing each person to go her own normative way as much as possible as long as she respects the outcomes of democratic decisions in the public sphere.

17 Majoritarianism is a particular political theory that rests on presuppositions all of which require defense (a task quite beyond the scope of this chapter). Some institutions require unanimous decisions instead (e.g., some decisions taken by the Council of Europe; and in the United States, juries in criminal cases are required to reach a unanimous verdict). In later pages I advocate expert committees (which usually seek consensus) and in this way qualify my support of democratic majoritarianism, which should be carefully circumscribed in other ways as well. For example, legally guaranteed rights of minorities – especially rights protecting minorities from majorities, including majorities generated by voting – are norms governing the acceptability of procedural outcomes. Such norms include respecting all participants' legal equality and civil rights as well as protecting society's general welfare from majorities that would threaten it. A different issue (also beyond the scope of this chapter) concerns which among different types of majority (such as simple, absolute, or effective) would be most appropriate for this or that bioethical question.

18 See Gregg (2003b).

particular policy commitments and values of each of the political parties competing for votes. In a fair system of voting,[19] a procedure establishes which party has received the most votes without influencing that outcome.

Another example: the constitution of a modern, liberal democracy guarantees its citizens the freedom of religious belief and practice. Any particular faith is normatively thick as a particular belief system. Hence if a nation state were to require all citizens to adopt one particular religion, it would thereby *violate* the thick norms of all citizens of other faiths because each faith has its own belief system (even as some of them may overlap in some ways). Guaranteeing the equal freedom of all faiths neither favors nor disfavors any one faith. In that sense, the rule of freedom of religious belief and practice is normatively thin. It does not violate the thick norms of any faith. In this way it may facilitate their peaceful coexistence. Or more generally: proceduralism can facilitate life within normatively heterogenous communities. It allows for reaching decisions that are binding on members of a society without presupposing some end or value prior to or independent of the goals in any given case.

To be sure, proceduralism allows for outcomes that are thick not thin. But participants need not identify in any way with the thick norms they nonetheless recognize as legitimate because they can recognize those norms as having been selected on a legitimate basis. Such is the idea of the losing party recognizing the winning party's right to form a government. Or the notion of recognizing the legitimacy of a judicial system even when one disagrees with a particular judicial holding.

To allow for difference in normative viewpoint or moral commitment is to allow for a kind of individual autonomy vis-à-vis other members of a society. In modern, pluralist, societies (and across different societies), groups and individuals regularly need to be able to interact on a normatively thin basis. The normative diversity within the population, or across different populations, in many cases is quite irrelevant to the tasks of modern life.[20] Here individuals, in their respective normative thickness, are *functionally interrelated* even as, in many respects, they are *normatively autonomous* of each other.

The notion of autonomy is a core feature of political liberalism. It values the individual's uniqueness vis-à-vis other persons. The bioethical notion of *patient autonomy* reflects this value. Autonomy should not mean *separation* from others but rather an appreciation of how the individual is involved in various group memberships yet is reducible to none.[21] Medical practice and biomedical research may in some cases regard persons as "isolated individuals, who

[19] I discuss what I mean by fairness below.

[20] To be sure, some groups and individuals – paradigmatically: ones of orthodox forms of religious belief – may reject some modern aspects of daily existence as ways of life that do not adequately isolate the sacred from the profane.

[21] I urge a particular understanding in view of the fact that different communities conceive of patient autonomy in different ways. To overgeneralize, it may be that Americans generally are

consent, or refuse to consent, to participate in research" (Childress 2003: 52). In other cases, it may regard them as members of "various nongovernmental communities, such as the family" or "racial and ethnic groups" (2003: 63).

How do we best conceive of patient autonomy? This, too, is a political question. A normatively thin standpoint does not regard the individual in terms of her communal memberships. Or at least: it does not attempt to determine her wishes and choices simply by "reading them off community traditions, beliefs, and values" (2003: 52). Rather, it views patient autonomy in terms of "uncoerced choice in accordance with the individual's subjective perception of her particularistic interests" (Jennings 1990: 216). Whatever their differences, all approaches in bioethics regard the individual as a "distinct locus of moral value" (1990: 216).[22] In most cases, the individual's interests would take precedence over the interests of the wider community and over those of scientific and medical research. But maybe not in *all* cases and, if so, then (from a patient's or physician's or family's perspective) no single understanding of patient autonomy would seem to be the best for all persons in all cases.

One familiar question about patient autonomy concerns the relationship between professional expertise and its individual addressee, as in the doctor–patient relationship. On the one hand, in the interests of her health, the patient may need and want professional expertise. On the other hand, she is vulnerable to medical paternalism precisely because she lacks professional expertise. Patient autonomy seeks to protect and preserve the vulnerable individual's freedom vis-à-vis the power of professional knowledge and practical skill.

Bioethics might frame this issue as one of *balancing* patient autonomy and medical expertise. Balancing here is not a matter of objective measurement. Determining an *acceptable* level of risk (or a *necessary* level of safety) is contingent, context relative, and depends on particular value commitments. Consider chemical therapies to treat cancer. How is the risk of their high toxicity best balanced against their power to subdue cancer? The risk is so great that, "unlike most other pharmaceuticals licensed for human use," chemical therapies "have never been tested on 'healthy adults' before clinical adoption" (Harris 2015: 30). Yet their benefits, measured against the lethal nature of cancer, may persuade some patients, and some clinicians, that the risks are acceptable. But not all patients and physicians will be so persuaded. Persons of different thick values will balance the risks and benefits differently.

Consider another example. Mitochondrial disease causes conditions like Leigh's disease, a fatal infant encephalopathy. And it causes other illnesses "that waste muscles or cause diabetes and deafness" (2015: 30).

more inclined than many Europeans to construct patient autonomy as embedded in the family. Such differences in viewpoint pose a challenge for my theory of thin proceduralism.

[22] That locus might be interpreted one way in human medical research and another in life-sustaining treatment: medical risk appraisal is consequence-oriented and seeks to secure patients against health hazards; medical research is truth-oriented and seeks to establish empirical facts.

Mitochondrial replacement therapy (MRT) inserts the healthy mitochondria of an unrelated person into an embryo containing the nuclear DNA of two other people. In one estimate, MRT "will enable some 2,500 women in the UK to have children genetically related to them" while avoiding terrible diseases (2015: 30). But risk–benefit analysis in this context must address the fact that, currently, there is no "alternative for women who want their own genetically related offspring" and that "many women will continue to desire their own genetically related children and will continue to have them if denied or unable to access MRT" – and that, without MRT, these women will "perpetuate the occurrence of disease" (2015: 30). Again, we interpret balancing as a matter of coping with competing values that different people may well weigh differently. In this sense, balancing is political as a means of coping with irreconcilable differences under social and legal conditions in which an authoritative decision must be made.

1.2.2 Substantive Constraints

I turn now to how proceduralism is constrained in several substantive ways. After all, the thin normativity of proceduralism does not mark the absence of all normativity; thinness is not neutrality, nor is it indeterminacy. On the contrary, proceduralism must be sufficiently thick, normatively, to generate answers to difficult questions about the good, the right, and the just. Yet it must be sufficiently thin to appeal to people who disagree about the *nature* of the good, the right, and the just. For that reason, no proceduralism can operate without introducing into itself at least a few substantive norms.

First of all, a commitment to proceduralism is not normatively neutral. Proceduralism is itself a norm that entails an obligation to recognize and abide by its outcomes. This is a significant obligation, normatively, because proceduralism does not generate normatively neutral outcomes. Any procedure that has "winners" and "losers" is hardly neutral in its results. So an obligation to recognize and abide by procedural results is an obligation to respect some norms that one may not share.

Furthermore, proceduralism entails various norms of fairness, including those regulating access to participation, conditions of participation, and sincerity of participant behavior. Norms of fairness give the individual who accepts such norms good reason to trust the group or institution in which the procedure is embedded. A patient's *informed consent* is a matter of fairness, a matter of the patient's being able to participate in making some of the decisions affecting her case. Such fairness provides the patient with reason to trust the medical professionals or scientific researchers involved.

What about the interests of third parties, for example a patient's parents or spouse or children? How are such third-party interests to be balanced against the patient's interests? In many cases, one might expect them to be subordinated to the patient's interests. But maybe not in *all* cases – for example, with respect to infants in intensive care. How are *its* best interests balanced against those of its family? The infant cannot participate, of course, but the question still poses itself where a proxy defines and advocates for the child's best interests. The attending physicians might be such a proxy. Consider cases in which the physicians do not share the family's view of the child's best interests. Each side may regard the other as subordinating the patient's interests to its own but neither side will regard itself as doing so.

Proceduralism in such cases involves substituted judgment, "where another must represent" the "autonomy of the self" who cannot "choose and act independently" (Jennings 1990: 217). Issues involving future children, such as those subjected to germline gene editing, require substituted judgment in lieu of the affected person's consent. Do the benefits enjoyed by the individuals, once born, weigh heavier than the risks to which the procedure exposed them? Not if germline gene editing "causes side-effects so severe as to make an individual's life not worth living" (Gyngell et al. 2017: 507). But the question of what makes an individual's life *not* worth living is political: any given answer will depend on particular value commitments that compete with those held by others.[23]

1.3 COMBINE TWO PROCEDURALISMS: EXPERT COMMITTEES AND DELIBERATIVE DEMOCRACY

To render political bioethics practical, I propose combining two types of proceduralism in mutually reinforcing ways: (a) the proceduralism of "expert" committees or commissions and (b) the proceduralism of deliberative democracy that carefully and systematically renders *lay opinion* better informed and more thoughtful. Both types of procedure are well known and much analyzed.[24] Both have been applied, separately, for some time now.[25] But neither have been applied, as I propose, in combination and toward a political bioethics.

1.3.1 Expert Committees or Commissions

I begin with bioethics committees.[26] They claim a special expertise in making normative decisions that endow their recommendations with normative

[23] Tellingly, Gyngell et al. (2017: 507) do not identify their own value commitments. Thus the reader cannot know on what normative basis they conclude that the "existential benefits will outweigh the risks" as long as germline gene editing is "sensibly regulated so as to mitigate risks."

[24] For example, Fishkin (1997), Bohman and Rehg (1997), and Gastil and Levine (2005).

[25] See, for example, Goold et al. (2012) and Kim (2016).

[26] Such committees take many different forms. For example, the Nuffield Council on Bioethics in the United Kingdom and the German Ethics Council are formal bodies dedicated to bioethical

authority.[27] But I would claim that public commissions cannot "operate on a plane above politics" (Powers 2005: 320). To clarify this claim, I draw on Mark Sheehan and colleagues (2017). They locate an expert committee's authority partly in the political community's stake in scientific research. According to these authors, it is this stake that justifies a procedural framework for research governance. They regard this stake as fundamentally democratic, situating "enquiry and research *within* the grasp of society rather than removed from it" (Sheehan et al. 2017: 712).

Yet they caution that a "specifically democratic location misses something important about the nature of enquiry," something that "transcends politics" (2017: 712). They argue that "insofar as the committee members operate *within* this framework, there is no distinctive *ethical* expertise relevant to the justification or practice of ethics review that exists independently of this process" (2017: 720). Thus "it is the *decision-making process* that is authoritative, not the committee." Indeed, "any committee member, or social researcher, who puts themselves forward as an ethics expert in this context would be at great risk of undermining the legitimacy of a fair process model of research ethics governance" (2017: 20).

In fact, to say that proceduralism's authority comes in part from the institutional status of the committee itself, both as a process and in the appointment of its individual members, obscures a political element here: the presence of different persons in the committee, accompanied by their respective value commitments, some of which may vary and compete with each other.

Expert bioethics committees are political along other dimensions as well: as a particular commitment to proceduralism as a means of public policy formation; in selecting criteria of membership appointment;[28] and in choices about whom to invite to provide testimony. These criteria may themselves include political calculations, such as seeking a range of viewpoints.[29]

issues. The American Society for Reproductive Medicine seeks to advance science in general but with a focus on the practice of reproductive medicine in particular. The World Health Organization is a specialized agency of the United Nations that promotes public health internationally.

[27] Compare Singer's (1972: 117) notion of such expertise as familiarity with moral concepts and arguments. Expertise so construed is based on adequate information and reflection upon that information, allowing one to "reach a soundly based conclusion more often than someone who is unfamiliar with moral concepts and moral arguments and has little time" to gather sufficient information and reflect on it.

[28] One problem: ethics committees that regularly seek a consensus might pursue that goal by limiting membership; another problem: committees that fabricate consensus when actual consensus proves unreachable.

[29] By contrast, Gutmann and Wagner assume what is impossible: some kind of "ideal speech situation" (Habermas 1990) in which anything extraneous to the arguments being made is excluded from influencing the discussion, such as participants' sex or social status or ethnicity or rhetorical facility: "For us, deliberation paved a path of inclusive discussions where each

1.3.2 Deliberative Democracy

The proceduralism of expert committees needs to be supplemented with, and integrated into, another kind of proceduralism, one that generates informed and reflected *non-expert* opinion: deliberative democracy. Why include lay opinion? To avoid what Alexis de Tocqueville (1981: 385) describes as the soft despotism that precludes popular control, namely the paternalism of expert tutelary powers. Tocqueville advocates participatory politics at various levels of government and beyond, in voluntary associations. Or to speak with Charles Taylor (1991: 10), who advocates popular rather than elite control of great social debates, "what we are in danger of losing is political control over our destiny, something we could exercise in common as citizens" – the "loss of political liberty" such that the "choices left would no longer be made by ourselves as citizens" but by some "tutelary power." This would "undermine the will to democratic control" despite "protest, free initiatives, and irreverent challenges to authority" (Taylor 1991: 112).

Deliberative democracy chooses participants randomly rather than selecting for affinity. It allows participants to draw on balanced expert information toward vetting competing perspectives carefully. By consulting with "experts representing diverse viewpoints and deliberations with peers" (Kim 2016: 178), participants "develop, examine and challenge their own views" (ibid.) while mutually influencing each other by reasoned argument that they themselves evaluate. This procedure encourages discursive argument based on views informed by exposure to scientific fact – as well as exposure to a range of normative thinking.[30]

Like expert bioethics committees, the deliberative process begins with certain norms, norms that can always be placed into question. Earlier I examined several of these kinds of norms: risk–benefit analysis, to minimize patient harm, and informed consent, to provide decisional autonomy to the individual. The deliberative process also begins with another norm: a commitment to deliberation, on terms of mutual respect. That commitment reduces the range of possible relevant reasons to only those "that can be accepted by others" (Gutmann and Thompson 1996: 101) or "on terms that all can accept" (Gutmann and Thompson 1997: 41).

To be sure, reasons acceptable to other persons often may be difficult to identify where the reason in question is an artifact of "contested background assumptions" such as what constitutes the good life or how best to organize a just political community (Powers 2005: 319). Furthermore, an approach based on giving and evaluating reasons makes definite demands on participants. It

commission member and all stakeholders could effectively bring individual expertise, experiences, and values to the table" (Gutmann and Wagner 2017: S37).

[30] Democratic deliberation is more than debate: it pursues actionable decisions; it does not avoid but rather seeks out a broad array of perspectives; it values rather than rejects dissent.

requires that they be able and willing to "change their minds based on giving reasons and evaluating" the reasons of others (Powers 2005: 189).[31] It requires that they be able to "consider trade-offs that are necessary in public policy" rather than assuming that their role is only and always to protect and preserve their particular interests. And it requires participants to be "respectful of minority views" (ibid.).

Not all participants, whether in the minority or majority, will be able or willing to meet these requirements. Indeed, proceduralism will fail to speak to some members of society for various reasons. For example, someone who would be guided politically by religious faith in revealed truth will reject normatively thin proceduralism. Another example: people who cannot subordinate their thick norms to thin ones will reject thin proceduralism because it confines, to thin norms alone, the bases on which public policy can be made. A third example: sources of conflict that are "inextricably interwoven with individual self-descriptions of persons and groups, and thus with their identities and life projects" (Habermas 1993: 59) challenge the coexistence of competing worldviews and ways of life. They will not yield to normatively thin proceduralism. In such cases, proceduralism runs up against its own limits; at such points, its fairness is compromised.

1.4 DEFENSE OF MAJORITARIAN PROCEDURALISM

I turn now to a defense of proceduralism as a *sufficient* condition for generating legitimate decisions in the face of profound and abiding disagreement among members of a society on any number issues of social significance (from general issues of legitimacy, fairness, and justice to the particular bioethical issues that I focus on). What renders proceduralism sufficient? A combination of features: (a) fairness, (b) wise outcomes, (c) liberal justification, (d) majoritarianism, and (e) a practical willingness to undertake the problematic task of distinguishing acceptable forms of reasonable disagreement from unacceptable forms.

(a) *Fairness.* A deliberative procedure for bioethical questions can be fair to all members of society even as it accepts some points of view (some reasonable ones, but not all) and rejects others (all unreasonable ones). Grounds that are unreasonable (because of ignorance, say, or stupidity, unfairness, or bad faith) are unacceptable and may be discounted without unfairness.[32] Because proceduralism so conceived distinguishes

[31] Not all communities are prepared to regard "reason" as a neutral platform for communication (e.g., some persons of religious faith). The ideal of a rational platform for debate is not, in fact, culturally neutral but presupposes commitments to European Enlightenment rationalism (exemplified in the ideal, if not always the actual, practice of natural science).

[32] To be sure, stupidity, unfairness, or bad faith are hardly self-evident, or objective, or a-cultural, or transcendental criteria. They are criteria always embedded in one or the other understanding of "reason." The history of philosophy (among other disciplines) offers a very wide array of

between reasonable and unreasonable grounds, it differs from other kinds, such as equally weighted votes with the majority trumping the minority. A fair procedure produces fair outcomes because the qualities that make a procedure fair convey to the outcomes. But an outcome is not legitimate *simply* because it is fair. A lottery or a coin-toss might be more robustly fair than majoritarian proceduralism (which favors the majority) because of its randomness, which favors no one. Even a majority of equally weighted votes might be fairer than my notion of proceduralism, which does not weight reasonable and unreasonable votes equally.

(b) *Wise outcomes.* A deliberative procedure for bioethical questions also seeks to generate "wise" outcomes: intelligent, informed input and deliberation, displaying keen discernment and deep understanding, for example by including a range of expert opinions. Proceduralism so conceived differs in this respect from fairness via randomness or equally weighted participants.

(c) *Reasonable disagreement and liberal justification.* Fairness and wise outcomes cannot require that only those procedural outcomes are legitimate that are beyond all reasonable disagreement. Such outcomes do not require that there be *no* such disagreement whatsoever. After all, likely no procedural outcome is beyond all reasonable disagreement. Still, procedural outcomes are not *necessarily* illegitimate, given reasonable objections. Nor need the fact that members of any society do not all share views on important matters consensually defeat the goal of seeking wise outcomes. No normative standpoint is likely to be entirely uncontroversial; reasonable disagreement may arise with regard to any normative judgment (including the value of majoritarian proceduralism for adjudicating difficult bioethical issues). Still, anyone who believes that procedural legitimacy is possible at all must believe that there can be reasonable agreement on *at least one* basis of legitimacy. Such belief marks faith in liberal justification, that is, in justification that is liberal in the sense of respecting all participants and all viewpoints to the greatest possible extent. Such respect for individuals entails respect for a majoritarian deliberative procedure (whereby respect by dissenting groups depends in part on the extent of leeway allowed them). Procedural legitimacy entails in turn the legitimacy of the authority that constrains participants and other affected persons to accept the procedural outcomes. In the spirit of liberal justification, the project for procedurally generated legitimate decisions attempts to define the category of

competing understandings. Reason as a culturally neutral and universally available platform is a conceit (one unusually promising but not entirely unproblematic) of the European Enlightenment.

reasonable disagreement as narrowly as possible, toward including as many persons and viewpoints as possible.

(d) *Majoritarianism.* With regard to the terms *reasonable*, *wise*, and *legitimate* as characteristics of proceduralism: there is no free-floating or independent standard by which to measure a procedure's "epistemic value" (Haddock et al. 2009). Just as people will disagree about the meaning of these terms, so they will disagree about the meaning of "reasonable." Not for this reason alone, no procedure is beyond reasonable objection. So while proceduralism must take all reasonable disagreement seriously, it must do so without automatically granting it veto power over procedural outcomes. The goal is a procedural outcome that is beyond reasonable disagreement for a majority of participants and other affected persons. A deliberative procedure for bioethical questions is majoritarian. Majoritarian proceduralism cannot end *all* reasonable disagreement about its outcomes; no method can do that for itself. So to make the goal of legitimate decision-making under conditions of severe and abiding disagreement possible, society must relax any requirement that any decision is freely embraced by *all* reasonable members. For any notion of legitimacy that made *any* reasonable objection fatal to procedural justification would undermine the very project of justification in general.

(e) *Distinguishing acceptable from unacceptable reasonable disagreement.* Majoritarian procedural outcomes can be legitimate even for some perfectly reasonable persons with perfectly reasonable disagreements: for an outcome to be legitimate, it need not be embraced as correct by *all* reasonable participants and other affected persons but only by *some*. In such cases, justifiability is decoupled from reasonable acceptance by *all* persons. Still, fair procedural outcomes must bind *all* addressees, even those who believe that the procedure led to the wrong outcome (and even those who reject majoritarian proceduralism as such).[33] The question remains. How can a line be drawn between acceptable and unacceptable disagreement when both are reasonable? In fact, humans have no independent access to some truth that would allow them to determine the epistemic value of one reasonable disagreement vis-à-vis another. Neither correctness theories nor pure procedural democracy can balance the competing demands of legitimacy with a search for the common good.[34] So there can be no proper account of reasonableness in terms of which we can reassure ourselves that we are rejecting only those reasonable

[33] Compare Honneth and Farrell (1998), who argue that proceduralism – unlike public opinion formation in the democratic public sphere – has the political power to make decisions universally binding within a political community. The questions they do not address: Just how much space should be left for dissenters willing to shoulder some sacrifice? Just how great a sacrifice may reasonably be expected of dissenters?

[34] Compare Estlund (2008) with respect to his alternative: "epistemic proceduralism."

disagreements that are "properly rejectable." A common epistemological experience: a community or society cannot agree on what counts as the right answer even as different persons and groups are confident that their particular answer is right. Under the circumstances, the best a society can do is to combine the proceduralism of deliberative democracy with that of expert bioethics committees. That combination does not homogenize participants but, at best, increases the diversity and number of participants. Doing so should enhance participants' respect for and faith in the procedure and its outcomes – even given abiding, reasonable disagreement, including disagreement about an expert committee's putative moral expertise.

1.5 CONCLUSION: THE KIND OF POLITICS PRACTICED WILL DETERMINE THE KIND OF BIOETHICAL REGULATION GENERATED

Political bioethics is *less* plausible, the *more* it presupposes shared common values or insists on creating them as the only acceptable grounds for regulation and public policy.[35] By contrast, political bioethics *is* plausible by means of decisions that are acceptable to all participants and affected persons – if not necessarily to society as a whole – to the extent that those decisions are *procedurally* legitimate. And bioethical decisions are *political* if made on the basis of procedural legitimacy.[36]

In this way, political bioethics, sensitive to moral diversity within human groups, recognizes the lack of convergence among moral experts as inescapable and, in the sense in which I use the term, inherently political. *Inherently political* means that there is no particular method of moral reasoning that can eliminate all normative disagreements. Hence the need to stipulate that many bioethical issues have a distinctly political quality. There is no external standpoint that would allow one to adjudicate – in a manner objective, neutral, or disinterested – among competing bioethical presuppositions or understandings. By itself, even reasoned debate all too often will fail to generate an answer equally acceptable to all participants and affected persons.[37]

[35] While proceduralism may increase the degree of agreement on a given bioethical issue, it will hardly discourage single-issue advocacy groups and other constellations of narrow, special interests that resist democratic deliberation.

[36] Geuss (2008: 36) warns that the "beliefs that lie at the base of forms of legitimation are often as confused, potentially contradictory, incomplete, and pliable as anything else, and they can in principle be manipulated." While this warning is cogent, his scholarship generally underestimates the quality of belief possible through deliberative democracy informed by expert committees.

[37] Proposals for the moral enhancement of the human species (e.g., Persson and Savulescu (2012)) raise a question they typically cannot answer: Of the myriad moralities at any time in all the millennia of human civilizations, which morality should any given society choose and why that

To view bioethics as politics is to ask, Given disagreement in the public sphere about bioethical issues that require decision for regulation, legislation, or public policy, how should bioethical questions be decided? On what basis? In liberal democratic community, at least, such decisions should be considered a heightened form of opinion. *Heightened form* means: informed by expert opinion of committees as well as by input from the general populace that has benefitted from democratic deliberation. Basing political, legal, or regulatory answers on expert opinion may not always be easy. Basing them also on democratic opinion is surely very difficult and always full of risks.[38] Deliberative democracy requires experts to provide several different domains of highly specialized information to a lay person in ways both comprehensive and understandable. Participants' "informed opinion formation, revision or refinement" requires an understanding of the "nature and purpose of scientific procedures in ... research, the rationale and structure of the current human subject protections system," as well as the state of current research (Kim 2016: 183). And the goal of extending participation to the general public to the greatest extent possible is itself fraught with dangers, such as reproducing popular prejudices or ill-informed viewpoints. For reasons both moral and political, not all issues should be available for democratic deliberation. Just as slavery is incompatible with a liberal democratic polity, so, too, would be the instrumental use of any individual for the purposes of another (such as organ procurement). In such a polity, neither should be open to referenda or other popular decisional methods.

So what difference does the adjective *political* make when conceptualizing bioethics? What difference would it make if a society were to adopt a viewpoint of political bioethics? It might make a practical difference. If bioethical questions cannot be resolved in a universally acceptable and compelling manner by rational argument, and if such questions can be regulated only on the basis of political decision-making, then the particular *kind* of politics practiced in any given society matters greatly. The kind of politics practiced will determine the kind of bioethical regulation, legislation, and public policy generated there.[39]

one in particular? "Moral enhancement" of any kind cannot but impose a particular worldview on people, many or most of whom do not share it. And from any standpoint that rejects coercion, moral enhancement by coercion cannot itself be moral.

38 And a sufficient understanding of the complex science involved may not even be the most difficult aspect of generating informed public opinion on bioethical issues. According to Hurlbut (2015: 13), "informed deliberation on genetic engineering research and its applications need not depend on comprehensive public understanding of the science behind CRISPR/Cas9 gene editing."

39 My focus on domestic regulation does not detract from the fact that decision-making is always an urgent need internationally as well (and one that may call for forms of proceduralism beyond those I discuss here). For example, with respect to somatic and reproductive genome editing, Chan and Arellano (2016: 426) discuss the possibility of medical tourism and "rogue therapies," especially in countries with inadequate regulation and where unlicensed therapies are readily

Attempts to meet that difficult and dangerous goal may never be more than modestly successful – if that. But a goal impossible to meet may still function in a regulative sense.[40] It may provide a society practical orientation as it continues to seek the best ways to frame and decide difficult bioethical issues. That orientation should be informed by a *democratic* spirit: to extend the discussion, and sometimes even aspects of the decision-making, to the general public, to the extent possible,[41] at any given time – and hopefully to ever greater extents[42] over time.[43]

This chapter introduced a core question of political bioethics: How can a liberal democratic community best decide contentious issues related to human genetic engineering – such as whether parents should be allowed to genetically modify their offspring and, if so, within what limits? A core element of this question is the claim that bioethics is politics: that it involves decisions that cannot be "correct" in the way natural scientific questions have, in principle, a right answer. Such questions can be answered politically. I propose ways to provide answers, ways that endow those answers with procedural legitimacy. The next chapter continues a political bioethical approach to questions of how best to regulate the genetic editing of human beings. Regulation in complex modern societies, marked as they are by significant value pluralism, challenges

available. Market demand from patient groups confronting the unavailability of effective treatments may lead to clinical treatments before safety and efficacy criteria have been met.

40 The same may be said for the problem of distinguishing therapy from enhancement discussed in earlier pages.

41 The phrase *the extent possible* should anticipate what may not be possible for some groups within the liberal democratic political community. In such cases, the phrase should allow exceptions for at least some of those minorities to somehow retain their moral integrity even in the face of procedurally just majority decisions.

42 The phrase *to ever greater extents* may have a democratic meaning in a national context but probably not in international contexts, for three reasons, among others. (a) While it may well be that "all humans have a common interest in the human genome" (Baylis 2017: 3), the ideal of "broad-based participation by people from around the world" in deliberations about how best to regulate gene editing (Baylis 2016: 22) remains implausible today. (b) Experience with proceduralism at *local* levels may provide insights about proceduralism that can be deployed at *national* levels, and at *national* levels for proceduralism deployed at *international* levels. Whatever difficulties proceduralism poses locally, difficulties will be more challenging as group-size increases. The democratic element may well drop out after the domestic level. (c) Urgent issues at an international level – from access to certain medicines, to regulation of transnational clinical trials, to intellectual property laws that disadvantage generic pharmaceuticals manufactured in developing countries – demand immediate attention (compare Jasanoff et al. (2015)). Urgent responses are unlikely to be democratic in nature because democratic procedure tends to be time-consuming, uncertain in result, and generally inefficient.

43 A next step in the project for a political bioethics would be designs that combine and deploy the two proceduralisms in specific venues under particular conditions for local questions. This effort might draw on projects such as that of MacGillivray and Livesey (2018).

the possibility of non-arbitrary regulation. Regulation by universally valid standards appears all the more challenging. Any particular cultural understanding of the problems and prospects of human genetic engineering may never be able to achieve trans-local legitimacy. If so, national political organizations are a more plausible source of regulatory norms.

2

Regulation Guided by Less-than-Universal Standards

Genetic engineering refers to the genetic editing of living systems – to the specific addition, removal, or modification of DNA sequences, for example to correct a particular gene's defective functioning in a specific biological context. Genetic engineering targets somatic cells, germ cells, and embryos.[1] Although genome editing by these new tools does not generate fundamental biological risks not already generated by previously available technologies, it is easier, quicker, more precise, and more powerful. Unlike them, the new techniques constitute a socially disruptive science and technology by posing profound and difficult moral issues, such as the moral evaluation of our species editing its own genome. The term *disruption* refers to challenges that can only be addressed politically: weighing the benefits and risks of genetic engineering is a political endeavor, not a scientific or technical one. As such, ordinary members of a political community should not abdicate all decision-making to experts in the natural sciences, the social sciences, medicine, or ethics – or, as Chapter 6 urges, to artificial intelligence. After all, such experts are not elected and cannot represent citizens, let alone particular cultural and political commitments. Different cultural and political commitments invite different problem-solving approaches, and complex modern societies are marked by significant value pluralism. The political goal of broadly shared agreement on how best to regulate human genetic manipulation is difficult already at the national level. More than a few observers call for agreement on a global level.

Current literature on universal standards betrays the problematic nature of a global standard for regulation, let alone standards universally valid. But given their intuitive appeal, they still merit consideration, as follows. (a) Many authors regard the diversity of current national policies as one reason why

[1] Genetic therapy targets somatic cells but not embryos.

global policy is needed. (b) A variety of notions of universal regulation is on offer. (c) These notions fail to develop a workable model of global regulation and some advocates offer notions of internationally coordinated domestic regulatory regimes instead. (d) This offer leads analysis back to competing constructions of national-level agreement. I now examine each of these points.

(a) National policies governing the manipulation of the human germline differ significantly from each other. For example, legislation in some countries – Australia, Belgium, Brazil, Canada, France, Germany, Israel, The Netherlands, the United Kingdom – prohibits germline interventions and imposes criminal sanctions (Isasi et al. 2016: 337).[2] Whereas some countries – including Germany and Canada – enact "upstream limitations" that "outlaw a technology or an application regardless of its purpose," other countries – notably France, Israel, Japan, and The Netherlands – forbid "specific downstream applications ... such as attempting to initiate a human pregnancy with an embryo or a reproductive cell whose germline has been intentionally altered" (ibid.). Each approach is problematic in its own way. Belgian law, for example, prohibits the genetic "selection or amplification of non-pathological genetic characteristics of the human species" (ibid., 338–339). Yet science cannot always identify the distinction between pathological and non-pathological.

Where it is reflective of particular cultural values, for example in the classification of congenital deafness, the Belgian law cannot be applied neutrally among cultural groups that differ on the issue. French law specifies that "no person may undermine the integrity of the human species" by genetic manipulation (Isasi et al. 2016: 339) yet it nowhere specifies those features that supposedly constitute the species' "integrity" (let alone explain how those features do so). And without defining the contested term "eugenics" – for example, does it necessarily imply the moral abuse of science and technology? – French law also prohibits "carrying out a eugenic practice aimed at organizing the selection of persons" (ibid.).

(b) Despite such problems, many observers invoke universal standards for regulating clinical germline editing, often in ways vague, undefined, and unsupported, and giving little thought to possible institutional mechanisms for international compliance with global guidelines. For example, the leaders of the British Royal Society, the United Nations National Academy of Medicine, and the American National Academy of Sciences imagine and expect – hence anticipate using as a standard for

[2] About thirty countries directly or indirectly ban all human germline editing (Araki and Ishii 2014: 108) and do so as they "follow separate paths" (Lander et al. 2019: 165).

decision-making – some kind of global agreement on guidelines (Reardon 2019: 445).[3] These leaders tend to assume that, because heritable genome editing has "global implications," universal regulation must be possible (Dzau et al. 2019: 175). One finds this approach in the scholarly literature as well. Thus Motoko Araki and Tetsuya Ishii (2014: n.p.) argue that each country must decide for itself whether to permit corrective genome editing. And if it decides to permit it, the "country would be required to express preventive measures against abuses of germline genome editing, and a global consensus will need to be formed, because thinking about germline gene modification involves ethical, social, and evolutionary considerations for all of humankind." Unclear is what or who would enforce this requirement on sovereign nation states or how a global consensus might be formed. For his part, Johannes Rath (2018: 110) asserts that "Current national and international risk management approaches to biosafety and biosecurity" are incapable of adequately mitigating "novel risks for both safety and security, which are not restricted by national boundaries," hence that "risky experiments might be carried out in countries with no legal framework" or in countries "where, although legal frameworks exist, their implementation cannot be achieved due to limited resources" (ibid., 108). This argument would seem to entail that domestic regulation can never be adequate and that global regulation is necessary. The question is: just *how* is it possible – if at all?

(c) Visions of international regulation common in the literature tend to collapse into visions of less-than-universal regulation. Representative of this literature is Eric Lander and colleagues' call for a moratorium on heritable human genome editing until an international regulatory framework is in place. The authors describe a voluntary international protocol: any given country might "allow specific applications of germline editing" only if it first "gives public notice of its intention to consider the application," "engages for a defined period in international consultation about the wisdom of doing so," "determines through transparent evaluation that the application is justified," and "ascertains that there is broad societal consensus in the nation about the appropriateness of the application" (Lander et al. 2019: 165–166). But why would any sovereign nation state choose to self-regulate in this way? On this approach, a country that chooses not to self-regulate would face no sanctions. Regulation then remains at the national level.

[3] Other internationally prominent organizations that entertain cross-border regulation include the Nuffield Council on Bioethics in the United Kingdom, the German Ethics Council, the American Society for Reproductive Medicine, the Council of Europe, and the World Health Organization.

Lander and colleagues (2019: 166) concede that "nations might well choose different paths" – a concession in tension with their subsequent assertion that countries "would agree to proceed openly and with due respect to the opinions of humankind on an issue that will ultimately affect the entire species." The term *opinions of humankind* is a hollow rhetorical device: it gestures vaguely toward a nonexistent species-wide consensus "on the appropriateness of altering a fundamental aspect of humanity for a particular purpose" (ibid., 167). The term *fundamental aspects of humanity* suggests a human essence, a notion meaningless in biology and of such indeterminate meaning in politics that it renders unlikely any communal agreement on what those aspects might be.[4]

By contrast, Natalie Kofler and colleagues (2018: 527) advocate "locally based, globally informed governance": a deliberative framework that "connect[s] deliberations around the world" and "report[s] on the outcomes of deliberation to inform global governance of gene editing" (ibid., 528). To be sure, the coordination of national-level regulation in different countries, by entities such as the World Health Organization or the United Nations Environment Program, does not rise to the level of universal regulation.[5] Nor is a "global coordination task force" "charged with coordinating multiple communities, nations, and regions to ensure successful deliberative outcomes" (ibid., 529). Neither national-level regulation nor a global task force would generate deliberative outcomes that could "shape gene-editing governance on a global scale" (ibid.).

Hervé Chneiweiss and colleagues (2017: 712) envision international legislation but only at a regional level: "European research institutions and political decision-makers should cooperate in the definition of ethical standards and guidelines which determine what kinds of translational research and application of genome editing are admissible." A European Steering Committee would evaluate the "benefit-to-harm balance of any potential clinical application," where harms include mosaicism at the on target location as well as potential off-targets (ibid.).

[4] As Chapters 3 and 4 will argue at length.

[5] Similarly, Jasanoff and Hurlbut (2018: 436) replace the goal of international regulation with that of internationally generated advice for domestic regulation. They do not advocate global governance or international standards but rather an "international network of scholars and organizations similar to those established for human rights and climate change," oriented on "gathering information from dispersed sources, bringing to the fore perspectives that are often overlooked, and promoting exchange across disciplinary and cultural divides." They call this approach a "global observatory for gene editing," with three functions: to "consolidate and make universally accessible the global range of ethical and policy responses to genome editing and related technologies" (ibid.); to "enable the tracking and analysis of significant conceptual developments, tensions and emerging areas of consensus around gene editing" (ibid.); and to "serve as a vehicle for convening periodic meetings, and seeding international discussion informed by insights drawn from data collection and analysis" (ibid.).

According to Victor Dzau and colleagues (2019: 175), "international consensus on standards that should apply to decisions about germline editing" might be achieved in part through the coordinated recommendations of various commissions, including the organizing committees of the 2015 and the 2018 international summits on human genome editing; a 2017 report by the American National Academies of Sciences, Engineering, and Medicine; a 2018 recommendation by the British Nuffield Council on Bioethics; as well as efforts by the Royal Society. But just as international commissions cannot generate binding international law, they are unlikely to contribute to any kind of universal agreement.

(d) Other authors eschew universal standards for human genetic engineering and propose nation-state-level regulation. They seek ways of creating a broad societal consensus within a single political community. The authors of the 2015 *International Summit on Human Gene Editing* assert the moral irresponsibility of proceeding with "any clinical use of germline editing unless and until ... there is broad societal consensus about the appropriateness of the proposed application" (National Academies of Sciences, Engineering, and Medicine 2015: 7). Similarly, Dzau and colleagues (2019: 175) maintain that a political community "must achieve broad societal consensus before making any decisions, given the global implications of heritable genome editing." Lander and colleagues (2019: 166) insist on the necessity of a "broad societal consensus" at the national level.

Given the challenges of creating wide-ranging agreement on difficult issues in complex modern societies, authors expectably disagree on how best to construct national-level consensus. In promoting informed cross-border public consultation on balancing the potential risks and benefits of human gene editing, the World Economic Forum (2017: 41) regards stable domestic governance as a necessary condition for regulation, requiring that the "various stakeholders likely to be affected are involved in the thinking about potential regulatory regimes and given the knowledge to enable them to make informed decisions." The Forum construes the term *stakeholders* broadly: "given the power of public opinion to shape regulatory responses, the general public must also be included in an open dialogue about the risks and opportunities of emerging technologies through carefully-managed communication strategies" (ibid.).

Confronting the challenge of engaging citizens with regard to complex and controversial science and technology, Simon Burall (2018: 438) advocates the formation of regulatory standards to connect "people to the science and policy debates" with "scientists and policymakers to other people." Franćoise Bayliss (2016: 22) advocates national-level standards, constructing national consensus not as unanimity or majority rule, nor as agreement that the "decision made is necessarily the best one possible," but merely the reassurance of each participant that, in coming to national agreement, her position was given a proper hearing and was not misunderstood.[6]

As a practical guide, this approach is weak. It requires a moral selflessness and humility implausible in practice: if dissenting participants "have had a fair hearing and others have not been swayed by their arguments, then they ought to recognize their own fallibility and step back instead of blocking emerging consensus for personal as contrasted with principled reasons" (ibid.). Participants will easily disagree as to which reasons are principled. They will not easily agree on how to understand compromise, whether as "evidence of commitment to procedural fairness" or as an "erosion of personal moral integrity" (ibid.).

These various efforts to regulate the biotechnological manipulation of humans through fixed, universal standards remain unpersuasive. They underestimate the difficulties of forging normative agreement at levels above and beyond the nation state. The question, How should a political community regulate the practice of human gene editing, whether somatic or germline?, confronts two questions: Can that capacity be regulated universally, across national boundaries? Could any particular cultural understanding of the problems and prospects of human genetic engineering achieve trans-local legitimacy?

I argue in the negative, in several steps. (§2.1) I identify the political quality of human genetic engineering and (§2.2) argue that, in democratic communities, answers to political questions must draw on the available science and, at the same time, they need to be plausible to local addressees. But because differences among different political communities cannot be bridged by the universal epistemic community constituted by science, trans-local political consensus on normative questions (including regulation) is unlikely. (§2.3) Under these circumstances, I propose one standard for the regulation of human genetic engineering: a non-universalistic notion of human nature. I construct human nature as the product of contingent and particular social learning processes. (§2.4) I then show how non-universalistic normative standards can be generated in learning processes,[7] toward normative agreement locally but not universally. (§2.5) I show that such standards are possible if they practice non-universalistic interpretive pluralism, ambiguity, and political compromise. I conclude that national political organizations (and sometimes even regional ones) are more plausible as a source of regulatory norms than the global citizen assemblies I examine in later pages.

[6] To be sure, like many other authors, Bayliss (2016: 22) invokes as an "important feature of the consensus building exercise on human gene editing" a notion, not further specified as to operationalization, of "broad-based participation by persons from around the world with a range of perspectives and interests." Her invocation provides no practical guidance.

[7] The Coda analyzes political community as a learning process as well as political bioethics as an ongoing, open-ended learning process in rational, secular argumentation.

2.1 THE POLITICAL QUALITY OF HUMAN GENETIC ENGINEERING

Human genetic engineering concerns the somatic or germline modification of aspects of the evolved human body. Its legal regulation is a political phenomenon insofar as regulation involves issues concerning competing normative commitments. Regulation is "not only about facts" but also about "ethics and laws; not only about science, but automatically about politics and governance" (Kersten 2013: 41). A commitment to increasing social equality might justify, as therapy, the engineering of "harmful" or "below average" genetic traits into ones "no longer harmful" or "average."[8] It might promote "universal access to interventions that improve cognitive performance" by analogy to universal access to "public libraries and basic education" (Sandberg and Savulescu 2011: 93).

Yet that same commitment might reject human genetic engineering on the argument that "repairing" "bad" genes in some cases might be indistinguishable from enhancing normal genes to a state "better" than just "healthy," or even enacting cultural preferences (such as a genetically more homogenous population) quite beyond plausible concerns of health.[9] Or a political commitment to individual free choice, for example in the form of parental autonomy with regard to rearing one's own children, might seem incompatible with genetically engineering one's own children inasmuch as the parents make decisions, highly consequential to the child's entire life, yet without the child's input or consent and which the child (or later adult) has no way to reject after the fact: the parents' autonomy might be thought to violate the child's autonomy, her body now the imprint of the will and preference of parents or guardians.

Another political dimension concerns the moral status of the difference between conventional forms of "therapy" for genetically based disabilities and genetic engineering as "therapy." Justice in this context entails reversing unwanted genetic conditions. For example, conventional means to overcome "natural" disadvantages such as blindness or mental retardation include transferring information into a form accessible to the blind or deaf, or special schools for mentally disabled persons. By contrast, biotechnological efforts include manipulating, say, an embryo indicating a genetic predisposition to blindness or mental retardation. Again, justice here entails overcoming the natural distribution of "poor" or "abnormal" genes by "upgrading" to "better" genes.[10] Whether conventional forms are to be preferred to genetic

[8] To be sure, conceptions of "harmful" and "average" are tied to specific cultural preferences, a fact that adds another layer of difficulty to the overall analysis.

[9] Health concerns can also be cultural in the sense, for example, of defining health and illness, normal and abnormal conditions, or even the notion of a healthy lifestyle.

[10] To speak of genes in this way is to invoke the metaphor of a lottery. If a social lottery based on the unequal distribution of wealth is ethically and politically objectionable, then perhaps a natural lottery might be no less objectionable if the unequal distribution is a consequence of

manipulation is a political question. It can only be answered on the basis of particular normative commitments, not on the basis of science.

Human genetic engineering is political for additional reasons. First, whereas not all normative claims are matters for the public sphere, all political claims are. Second, many claims about the possible regulation of human genetic engineering are not well grasped simply as a "technocratic problem to be effectively managed" (Neimanis et al. 2015: 75). Here regulation exceeds the merely technical and constitutes a normative issue as well: a matter for politics. Third, for political questions, there is no standpoint except the human: that standpoint concerns power and mastery and is oriented on future persons and future generations. In its capacity to alter the human genome, genetic engineering betrays peculiarly human perspectives. If it poses a threat to human life, then it does so from a perspective *only humans* define as a threat. If human genetic engineering threatens humankind in some way, then only because humans construct moral or legal personhood as vulnerable to human genetic engineering. And the task of "saving nature" is a distinctively human one, whether nature refers to the human genome or to planetary life in general.

2.2 POLITICAL QUESTIONS REQUIRE STANDARDS NEITHER UNIVERSALISTIC NOR NORMALIZING

Claims about adverse consequences of human genetic engineering presuppose a normative standard to determine whether any consequences are "adverse." On the one hand, a normative standard is a cultural construct (and not a natural scientific claim). On the other hand, the capacity to make cultural claims has a basis in human biology.[11] The human capacity for normative thinking – critical to our moral estimation of human behavior toward the natural world (including our biological selves, of course, and including potential future persons) – is not independent of our evolved nature.

The ancient notion of "human nature," defined over the millennia in many different ways, is one way to frame the sociobiological basis for the human capacity to make normative judgments. But the notion can do so only in a form that does not contradict natural science, hence only if divested of theological, metaphysical, and mythical elements present in many of its widespread versions.

unequal access – say, because one's parents did not have the economic power to purchase a particular enhancement, or because of a political community's regulations, or because of a religious tradition's objections.

11 A thesis often described as "sociobiology," a term Wilson (1975) coined to refer to the social and ecological forces driving the evolution by natural selection of animal behavior: behavioral ecology in the sense of methodologically adaptationist approaches to understanding the nature and causes of animal behavior. It acknowledges the significance of phenomena studied by neuroscience.

Two standards at work in common notions of "human nature" are "normal" – as in the phrases *a normal person* and *normal environmental conditions* – and "universal," as in the notion of *universal features* of species-membership. Across time, geographies, and cultures, humans have engaged in a "relentless search for human universals," excited "at the prospect that we may thereby unlock something at the core of our being" (Gould 1986: 6). The quest has never succeeded.

My alternative is a non-universalistic, *non-normalizing* notion of "human nature." It rests on two propositions. First, any plausible idea of a human nature must operate in part with biological data even if that idea cannot be reduced entirely to those data. Still, any notion of human nature is incoherent at any point where it is incompatible with biological data. The upshot is that human biology does not itself yield a notion of some universal human nature. A universalistic notion of human nature is incompatible with human biology.

Second, from a naturalistic standpoint – compatible with the natural science that generates biological data – all normative claims can only be a product of human imagination, embedded in particular cultural visions. Significant for my proposal is the claim that a norm is cultural not natural. In phrases such as "normal human being," "normal human traits," or the "normal functioning of a human trait," the term *normal* is a social construct. It is not a natural scientific description of our species but rather an expression of particular cultures or traditions.[12]

2.3 A NON-UNIVERSALISTIC NOTION OF HUMAN NATURE

If there were a universal human nature in the sense of an identical set of features with identical functioning in all members of the species, it would be identifiable by one or more of those supposedly universal traits.[13] In fact, various traits are present in human populations at various frequencies, from low to high. Evolutionary sciences draw on the same processes – natural selection, mutation, migration, and genetic drift – to explain this fact.

From an evolutionary standpoint, the universal presence of a trait has no particular significance: "Perhaps a claim like 'trichromatic vision is an element of human nature' commits us to nothing more than an assertion of widespread presence and its evolutionary rationale" (Lewens 2018: 3). But to say that

[12] But particular origins do not necessarily preclude an eventually universal embrace. In normative contexts, such as claims to human rights, universal validity is possible as a contingent, historical achievement of politics, society-wide learning, and cultural invention.

[13] Problematic is the assumption that such traits are necessarily universal among humans. Yet the possible status of a trait's universal presence is without evolutionary significance. Further, one can more easily exclude possible traits than identify possible ones. A trait widely shared among members of the species is not for that reason an "essential" trait. All humans have mass and breathe oxygen, yet neither trait is specific to humans.

"trichromatic vision is part of human nature" does not imply that "literally all humans are trichromatic," nor does it imply that "colour-blind people are not members of Homo sapiens" (ibid).

Two further generalizations about humans are relevant here. First, all human traits, possessed to different extents and in different measures by different individuals, are evolved. They continue to evolve. Second, some of these traits are shared with other species (without thereby undermining distinctions among species).

Upshot: human nature is not what makes the individual a member of the species because no particular trait is either necessary or adequate to determine membership in the species. For example, if blood type were a trait relevant to the question of human nature, it remains that not all humans have the same blood type – and yet persons with different blood types are equally members of the species. Consider linguistic capacity, a trait not universally distributed among human beings. Even persons who cannot speak or understand language are *Homo sapiens*.

A person is not capable of learning language if she lacks the necessary neuronal system (whether for genetic reasons or because of extreme environmental deprivation). She might have been capable of learning language if she had a different genetic inheritance or if she had experienced adequate environmental stimulation. Nonetheless she is a member of the species; if there is a human nature, she has one. A chimpanzee by contrast has a capacity for language learning yet it is not a member of our species; it does not have a human nature.[14]

In short, human nature is not singular; it varies among members of the species. Hence no particular trait determines human nature. No trait can fulfill the traditional function of a conventional account of human nature, such as the metaphysical notion of a human essence. Further, every trait tends to variation. Not only are most phenotypic traits variable; in "some species there is more intraspecific variation than interspecific variation" (Hull 1986: 7).

As Darwin (1854: 155) notes, "Not only does every external character vary greatly in most of the species, but the internal parts very often vary to a surprising degree," whereby no part or organ is "absolutely invariable in form or structure." Indeed, species evolution through natural selection requires genetic and phenotypic variation. Which particular variations occur depends both on regularities of selection processes and on any number of contingencies

[14] And "distribution of language use or the capacity for language use" implies nothing "about any 'genetic basis' for language capacity" (Hull 1986: 5). Consider the rare example of children "raised in near total social isolation until adulthood" who "cannot speak or understand any human language" and who "at this late date are taught one," where the capacity for language is no longer present (ibid., 7). Or consider the rare case of babies "born with little in the way of a cerebrum," with no "significant sense in which they nevertheless retain the potentiality for language use" (ibid.). Even then, they belong unproblematically to the human species.

and accidents. The very possibility of biological species requires the process of variation. What we are as humans varies over (very long periods of) time. This is one trait that makes us humans.

If no single biological trait – biochemical, morphological, or psychological – distinguishes humans from nonhumans, then none can be used to identify a nature that is uniquely human. The same can be said of *cultural* traits where cultural traits are understood as persisting universals. For example, the claim that all cultures prefer health to illness is unhelpful inasmuch as concepts of health and illness are plastic: they may vary within one culture and across different cultures, and within one culture over time. Indeed, the idea of culture as a set of unchanging traits generating cultural universals presupposes some kind of universal human psychology.[15] Yet evolutionary psychologists do not agree on a universal human psychology. Anthropologists cannot identify universal cultural characteristics.[16]

From a standpoint somehow independent of our cultural constructions, we humans cannot describe the nature of our own species. We cannot consider human genetic manipulation from such a standpoint. Because human nature cannot be separated from human culture, human culture cannot be separated from human nature: "there is no such thing," according to anthropologist Clifford Geertz (1973: 49), "as a human nature independent of culture."

So understood, most any notion of human nature is contingent on culture. As a product of natural evolution, human biology is contingent on genetic mutation within changing natural environments. But human biology is also affected by some cultural developments, as I discuss below. For the effort to formulate standards for the legal regulation of human genetic engineering, two conclusions follow.

(a) Legal regulation is a normative concern. Normative thinking is contingent on the cultural presuppositions that inform it. It is also contingent because human nature, as a sociocultural product, is contingent. Independent of genetic adaptation, the development of culture requires certain socio-cognitive conditions. It requires those conditions inasmuch as human consciousness is communicatively socialized. And communication involves cognition entwined with understanding, inasmuch as understanding is a cognitive act, as is intentionality.

Self-regarding intentionality of the very young child widens into a kind of "group mind" of participants in common practices of daily life. It widens into a cognitive focus; it is intentionality shared by multiple persons simultaneously (or even asynchronously, as in the case of cultural transmission between generations).

[15] Compare Kaplan and Manners (1972: 151).
[16] Compare, e.g., Buller (2005) with Pinker (2002).

Further, the social construction of culture, society, and political community – all of which are types of "group mind" – requires the development of human socio-cognitive capacities and abilities. That development traces aspects of the species' long evolution. One example is the species' gradual movement from gestures to language and the consequent, massive increase in communicative possibilities, with profound consequences for developing diverse forms of sociocultural life. Language makes possible the coordination of behavior in communities and cultures, such as cooperation in the division of labor and in the socialization of individuals.

(b) To a degree, normative thinking is biologically influenced inasmuch as humans are biological creatures and human cognition has biological predicates. From the standpoint of evolutionary science, what for nonhuman organisms may be a developmental niche is, for humans, a cultural product and social construction. Kim Sterelny (2018: 120) notes for example that literacy physiologically alters the brain and "transforms the mind of the literate." For its realization, the human capacity for quantitative reasoning depends on culture in the form of "environmental scaffolding," such as the "collective invention and transmission of representational systems" (including numerals as well as the "social organization of the learning environment of young humans" (ibid.). Even the modern market economy requires the cultural formation of biological nature in the sense of displacing drives for immediate gratification with a slowly acquired capacity for delayed gratification. Some characteristics of our evolved species, indeed evolution itself, affect the evolution of culture in many significant ways.

To be sure, biology generates no norms of human conduct, let alone norms for the organization of political community.[17] Further, no normative system can be any more stable than human biology. Human thought systems and cultures change constantly, indeed at an ever more rapid rate that far outpaces the velocity of species' evolution. Normative thinking will never issue into some final form; it is forever open-ended. The only finality the species could know would be species extinction.

In timescales short and long, cultural environments contribute to the formation of individual traits just as individual traits contribute to the shaping of social environments. In this way, human nature and human culture are always already entwined as phenomena that evolve and that evolve together; each is a particular kind of evolutionary process. Social learning is a prime example. As one of the ways in which human culture evolves, social learning bears analogy to biological evolution: learning from others to adapt, transform, even to create

[17] On the question of whether moral norms themselves can be changed by genetic evolution, see Ruse and Wilson (1986: 186).

our various environments, from the physical and social to the economic and political. Learning in this sense is a constant feature of human evolutionary history. The mechanisms that ground the human capacity to learn are both biological and cultural inheritances: "genetic evolution has made human infants receptive to teaching" and cultural evolution is important in shaping human nature (Heyes 2018: 76).[18]

Culture is itself an inherited environment: "organisms inherit their environments as much as they inherit their genes: a fish inherits not only fins but also water" (Tomasello 2019: 7). Human children inherit cultural contexts rich in understandings, practices, symbols, institutions, and other artefacts. They trigger and promote the child's maturation. Without them, the child's capacity for culture and maturation would remain inert.

Social learning presupposes the human capacity for normative plasticity (directly relevant to standards for the legal regulation of human genetic engineering). Individuals can acquire the beliefs, values, and motivations of other persons, groups, and cultures. Acquisitions can be preserved and passed on to others.

Given human plasticity along multiple dimensions, human nature is complex not simple. Human nature includes the fact that it admits of many different generalizations and that human nature possesses no unchanging characteristics. The individual human organism is a set of processes and subprocesses, and the species as a whole is a sequence of multiple, evolutionary events with no fixed endpoint. If normative standards to regulate human genetic engineering were to be grounded in some quality of human nature, such a nature could not possibly be something permanent and unchanging.

2.4 NON-UNIVERSALISTIC NORMATIVE STANDARDS GENERATED BY LEARNING PROCESS

Social learning in a broad sense refers to the cultural patterning of the individual: the cultural formation of the individual's evolved cognitive and emotional capacity. Social learning is a form of socialization, a life-long process. The individual learns to construe "pedagogical communication as reflective of culturally universal and objective knowledge" (ibid., 341). Such knowledge is not universally valid *as such*; it is not objective in the sense of natural scientific propositions universally valid regardless of the particular cultural communities from which they emerge.

Rather, the individual *learns to regard* her particular cultural standpoint not as limited and relative but rather as universal and objective. What appears within the community as culturally *universal* knowledge, and perhaps therefore is regarded by communal members as *objective* knowledge, is in fact the

[18] See Csibra and Gergely (2011).

intersubjective viewpoint from within one or more cultures. To be sure, that viewpoint is not subjective in the sense of an individual's opinion. Rather, it is *intersubjective* in the sense of being valid for the community that has persuaded itself of that validity. In the sphere of moral learning – ultimately, the source of standards for the possible regulation of human genetic engineering – the individual comes to identify this intersubjective viewpoint with her own feelings of fairness and impartiality.[19]

Social integration within a community is supported and furthered by shared belief systems. They include normative attitudes embraced by many members of the same community, thereby constituting an intersubjective viewpoint. The attitudes' quality of being shared within the community lends them a sense of impartiality or fairness, of universality and objectivity. This normative attitude facilitates social integration in terms of cooperation by encouraging the child to common commitment to perform her role as best as possible. It facilitates integration by encouraging and reinforcing conformity with respect to a shared embrace of the same social norms.

In this context, the term *human nature* could serve the cultural pursuits of generating answers to moral and legal questions embraceable from an intersubjective viewpoint, as a moral framing and as a socially constructed worldview. For human nature so understood, biological nature ceases to be an indispensable reference point for cultural interpretation. With regard to human genetic engineering, political community no longer appeals to this or that particular understanding of nature to answer such questions as: Does a fertilized human egg cell "possess" dignity and rights? Can morality (in the form, say, of dignity and rights) be ascribed to nature when by *nature* we mean life at stages before birth, for example as an eight-celled embryo? If a fertilized human egg cell does not immediately possess "human dignity," then at what point on the developmental continuum does it acquire it – and how? Is a political community just if its laws allow the genetic engineering of an embryo that the state or community regards as possessing dignity and rights? To answer these questions without recourse to nature is to recognize the regulation of human genetic engineering as a thoroughly cultural project, one involving cultural evaluations that follow from the learning processes undergone by participants in the course of life-long socialization. Evaluations change when, and only if, learning processes change.

By *learning processes* I refer to three processes in particular: coordination, adaptation, and transmission. First, culture is a means by which participants coordinate within self-created cooperative structures. Culture is a means for deploying norms, conventions, and institutions to secure, within human communities, trust, commitment, and fairness. Culture has a capacity to coordinate individuals in thought and action, and members of a cultural group can

[19] See Tomasello (2019: 341).

coordinate themselves synchronously within social structures that encourage and facilitate cooperation. Examples include norms, such as moralities and laws; institutions, such as marriage and family life; and conventions, such as languages. Individuals coordinated by cultural means can then relate to each other cooperatively in terms of trust and fairness, on the basis of shared understandings and commitments. They can coordinate with each other cooperatively in unique ways, in ever-new forms, in the immediate present or in the long run. The human capacity to coordinate follows from the confluence of biological evolution and cultural evolution.

Second, culture provides an evolutionary adaptive advantage. Under evolutionary conditions, "individuals who could best cooperate with others – individuals who were both capable and motivated to put their heads together with others to collaborate or form a culture – were at an adaptive advantage and so proliferated" (Tomasello 2019: 5). On the one hand, culture adapts to social evolutionary challenges. On the other hand, culture is itself an adaptation to those challenges. In the form of social organization, culture responds to particular adaptive challenges faced by humans, as it has done so across the history of the species. To be sure, human cultural development outpaces human biological evolution by a very large factor, indeed one that accelerates over time. Group-level cultural learning similarly exceeds genetic adaptation in pace and diversity.

Third, communities can transmit their cultures and acquired abilities to later generations. Cultural practices and products tend to "evolve" in transmission (languages, for example, tend to simplify in the sense of complexity-reduction). In the form of norms, conventions, and institutions, cultural constructs and practices may develop a kind of trajectory over time, sometimes even "improving" themselves in function and consequence. Andrea Migliano et al. (2020) suggest that the global expansion of the human species was only possible on the basis of cumulative cultural adaptation by hunter-gatherers. Cultural evolution required the concentration of cultural groups, through the clustering of kinship networks within camps, and then the clustering of camps within regions, as well as cultural transmission within those networks. It also required exchange among different cultural groups through high intercamp mobility. Maxime Derex and Alex Mesoudi (2020) show that our species' ability to acquire adaptive social information selectively allows us to accumulate cultural innovations gradually. Multiple generations of individuals, effecting incremental improvements over centuries, develop technologies and other sophisticated cultural practices and artifacts that far exceed the inventive capacities of any one person.

Culture so understood is a learning process. Political change occurs through changes in learning processes – for example, cultural cues that support the project of intersubjectively shared viewpoints that regard women as intellectually, morally and, in potential, equal to men.

The political project of regulating human genetic engineering engages the human capacity for learning, a capacity at once biological and cultural. Culture itself can enhance the biological capacity for culture, for example through institutionalized educational systems, by a robust economy, by good nutrition especially in the first decades of life, and by infrastructure (such as schools as well as transport to and from schools) – as well as by cultural cues that encourage learning as a collective value widely shared throughout a community.

This inextricable relationship between human biological nature and human culture suggests that there is no "pre-cultural human nature" and no "culturally overlaid 'superorganic' realm" (Lewens 2018: 15). Again, the human develops as a product of the interaction between biology and culture. One example: human imagination is in part a biologically evolved phenomenon with culturally mediated contents acquired through learning.[20] Biological humans cannot become humans in a rich sense without culture to unlock the potential of the biological human. Cognitive and social capacities, unique to our species, enable individual communicative and collaborative experiences with others. They enable experiences guided by cultural structures such as social norms.

Not only are human biological nature and human culture deeply interrelated. They are also similar in that neither a particular genome, nor a particular culture, is universally present: members of the species are not identical to each other, biologically or culturally. The individual's cognitive and social ontogeny depends on transactions between her personal and her cultural environment. The transactions generate variations both in the individual and in her cultural environment. They are "necessary for normal human development" and they are "responsible for many cultural and individual variations" (Tomasello 2019: 8).

Members of the species are not identical to each other but they share traits unique to the species, traits involving a uniquely human psychology and uniquely human forms of cognition and sociality, and generated by species-specific cultural behavior. We again see how nature and culture entwine: one form of "human nature" – human biology – prepares, equips, and conditions our species for another form of "human nature": cultural behavior. Without uniquely human biology, there would be no human culture and the experiences it makes possible. Indeed, human nature can be an object of human study only because of the evolution and inheritance of human culture. Conceptions of nature, like conceptions of culture, are products of earlier generations and communities.

[20] Another example: the processes of acquiring and transmitting natural scientific knowledge follow cultural dimensions such as the state of technology, or the particular research agendas of scientists at any given time, or the interests of funders or governments or of other groups, organizations, and communities. Correspondingly, patterns that compose human culture are the patterns of which a biologically evolved organism is capable – which is why one might argue that "patterns that make up human nature can be discerned in traits of all kinds" (Lewens 2018: 11).

2.5 REGULATORY QUESTIONS NOT ANSWERABLE BY SCIENCE ALONE

Even as human biology and human culture are intertwined, the cultural phenomenon of politics cannot accomplish its tasks simply by invoking science, for three reasons. First, science cannot avoid playing a role in struggles in the political sphere over competing value commitments. In playing that role, it is perpetually vulnerable to abuse. Karen Litfin (1994: 197) for example argues that "inasmuch as scientific discourse permeates political debates, as often as not it serves to articulate or rationalize existing interests and conflicts." Even if not abused in political debates, scientific epistemic communities cannot save political communities from themselves. They cannot, for example, solve social and political problems of institutional uncertainty and lack of trust between a citizenry and its elites. Science's cognitive authority cannot settle policy disputes, for example when deployed in the public sphere for purposes of debating and formulating public policy. By itself it cannot establish acceptable thresholds of safety, or unacceptable levels of risk, in bioengineering. By itself, it cannot tell us how best to regulate human genetic engineering.[21]

Second, even if, in some political conflicts, "science is seen as an important tool in attempts to globalize normatively contested concepts" (Gupta 2004: 129), successful politics is more likely facilitated by some degree of normative ambiguity than by the technical precision, value neutrality, and universal validity of science. But the global validity of science cannot be transferred to particular political values and preferences. Science cannot provide a "discursive and institutional framework for creating globally convergent understandings" about how best to regulate human genetic engineering (Jasanoff 1998: 84). And yet when it plays a role in the public sphere by informing public policy, science can hardly isolate itself from its political environment.[22] But it cannot solve political problems or normative questions – questions that do not admit of the rigor in reasoning, freedom from ambiguity, and value-neutrality to which science aspires.

Third, ambitions to global normative regulation confront the localist logic of a great deal of politics. Politics works best if sensitive to local understandings. It works best if it resonates in local application. The beliefs and behavior of elites and ordinary citizens alike are more consequentially normed locally than at national or supranational levels.

The political dimension in deciding questions of biotechnological applications, including the regulation of human genetic engineering, requires interpretive pluralism that allows for differences among different venues. And it requires deliberately ambiguous compromises among different political communities. It requires defining matters so as to allow for multiple, competing interpretations. Disputed interpretations can function as placeholders for an

[21] Compare Jasanoff (1987).

[22] See also Jasanoff (1998); Herrick and Sarewitz (2000).

agreement that, even if unlikely, may provide political orientation nonetheless. Disputed interpretations may allow for political compromise that in turn links elite or expert opinions with particular local contexts precisely by leaving relevant issues open to competing interpretations.

2.6 CONCLUSION: GLOBAL REGULATORY NORMS ARE IMPLAUSIBLE

The project for regulating human genetic engineering is unlikely ever to forge norms capable of global embrace. The project more realistically aims at regulation that enjoys at least some degree of local legitimacy. Regulation is plausible in the form of discretion at the nation-state level, recognizing differences in interpretation, preference, and value commitment.

One notion of developing globally shared norms emphasizes inclusive participation, including the "meaningful participation of citizens from around the world" in some form of public deliberation on regulating human genetic engineering. A global citizens' assembly is one example. As an alternative to unreflective mass responses to survey questions, it seeks to generate public opinion "as a provisional and dynamic outcome of inclusive and competent public discourse supported by evidence-based science that connects to public values" (Dryzek et al. 2020: 1435).

Such an assembly "would at a minimum be composed of 100 people. Participants would be recruited throughout the world. Stratified random sampling would yield a broad spread in terms of nationality, cultures, level of education, age, income, religion, and gender" (ibid.). Imagine an assembly exploring questions about regulating human genetic engineering and genome editing technologies. For example: Should regulation take place at a level national or international? The assembly would facilitate broad, informed participation[23] by persons selected from civil society, selected to yield greater cognitive diversity than otherwise likely. Participants would be exposed to information from opposing viewpoints of experts in science and technology, in public policy, and in other relevant fields.[24]

A citizen assembly would not legislate. It would not formulate public policy. Its conclusions would be widely available to the general public through various kinds of media, in the hope and expectation that nonparticipants might benefit from the perspectives of persons who were able to participate. Participants and nonparticipants influenced by informed, thoughtful conclusions – informed because based on listening to, and questioning of, representatives of different perspectives within expert groups, and thoughtful because developed through discussion and debate among fellow citizen participants – might contribute positively to public opinion. These conclusions might be somewhat more

[23] See Chneiweiss et al. (2017). [24] See Grönlund et al. (2014); O'Doherty and Burgess (2013).

inclusive because somewhat less wedded to particular cultural and political contexts.

At best, global citizen assemblies would generate trust between participants and experts (scientists, health-care professionals, policymakers) drawn from both public institutions (governments and international organizations such as the UN Food and Agriculture Organization and the World Health Organization) and private ones (corporations). Assemblies might generate popular legitimacy for public policy to the extent that popular trust in biotechnology can be secured through popular participation in deliberations about its regulation. By itself, expert knowledge cannot warrant its acceptability to a broad public. Nor can it legitimize particular value judgements for the community, or entail a specific agenda for the public sphere.[25]

But global citizen assemblies are implausible.[26] That implausibility adds to the reasons I earlier advanced for non-universal rules for regulating human genetic engineering. They are implausible for three reasons. First, all normative framings of questions related to human genetic engineering are problematic in one way or another. No global citizens' assembly can generate an unproblematic framing. So the framing of possible problems and prospects of human genetic engineering is unlikely ever to be consensual. Even if a consensual framing were possible, there are no multilateral regimes that might transfer it across diverse national and local contexts for application. Second, global citizens' assemblies cannot forge valid norms for an international regime of regulation, not only because of significant cultural and economic differences among the various participating communities. Whereas some degree of legitimacy may be generated within a nation state through popularly elected political representatives, the international level offers no corresponding mechanism of popular influence. Third, global citizens' assemblies confront the fact that politics require local interpretive flexibility, in two respects: in framing issues relevant to human genetic engineering, and in applying rules and regulations in concrete cases. So the cultural project of deploying norms, conventions, and institutions toward securing, within political communities, trust, commitment, and fairness, is unlikely at a global level. The types of cultural groups able to coordinate norms, conventions, and institutions with each other, and to generate bases for continued cooperation such as trust, fairness, and commitment, might sometimes rise above local levels to a national level, and in some instances even to a regional level, but likely never to a global one.

[25] Moreover, some expert participants may have viewpoints already committed to particular interests or values in ways that could restrict their ability to advance the public interest. Further, expert knowledge, whether scientific expertise or the expertise of professional ethicists, is not necessarily a public value, and the assemblies seek to generate public values.

[26] Still, plausible standards can be more than national even if less than global, as I argue in Gregg (2016a, 2016b, 2020c, 2020d, and 2020e).

To be sure, problems remain, particularly for democratic communities.[27] The biotechnology of human genetic engineering easily crosses national borders and other boundaries. Regulatory efforts will always need to reach beyond those borders even as they frustrate those efforts. Frustrated efforts will bring inconsistent, unsystematic, and incomplete regulation.[28] They will also see "ethics dumping." That is, researchers (often in high-income regions) avoid local legal and ethical restrictions on research practice by pursuing unethical research practices in other countries (often in lower-income regions of the world) marked by a persistent legal and regulatory void.[29]

Differences in regulatory standards will always disfavor poorer regions, countries, groups, and individuals. One consequence of such inequality is "medical tourism." Another is the inability of some countries to afford extensive and detailed regulatory oversight and enforcement. In a world of maldistributed wealth and uneven development, a global set of cost–benefit calculations is impossible. For these reasons, too, universal standards for the legal regulation of human genetic engineering are unlikely.

This chapter made a case for less-than-universal standards for the regulation of human genetic engineering.[30] In a world of significant differences in value commitments, less-than-universal standards are more plausible than global standards. National (and, in some cases, even regional) regulation is more plausible than global citizen assemblies. The next chapter examines the issue of regulation with respect to possible standards. It proposes one that provides a basis for the rest of the book: a naturalistic understanding of the human species. Because it is not deeply embedded in particular ways of life, it offers a basis for dealing productively with abiding competition among different normative understandings and commitments. By contrast, most notions of human nature are deeply embedded in particular cultural commitments. I propose an alternative: constructing a notion of human *nature* we have reason to prefer precisely by constructing the human *rights* we have reason to want. This political notion of human rights, linked to a political notion of human nature, offers a normative standard capable of wide embrace.

[27] See Warren and Gastil (2015). [28] See Isasi et al. (2016).

[29] See, e.g., Schroeder et al. (2018).

[30] When in Chapter 10 and in the Coda I speak of an aspiration to universally valid norms of regulating human genetic engineering, I speak of aspiration in a regulative sense: to orient progress toward a goal never to be reached.

3

Regulation Guided by Human Nature as Construction, Not Essence

No one argues for regulation-free biotechnological interventions into the human genome. But no one agrees as to which forms of human genetic engineering should be allowed, which disallowed, and in each case, for what reasons. While convictions about human genetic engineering are many and diverse, the addressee of human genetic engineering is one: every human being and, in principle, our species as such.[1] For a liberal democratic community, one that aspires to rational self-determination, the question poses itself: How might a community generate the widest possible agreement on appropriate standards for the legal regulation of human genetic engineering?

I propose several baseline presuppositions for decision-making that would create better conditions for greater agreement. These presuppositions rest on a specifically "political" understanding of both human nature and human rights. By *political* I refer to seven features, each of which I identify in the course of my proposal for a human rights-oriented human nature:

- a quest for free and wide agreement on normative questions in the public sphere;
- oriented on norms to which members of a particular political community aspire;
- deploying self-reflection as a capacity for normative self-constitution;
- linking a notion of human nature as social construct with a notion of human nature as political tool;
- focused on how humans co-construct and coevolve with their environments;

[1] But the species as a whole is neither political community nor collective agent. The human population is (self-)divided into many different groups, not least of all in different nation states. So I speak of political communities as the most administratively plausible addressee of the need to regulate human genetic engineering.

- oriented on how the human species adapts itself to its natural environments by constantly constructing and modifying its many cultural environments; and
- taking a pragmatic approach: that belief is not so much truth guided as behavior guiding.

What makes these features *political*? Each is a matter of self-consciously normative agency oriented on group self-determination:

- generating agreement;
- observing communal norms;
- self-consciously self-constituting;
- self-constituting along the dimensions of human nature;;
- conscious of the interplay between a community and its environments;
- conscious of how that interplay is heavily cultural rather than biological; and
- oriented on guiding communal behavior.[2]

This political understanding is compatible with a naturalistic understanding of the human species. A naturalistic understanding contrasts with metaphysical and theological understandings. It is this-worldly.[3] It is not deeply embedded in particular ways of life – or it is embedded much less in any particular way of life than are metaphysical and theological understandings.

The commitment of political bioethics to a naturalistic understanding offers a basis for dealing productively with abiding competition among different normative understandings and commitments. Political bioethics does not ask scientific questions but rather normative ones. It is political in its quest for free and wide agreement to those normative questions.[4] As possible answers, it admits only those that, while not themselves natural scientific, do not contradict a naturalistic understanding of the world. Here we have the first of seven features of a political approach. In this approach, the fundamental political question is not (as in natural science), What is true? The question is (as in normative spheres of law, morality, ethics), By what norms do we members of a particular political community wish to be governed by, and for what reasons and to what ends?

This is a second feature of political approach: to treat both human nature and human rights as social constructs. Social construction is a distinctively

[2] Whereas Hull (1986) argues against the notion of human nature as a matter of truth, I argue for the social construction of human nature as a means to political ends. In this sense, my approach is pragmatic.

[3] That self-understanding confronts the epistemological challenge of being both the subject and object of understanding. The challenge lies in the fact that humans cannot assume a neutral "view from nowhere" (Nagel 1986). They cannot escape a peculiarly human viewpoint or a peculiarly human way of being in the world.

[4] At least in polities more open than, say, authoritarian polities to reasoned debate, to public reason, and to politically free public spheres.

human activity. It involves multiple capacities: symbolic language, social norms (such as human rights), and the science and technology that lead to the biotechnologies with which humans can now genetically engineer embryos and, through the germline, the species.

The term *human nature* can be understood politically as the self-understanding of the human species. The species may understand itself in normative self-reflection, by responding to the question, What kind of moral beings should we aspire to become? Humans might respond by constructing human rights and, in political community, assigning those rights to themselves. The word *human* in the phrase *human rights* then refers to the only species we know to give itself rights because the only one capable of normative self-reflection and normative social construction.

The act of critical self-reflection is a core feature of human-rights thinking. The capacity for self-reflection may be unique to our species and, in any case, is evidence of how profoundly human cognition and human culture are intertwined in evolution. For example, on the one hand, humans have the genetic makeup and the physiology necessary for language creation and use. On the other hand, any given language itself is entirely a cultural construction. So while the capacity to create a language requires genetic endowments, the languages humans create are not themselves determined biologically. To be sure, in some ways what humans are capable of creating might be circumscribed by human biology.

Self-reflection (with multiple orders of intentionality)[5] is a capacity for normative self-constitution, a third feature of a political approach. Capacities for self-reflection and normative thought are at work in the very question of whether there is a human nature (and, if there is, what it might be). They are at work in the social construction of human rights and of human nature. The respective notions of human rights and human nature are interrelated in answer to the question, Might we humans construct the human *nature* we have reason to prefer precisely by constructing the human *rights* we have reason to want?

I answer this question in several steps. (§3.1) I argue for a non-essentialist notion of human rights and propose, as an alternative, (§3.2) a "political" notion of human rights. (§3.3) I then argue for a non-essentialist notion of human nature (§3.4) to advance, as an alternative, a "political" notion of human nature. I conclude by linking these two alternatives in the idea of human nature oriented on human rights. The linkage offers a normative standard which – if adopted as a presupposition by participants to debates on the legal regulation of human genetic engineering – could contribute to a wide embrace of any answer then produced.

[5] For example, knowing that one knows, thinking about how one would like to know, and creating new ways to know.

3.1 CRITIQUE OF HUMAN NATURE-ESSENTIALISM

There are more than thirty recent scholarly accounts of the term *human nature*. There are even more folk versions and religious accounts (Fuentes 2008). Many of them employ what I term *human nature-essentialism*. It posits human traits that are purportedly (a) innate, (b) invariant, (c) universal, and (d) unique.[6]

(a) Innateness is a notion of fixed, genetically based traits that do not vary across cultures (Griffiths et al. 2009). An innate trait is present at birth; it is not acquired through education or any other form of socialization. Innate traits come to expression through normal human development (Lindquist 2011). Even as that development depends on environmental cues or stimulation, the presence of an innate trait is independent of its environment. Genetic essentialism locates an innate trait in the individual's genetic makeup.[7] Philosophical accounts source it in metaphysical or theological notions of human existence.[8]

(b) Invariance refers to the historically unchanging "core" of human traits. This "core" constrains all possible diversity[9] and variation in traits and capacities. Some accounts of invariant human nature allow for greater malleability than others.[10]

[6] The conceptual overlap among these traits entwine them in any given account.

[7] A strain of evolutionary psychology practices human nature-essentialism as a biological phenomenon that largely excludes influences of socialization and other cultural phenomena. Such influences appear in a staggering variety of cultural forms yet all of them instantiate the same human nature. In one case, Tooby and Cosmides (1992) depict human nature as modules of the human mind; a module is a psychological universal. In another case, Pinker (2002) postulates an innate set of universal traits, such as reasoning, linguistic capacity, a capacity for morally normed behavior, and culture (from perceptions and understandings, to practices such as religion and music, to socially constructed institutions such as marriage). Products of evolutionary adaptation, these traits circumscribe the range of how all humans think and behave today. For a trenchant critique of Tooby and Cosmides (1992) and Pinker (2002), see Buller (2005).

[8] Scholars as diverse in their thinking as Annas (2005), Fukuyama (2002), and Habermas (2001) all confer an otherworldly normative status on humankind. They regard the human species as endowed with an objective, pre-political moral status in the sense of moral realism – a status presumably metaphysical or theological. They regard almost all forms of genetic engineering as infringement, interference, or violation of a human essence, and as a moral crime that should be a legal crime as well. Thus Fukuyama (2002: 4) fears genetic engineering will cause the "end of the human species as such." Annas (2005: 56) thinks that engineering "could lead us to commit species suicide." The philosophically richest account of human nature-essentialism is Habermas's (2001). He argues that human genetic engineering undermines moral equality because the engineered person bears the imprint of the intention of other persons (such as the parents who sought particular traits, or the scientists or physicians who undertook the engineering). That imprint destroys the autonomy of the engineered person inasmuch as he or she is then "predetermined" by means of that engineering rather than being the outcome of natural reproduction not influenced by human design.

[9] Diverse evolutionary processes, including drift, adaptation, and phylogenetic constraints, have contributed to widespread human traits. Such traits by definition cannot be necessary but only contingent.

[10] If one thinks of human nature as traits and behaviors that are shared in patterns, one confronts the question, To what extent are these patterns fixed, and to what extent, malleable? Human

(c) Traits universally present among members of the species (Brown 1991) must affect some aspects of all human cultures and, from an anthropological standpoint, lead to a limited set of cultural universals (Pinker 2002).[11]

(d) Traits that are unique to the species likely express themselves in most individuals. So the term *unique* refers above all to differences between humans and nonhuman animals.[12]

3.2 ALTERNATIVE: A POLITICAL NOTION OF HUMAN NATURE

The notion of an intrinsically valuable human nature would seem to entail that genetic engineering violates human rights – if one believes that engineering violates human nature because it involves changes that, from the standpoint of innateness as a moral quality, should be inviolable to almost any technical manipulation.[13] Against that notion, I argue that to construe a trait as having intrinsic value is not to objectively, dispassionately, or neutrally describe human nature but rather to assign it moral value. Such assignation is an act of social construction and cannot be value-free. It construes human nature as an essence.

Toward a general basis for the legal regulation of human genetic engineering, I offer an alternative to human nature-essentialism. It operates with a political notion of human nature and contains two propositions. Taken together, these propositions constitute a fourth feature of a political approach.

Proposition 1. Any notion of human nature is something learned in particular cultures. It is a contingent phenomenon,[14] historically and culturally embedded, plural, and one that changes over time. The traits of any given

nature-essentialism argues for strongly fixed traits and would regard an extremely malleable nature as no nature at all. By contrast, a non-essentializing account argues that abiding cultural patterns generate the cultural similarity that underlies so much of the variation within and among human cultures. The resilience of these patterns over time can be explained in a this-worldly way. While not itself naturalistic (the patterns are not biologically determined nor are they products of natural selection), this way does not contradict a naturalistic understanding of the world. The resilience of some cultural patterns does not require innate, invariant, or otherwise "essential" traits; it does not require an implausible otherworldly account.

[11] Yet traits universally present are not necessarily adaptations. An adaptation is not necessarily universal but could be local.

[12] Most notions of human rights are constructed on the claim that the distinctions between human animals and nonhuman animals are significant enough to entail human rights with no corresponding rights for nonhumans.

[13] E.g., Habermas (2001) grounds the moral equality of human beings as following from humankind not controlling the biological development of a human life (or an essential human nature) once a sperm fertilizes an egg. Annas (2005) makes a similar argument: engineering that changes an essential human nature thereby undermines human dignity and human rights.

[14] The question of contingency is one of the many ways that human nature and human rights intersect. If human nature is contingent (as Harris (2011)) argues) because evolved human genetic identity by definition is not fixed, then it can hardly ground human rights if human rights are construed as permanent not changing, necessary not contingent.

notion of human nature can be acquired through learning and teaching (Downes and Machery 2013). Teaching and learning pursue the transmission of culture, and notions of human nature transmit cultural patterns from generation to generation.

Cultural patterns contain more information than do genetic patterns about what it is to be human. Human groups display little genetic diversity[15] compared to other mammals, yet, unlike other mammals, extraordinary cultural diversity. Cultural diversity involves variations on a theme. Consider kinship structures, family organization, and norms about kin relations and non-kin relations. While these themes appear in tremendous variety across cultures and time, we know of no culture without some version of them. While humans construct these patterns in many different forms, they never construct a culture and community without any forms whatsoever. There are no cultures without patterns of kin relationships or patterns that regulate the relationship between clan and non-clan.

While the *capacity* and even motivation to acquire norms might be invariant across human populations, variations in normative *content* are not informed by evolutionary biology. The content of most if not all norms is cultural. Like all cultural phenomena, they tend to vary significantly within one community and even more so across communities. To understand the distinction between capacity and content, one might first analogize *what is learned* to computer software and programming, and then analogize the learner's brain to computer *hardware*. Programming here corresponds to socially learned behavior while hardware corresponds to genetically determined behavior. In terms of my example, the phrase *what is learned* refers to a particular culture's kinship structures, family organization, and norms about kin and non-kin relations. The term *hardware* refers to any genetic bases for the patterns of which any particular culture creates its own variations.[16]

Robin Dunbar's work (2014, 2016), which stresses the cognitive springs of much of human behavior, provides support to my idea that human nature is something learned. Politically and ethically relevant incentives, sanctions, and persuasion are forms of learning. And social learning – including learning by enculturation during childhood and throughout the life course – is cognitive.[17] In terms of culture, we humans *are* our socialization.

[15] Perhaps given some kind of bottleneck in evolutionary history?

[16] This (very rough) analogy reifies software and hardware as different in kind. By contrast, learning, cultural patterns, and human brains may be different levels of the same system (Dunbar 2016).

[17] Further, the experience of persuasion by good arguments finds biological reinforcement in the individual's endorphin system. That system may reinforce conforming behavior inasmuch as it can foster a sense of belonging to the community: for example, grooming among primates or religious rituals practiced in human communities.

Proposition 2. A political conception of human nature can guide some norming of human behavior. Human nature can be normed by any number and kind of ideas, of course. Hence Proposition 2 is unique only with respect to the *nature* of the norming idea: a specifically political conception of human nature, namely human nature as social construct and political tool. This notion of human nature (a) involves biological and cultural coevolution and (b) regards human nature as a social construct and as a political tool.

(a) Some forms of human nature-essentialism regard human traits as a product solely of evolution, without interplay of genes and their various environments, hence without exchanges between factors internal to the organism and social factors.[18] Against this view, I emphasize that all aspects of the human being are products of complex interactions between genes and their various environments, natural and man-made. Development of the human genome always involves internal and external factors – factors genetic as well as factors socially constructed – so much so that these factors often appear to be woven together.

Human nature so conceived is not a static essence with innate properties. It derives from a dynamic relationship between biology and culture. That relationship can be modeled in various ways. For example, changes in ecologies affect patterns, foci, and intensity of natural selection, which in turn affect ecological inheritance. Here I refer to the well-known niche construction model, according to which organisms influence their local ecologies and consequently their evolutionary trajectories. Organisms are shaped by their ecologies even as they shape their ecologies. According to the gene-culture coevolution model, also well known, human biology and human culture influence one another reciprocally. In both models, human agency is itself a source of variation in human genetics and in human culture. Variation is a significant means of evolutionary change just as cultural variation is a means of cultural change. Both human biology and human culture transfer phenotypic variations from one generation to the next (Jablonka and Lamb 2005).

A political alternative to essentialism in human nature, and a political alternative to essentialism in human rights, relies on the fact that variation can be constructed whereas essentialist accounts are static and involve no human agency. According to Kevin Laland and colleagues (Laland et al. 2014: 162), evolutionary processes involve more than just genetic material: "organisms are constructed in development, not simply 'programmed' to develop by genes. Living things do not evolve to fit into pre-existing environments, but co-construct and coevolve with their environments, in the process changing the structure of ecosystems" (ibid.). Here we have a fifth feature of a political approach.

[18] Wilson (2012) argues that human nature is strongly innate and entirely biological.

(b) A political notion of human nature gives primacy to cultural adaptation over biological adaptation. I draw on Francisco Ayala (2012) to argue that the human species adapts itself to its environments in ways not primarily biological but rather cultural. This political notion of human nature also finds support in Peter Richerson and Robert Boyd's (2008) characterization of humankind as a cultural species: it accomplishes most of its tasks in communal and individual life by means of cultural learning. This is a sixth feature of a political approach.

To be sure, cultural evolution is only possible given human intelligence, itself a biological phenomenon affected by cultural phenomena in the individual's environments. Humans adapt themselves to their environments by means of their intelligence, particularly in the form of teaching and learning.

I use the terms *teaching* and *learning* in the encompassing sense of behaviors designed to pass on information in ways that recipients can interpret, modify, build upon, reject, extend, and so forth. Teaching and learning are forms of human agency that are plastic and context-dependent. The evolved capacity to teach and learn is related to the plasticity or malleability in outcomes of human development.[19]

The capacity to teach and learn may have coevolved with some kind of biologically based "capacity for culture." Culture accumulates and expands the possible contexts of learning, generally increasing people's survival chances over what those chances might be if the collective store of knowledge teachable across generations were not available.

Cultural adaptation is possible at a pace tremendously more rapid than that of biological adaptations to the natural environment. And while the rate of biological adaptation may be more or less constant, the rate of cultural adaptation continues to accelerate over time. At any given time, the largest part of human adaptation is not biological, by means of natural selection, but rather cultural, by means of social construction.

3.3 CRITIQUE OF HUMAN RIGHTS-ESSENTIALISM

The human rights project[20] makes normative claims about the ethical treatment of individuals and groups. Most versions of human rights theory claim universal validity for themselves. Some invoke one or the other notion of a universal

[19] Evolutionary biology suggests that plasticity may be universal even as it is higher among vertebrates than invertebrates, and higher among large-brained animals than small-brained-ones.

[20] By the term *human rights project*, I refer to social, political, philosophical, and legal movements to advance human-rights thinking and practice as widely and deeply as possible. In that quest, the project contributes to broader social movements seeking to limit government and to restrain state sovereignty (by means of liberal constitutions and bills of rights, or by opposing racism, sexism, torture, and genocide).

human nature as the normative foundation for human rights. A universal nature so understood is an essence, as we see for example in the United Nations 1948 *Universal Declaration of Human Rights*. It grounds human rights in a human individual's "inherent dignity" where "dignity" functions as a trait of human nature.[21]

Some forms of human rights-essentialism source human rights in human biology. Human rights so conceived use biological traits such as "potentiality, life, sentience, consciousness, self-consciousness" to "establish our basic universal entitlements" (Cochrane 2012: 310). The philosopher Francis Fukuyama (2002: 172) does just that: "We do not want to disrupt either the unity or the continuity of human nature, and thereby the human rights that are based on it."

Other forms of human rights-essentialism ground human rights in various capacities such as rational and moral agency (Griffin 2008; Gewirth 1982); in particular capabilities (Nussbaum 1997); in a set of shared basic interests (Tasioulas 2010); or in kinds of vulnerability regarded as peculiarly human (Turner 1993).

Human rights-essentialism is vulnerable on multiple fronts. Consider the linked claims that some human capacities (language use, for example) may be "natural" and that they may be universally present in the species. These two claims do not entail a fixed human nature. Nor do they entail the moral status of those features. Even if one argued that moral capacity requires certain biological characteristics (such as a nervous system, sentience, cognition, and self-consciousness), one would still have to show that these characteristics have a moral status. No one has ever shown as much. And entitlement to human rights can hardly follow from biological traits that have no moral status.

Consider now a different form of human rights-essentialism, one that sources human rights in some kind of universal anthropology. In the face of cultural difference, this form of essentialism posits an underlying identity of all humans, however diverse their different enculturations. Cultural anthropology defeats this claim to an underlying anthropological identity inasmuch as it has never found underlying cultural elements universally present.

This result resonates with the institutionalized discipline's rejection of another form of essentialism I examine below: human rights-essentialism. From an anthropological perspective, human rights are an example of historically contingent normative culture. Cultural anthropology is a science of differences (even as it periodically faces external, political imperatives to stress what is shared across cultural differences).[22] As the United Nations drafted its human

[21] Universal Declaration of Human Rights, adopted 10 Dec. 1948, G.A. Res. 217A (III), U.N. GAOR, 3d Sess., U.N. Doc. A/RES/3/217A (1948).

[22] By saying that even *as it periodically faces external, political imperatives to stress what is shared across cultural differences*, I mean: fifty years later the AAA officially embraced the idea of human rights, finding the idea compatible with "anthropological principles of respect for concrete human differences, both collective and individual, rather than the abstract legal

rights declaration in 1947, the American Anthropological Association (AAA) – dedicated to the study of profound and enduring cultural difference – disputed the notion of rights valid across all cultural boundaries – even as many cultures overlap at points, and even as all cultures are hybrids to various extents. The AAA sought to discourage the drafting committee accordingly, querying the UN Human Rights Commission that drafted the Universal Declaration: "How can the proposed Declaration be applicable to all human beings and not be a statement of rights conceived only in terms of values prevalent in the countries of Western Europe and America?" For "what is held to be a human right in one society may be regarded as anti-social by another people, or by the same people in a different period of their history" (AAA 1947: 539, 542). In short, a rights claim is a cultural claim because all rights, including human rights, are cultural artifacts. As cultural artifacts, rights are valid only for the cultures that adopt them. They are contingent preferences with no necessary dimensions.

3.4 ALTERNATIVE: A POLITICAL NOTION OF HUMAN RIGHTS

Human rights-essentialism "entails that rights exist prior to membership in a community" and, in many versions, that human rights are "located in human nature, either human nature as such or in a characteristic or power ... thought to be essential to a human being" (Parekh 2007: 773). A political grounding of human rights offers an alternative to human rights-essentialism with respect to notions of both human nature and human rights.

A political approach is, first of all, pragmatic. This is a seventh feature of a political approach. Pragmatism is a belief system in which belief is not so much truth guided as behavior guiding.[23] Such an approach rejects human rights-essentialism to argue that human rights are not valid a priori or independent of membership in political community. They are constructed within political

uniformity of Western tradition." AAA, *Declaration on Anthropology and Human Rights, Committee for Human Rights*, (1999), www.aaanet.org/stmts/humanrts.htm. AAA's 1999 statement coheres with its 1947 statement: it maintains that irreducible cultural differences exist no less than tensions between such differences and the uniformity of any system of normative rules (including human rights). But now the AAA argued that human rights norms can be reconciled with irreducible cultural differences among different communities. Tellingly, it neglected to say just how. Likely it was unable to say just how; on this point, political imperatives "colonized" the discipline.

[23] The notion of belief as primarily action guiding derives from Peirce (1986: 21). He asserts, for example, that "Conviction determines us to act in a particular way." From Dewey (1981: 128) comes the search for valid propositions as an attempt at practical problem solving: "this is the meaning of truth: processes of change so directed that they achieve an intended consummation." Equally pragmatic is the spirit of Marx's (1998: 21) eleventh thesis on Feuerbach, the claim that philosophers have always only interpreted the world in various ways but that what matters is to improve it. The pragmatist understanding is distinct from Marx's in that it dispenses with the self that Marx elsewhere construes metaphysically. Resonant with pragmatism is Marx's emphasis on human agency.

community and are possible only within it, as decisions rather than propositions that can be shown to be true or false. Hence there are no legal (or other) rights outside of, or antecedent to, political community.

To be sure, one can always speak of a right aspirationally, in the sense of advocating for a right that does not yet exist. As Beth Singer (1999: 8) says, "Saying that 'there is' such a law states an ideal, which, rather than being a fact, sets up a standard for human society." But for a right to obtain in fact, it must be "operative in a community" (Parekh 2007: 772). Like positive rights, human rights are a social phenomenon. They are notions of the moral possibilities of human community and of the moral "requirements of social interaction" (Singer 1999: 34). They are norms of rightful behavior between and among persons and groups. And as social constructs, they are historically contingent, vary from locale to locale, change over time, and can be acquired only through learning.

Within any given political community, what resources offer themselves for developing human rights thinking and practice within and beyond it? The ascription of human rights to individuals is most plausible locally (Gregg 2012a, 2016a). Ascription can then expand from local venues outwards, to overlap with other local venues. The motivation to expand human rights ascription derives from normative convictions about standards of human behavior toward other humans. Human rights will appear necessary to anyone persuaded of their normative validity; they will appear necessary to anyone persuaded that local and extra-local conditions violate them.[24]

3.5 CONCLUSION: A POLITICAL NOTION OF HUMAN NATURE ORIENTED ON A POLITICAL NOTION OF HUMAN RIGHTS OFFERS A NORMATIVE STANDARD OF POTENTIALLY WIDE EMBRACE

A widely plausible notion of human nature might allow political communities to characterize humans as a homogeneous group, not only because of evolution but also because of a cultural commitment to human rights. This notion of human homogeneity, along dimensions both biological and cultural, offers a basis for the legal regulation of human genetic engineering. And the widest possible agreement on appropriate standards for regulation would be facilitated by (a) a common understanding of both human rights and the moral status of human beings compatible with a naturalistic understanding of the species; (b) an understanding of human nature as a matter of degree; (c) an embrace of

[24] The only configuration in which one could speak descriptively of "universal human rights" would be the community of all members of the species. Such a community is not political but biological and, as such, not itself a carrier of rights (which are grants of political, not biological community).

morally relevant capacities, not human biology, as the basis for human rights; and (d) a primarily cultural approach to constructing a human rights-oriented human nature.

(a) A widely embraced understanding – consensus across national borders – of both human rights and the moral status of human beings would aid international legal regulation of human genetic manipulation. Such a common understanding is possible, even if only problematically, by emphasizing legal norms that do not contradict a naturalistic understanding of the human species. Such an understanding operates with biological data but cannot be reduced to those data. That is, human biology does not yield a notion of universal human nature. This recognition offers a political advantage: norms based on a naturalistic approach to the human species need not be deeply embedded in particular ways of life. As such, these norms can be generalized across national borders, sometimes in the form of human rights.

From a naturalistic standpoint, normative claims are human artefacts, products of human imagination, embedded in particular cultural visions. Norms so understood replace human nature as a metaphysical essence with a naturalistic understanding of the human species. This view contradicts no claim of natural science or medicine. In this way, the international legal regulation of human genetic engineering might become more plausible than it currently is, because different political communities would then have means of agreement on defining both benefits and adverse consequences of genetic intervention. The political challenge is to facilitate a wide popular embrace, beyond elites.

(b) While most human traits are homologous to traits found in other species, humans display some traits that appear to be unique to our species, such as sophisticated speech, upright posture, great intelligence, dexterous hands, and a childhood of long duration. But how could traits peculiar to humans entail some essential human nature? The fact that only humans possess them cannot, of itself, render them an essence.[25]

The interest of some biologists, psychologists, and anthropologists in possibly uniquely human traits is not an interest in abilities that only humans possess. It is an interest in the capacities that make those abilities possible, above all a capacity for higher-level reasoning rather than, for example, a capacity for extraordinary sight, hearing, or sense of smell. Even in this respect, the difference between humans and other animals is not absolute; it is a matter of degree. Intelligence is something humans have in greater measure than other animals but not in distinction to them. Even a capacity that humans have in unique measure remains a matter of the degree in which the capacity is

[25] Compare Tomasello (2009) on distinctions between human and nonhuman animals.

possessed. If one calls such a capacity *human nature*, then human nature cannot be something absolute. It can only be a matter of degree. By contrast, the notion of essence is usually binary: it is either present or absent, not *present to some degree*.

(c) If human nature changes over time, both naturally and through human intervention (through biotechnology, for example), then the conditions for *what it is to be human* must also change over time. One might argue, for example, that human rights reflect a widespread contemporary understanding of what it means to be a human being: an animal that has developed normative categories with which it can persuade itself that all members are equally deserving of inclusion in standards of, say, medical care and treatment. This would not have been an understanding 200,000 or 300,000 years ago when *Homo sapiens sapiens* emerged as a distinct species. After all, the cultural resources for the kind of normative thought leading to the human rights idea might not have been possible much before 10,000 years ago, when the move from hunter-gatherer communities to settled agricultural ones allowed, materially, for the development of higher culture, such as sophisticated normative thinking, its transmission, and its institutionalization, magnifying its scope and power across generations.

Our species in the future will in some ways differ from what it is today. As various aspects of human life change, so, too, does the species. Any species endures only if it changes: only if it is resilient and adaptable with respect to its changing environments. Perhaps the cultural diversity among humans nonetheless rests on patterns that are resilient, in this respect contributing to the profound ways in which human beings are interestingly similar.

This conclusion is compatible with viewing morally relevant capacities, not human biology, as the basis for human rights. Those capacities are the products of cultural influences, not biological adaptations for survival and reproduction. Nor are they products of natural selection, biological determinism, or adaptationism.[26] They can be explained social scientifically at the level of cultures, institutions, and individual motivations.[27]

(d) The primary practical challenge of constructing a human rights-oriented human nature is cultural. It is a matter of constructing a particular self-understanding of the species: human rights as an aspect of species identity. Particular political communities might claim that their members

[26] The view that natural selection is the most central cause of evolutionary change.

[27] Human rights are not necessary in the sense that essentialism maintains; rather, they are one more idea that can contribute to human flourishing. This fact defeats Parekh's (2007: 774) claim that "Explaining why human rights are necessary is a limitation of all the non-foundationalist thinkers."

enjoy human rights as a matter of their human nature. Groups inside and outside political communities might someday claim the same thing. But what are the prospects for the idea that, someday, all political communities might reach consensus on a human rights-oriented human nature? According to Claude Lévi-Strauss (1983: 329), a

> concept of an all-inclusive humanity [that makes] no distinction between races or cultures [appeared only] very late in the history of mankind and did not spread very widely across the face of the globe . . . For the majority of the human species, and for tens of thousands of years, the idea that humanity includes every human being on the face of the earth does not exist at all. The designation stops at the border of each tribe, or linguistic group, sometimes even at the edge of a village. So common is the practice that many of the peoples we call primitive call themselves by a name which means "men"; [in other words, they claim that the] other tribes, groups, and villages do not partake in human virtue or even human nature.

While more or less all political communities today appear ready to recognize all "tribes" as members of *Homo sapiens sapiens*, none recognizes what I propose as a human rights-oriented human nature. In distinction to the claims of modern biology, that notion is peculiarly cultural (in Lévi-Strauss's sense).[28]

The task, then, is cultural – as is the solution. *Cultural* is *the social construction of human nature*, such as conceiving of the species as homogenous (that is, the same species distributed across different cultures over long periods of time); as more or less globally invariant along some dimensions (such as behavioral patterns of social interactions or language use); and as homogenous due to its evolution (what humans have in common *because* they are products of the same evolutionary processes). Also *cultural* is *the construction of human rights*: a human rights-oriented notion of human nature leads to human rights socially constructed to regard all human individuals as morally equal and as deserving of the same high moral regard and treatment.

A human rights-oriented notion of human nature is then political as a matter of self-consciously normative agency toward group self-determination: oriented on generating normative agreement in the public sphere; aligned with central normative aspirations of political community; self-constituting this normative vision in self-conscious ways; self-constituting along the dimensions of human nature as social construct and political tool; conscious of how humans co-construct and coevolve with their environments; conscious of how co-construction and coevolution are heavily cultural; and pragmatic, that is, less truth oriented than behavior oriented.

This chapter developed a non-essentialist theory of human rights that links a political notion of human rights with a political conception of human nature.

[28] After all, the human genome is more than 95 percent identical with that of the chimpanzee; further, each individual human's genome is 99.9 percent identical with that of every other human.

If adopted by participants as a presupposition in debates on the legal and social regulation of human genetic engineering, it could provide a basis for regulation wider than what alternative bases might provide. The next chapter develops the anti-essentialist approach of political bioethics further. It proposes the idea of dignity as a future person's decisional autonomy, held in trust by the current generation. This regulatory principle draws on the idea of a child's right to respect for its best interests to show that the future person's dignity is not necessarily violated by the genetic modification of the embryo from which she developed.

4

Regulation Guided by Human Dignity as Decisional Autonomy, Not Essence

We humans *have* bodies in a biological sense. By contrast, we *are* our bodies in the cultural context of how, normatively, we collectively regard our own bodies and the bodies of others. The biological is given; the cultural, socially constructed. With the rapidly increasing capacity to manipulate future bodies genetically, toward influencing some traits of future bodies, the distinction between nature and culture weakens but hardly vanishes. To be sure, the sphere of human nature has always shared a porous boundary with human culture. Consider several examples of how humans construct culture. Disease, pathology, and medicine have more to do with nature than culture – but they are not culture-free. Another example: "human nature" with respect to what is "normal," what is "illness," what is "harm," and what constitutes a physical disease or cognitive illness, involves elements both natural and cultural. A third example: notions of human freedom, equality, and rights have mostly to do with culture – but they are not nature-free.

My concern is with genetically based congenital diseases. Here, too, nature and culture are porous vis-à-vis one another. Medical practice works with a naturalistic conception of disease, defined as a pathology whereby a particular bodily system departs from "natural functioning" with adverse consequences for the individual. Even this naturalistic conception has a cultural element: the evaluation of a particular, natural, biological process as harmful.

Disease so understood is neither wholly empirical nor wholly normative (whereby I understand all social and moral norms to be social constructs).[1]

[1] I distinguish my concern with genetic disease from another category of concern, genetic disability. While the categories may overlap in the case of genetically based disabilities, genetic disability – in its complexity along social dimensions – cannot be reduced to genetic disease and merits separate treatment. Consider possible differences in standpoint between observers and disabled persons with respect to whether a particular disability degrades the individual's life significantly enough to

To the extent that abnormal functioning can be identified by science, it is something objective. To the extent that humans frame the abnormality as adverse – because resulting for example in the individual's diminished well-being – the term *disease* has a normative, hence inter-subjective component even as the phenomenon itself is objective. In other words, a biological abnormality may have consequences for the individual's life that human communities define in value-laden ways (for example, as something "bad" for the person). At an extreme, if humans understand a particular biological process to be harmful to its carrier, the process may then be understood to be dysfunctional (much in the way that human communities classify some flora as "weeds" and some animals as "vermin"). What humans regard as the negative quality of biological processes, and call *disease*, may in fact be a quality identified by human values, not natural scientific observation. Here, human interests (value judgements) frame natural phenomena in cultural ways.[2]

Thus the claim that abnormal functioning is not in the individual's best interest, that it degrades her potential well-being, that a particular bodily process is harming her in a particular way, is normative not natural. Such a claim does not require a notion of "human nature" but in fact is often accompanied by some such notion. Any notion of human nature can only be a culturally particular conception, such as the "genetic essentialism" that I analyze in later pages as a particular notion of human dignity.

I examine nature/culture porosity with respect to human genetics. The technical capacity to manipulate the human genome renders all the more porous the dichotomous quality of being human, that is, being an evolved organism with a capacity to socially construct aspects of its environment as well as itself. The back-and-forth flow between human biology and cultural norms increases as the *physical object* of genetic alterations intersects with cultural constructions of the *normative acceptability* of such alterations. At that intersection, a question poses itself: How might human genetic engineering

recommend genetic engineering toward preventing that disability in future persons. Kahane and Savulescu (2016: 774) argue that "disabilities such as deafness, blindness, paraplegia, and severe intellectual impairment are harmful and have a significant overall negative impact on a person's life." They conclude that "prospective parents have ... reason to prefer to create an able-bodied- ... child rather than a disabled one" (ibid., 775). Barnes (2014: 89), by contrast, argues that some adults with disabilities claim that these conditions are not globally bad and that they would not choose not to have them: "having a disability makes you nonstandard or different, but it doesn't by itself make you worse off." There is no comparable debate with respect to genetic disease.

[2] Glackin (2019: 260–262) distinguishes the question about the objective, physical basis of an individual's bodily condition from the question of why a particular bodily state is properly judged to be diseased. The framing of a particular corporal condition as diseased is the normative framing of an empirical phenomenon. For example, aging is a normal feature of organic life. That most elderly persons, but not most young persons, are frail, is hardly a disease. By contrast, Hutchinson–Gilford progeria syndrome is a disease: an incurable, randomly occurring genetic mutation that leads to a bizarrely rapid rate of senescence (such as slow growth and hair loss), beginning in the first year or two of a child's life and usually leading to death by age 17.

best be regulated? The question is vexed. On the one hand, some forms of genetic manipulation may eliminate, in human embryos, some genes that cause some diseases. On the other, the idea of rendering species biology fungible to human design is an abiding source of unease.

Consider CRISPR-Cas9,[3] one of the most powerful forms of genome editing technologies, possibly even a "magic bullet for generating customized gene and cell therapies, more targeted treatments" and maybe even for "direct editing out of disease-causing genes in human embryos" (Jasanoff et al. 2015: 28). It modifies an organism's genetic code by editing the order of DNA sequences, "adding, deleting, or altering genetic material at a particular location in its genome" (Alta Charo 2018: 344).

Political communities in coming years face the challenges of responding to issues raised by CRISPR and other forms of genetic manipulation. They confront difficult moral, legal, and political questions such as: Could genetic manipulation emancipate humanity from genetic disease – or might genetically modified persons be robbed of individual autonomy and personal freedom by the modifiers and thus rendered captives of others' preferences? What rights might be legislated to allow or disallow various forms of genetic editing? Should parents have a legal right to determine what, in their opinion, would be the "best" genetic inheritance for the lives of their future children? Or does a person not yet born, a future person, have a legal right to be free of irreversible genetic enhancement desired by her parents?

Normative questions demand normative answers; natural science cannot answer them. The widely deployed but often undefined term *human dignity* offers itself as one kind of normative answer. As I will show, it offers – at least from a consequentialist standpoint – a peculiarly political route to thinking critically about possible legal regulations of human genetic engineering: as the individual's decisional autonomy. But the term offers as much only if it can be defined in a way that is culturally plausible and does not contradict a naturalistic understanding of our species (hence one that does not contradict modern medical practice). Such a definition would capture the porosity of human culture and human nature. It would find expression in the human species taking increasing measures of control over its own evolution.

The notion of decisional autonomy might seem implausible in the context of human embryos at the point of genetic engineering, when there is no person present who could exercise autonomy through participation in deliberation about the problems and prospects of genetic manipulation. Here there is no person who could veto the planned manipulation of the embryo from which the future person will develop. Only when the future person becomes a current person is decisional autonomy present. But at that point she can only react to a

[3] Clustered regularly interspaced short palindromic repeats.

fait accompli – to her having been genetically modified – with no means to reverse it.

I draw on the idea of a child's right to respect for its best interests to show that the future person's dignity is not violated by the genetic modification of the embryo from which she developed. While the principle of the child's best interest does not engage the autonomy of the child itself, the child's circumstances are analogous in some ways to the future person: one day both will have interests that current persons, in deciding matters of genetic manipulation, should take into consideration today. They should consider how the planned genetic modification might serve the future person's future interests. Recognizing those interests *today* offers a placeholder for her *future* autonomy. Genetic manipulation of the embryo is like preventive medicine in that it can serve the future person's future autonomy.

I propose a way out of this political aporia in six steps. (§4.1) I begin by analyzing the notion of the human genome as invested with a moral status, which leads to genetic essentialism. (§4.2) I show that a critique of genetic essentialism is hardly a strawman and (§4.3) argue against defining human rights in terms of genetic essentialism. (§4.4) I develop an alternative to genetic essentialism: dignity as a future person's decisional autonomy, held in trust by the current generation. (§4.5) I articulate a future person's interest in decisional autonomy and (§4.6) sketch a form of deliberation, within political community, toward principled agreement on how the decisional autonomy of future persons might be configured at the point of genetically engineering the embryo from which that future person will develop. I conclude that a consequentialist notion of human dignity as the future person's decisional autonomy provides a plausible regulatory principle.

4.1 THE HUMAN GENOME INVESTED WITH AN INHERENT MORAL STATUS

Human biology and cultural norms sometimes intersect in the politics of health even as the respective spheres of health and politics pursue distinctly different objectives. (a) Health norms seek a path from illness to health whereas (b) political norms offer ways to evaluate that path in terms of socially constructed norms.

(a) If successful, human germline gene editing may offer heritable "therapeutic treatments of genetic disorders" (Kang et al. 2016). From a standpoint of health, the benefits of genetic "information manipulation" extend far beyond the "prevention of monogenic diseases" and "personalized assisted reproductive technology" (Ishii 2017: 46). Consider several examples.

- Some analysts regard gene editing as a "reliable molecular toolbox" (Bayat et al. 2018: 107) to "precisely alter genomes for numerous applications" (Batzir et al. 2017): from basic research to clinical application, and from developing "animal models for genetic disorders" to "gene therapy to combat virus infectious diseases," and even to "correct monogenic disorders in vivo or in pluripotent cells" (Huang et al. 2017: 3875).

- Germline genome editing in human embryos can program cells "for diverse applications, including regenerative medicine and cancer immunotherapy" (Ho and Chen 2017: 57).
- It can prevent parents' giving serious genetic diseases to their offspring (Ishii 2017: 418). It can correct "mutations in patient cells," and unique gene therapies can screen causative mutations and identify "rare genetic disorders and non-exonic mutation-caused diseases" (Miyamoto et al. 2018: 133).
- It can enhance the "efficacy of genome editing in the early embryo" and enable the "generation of allele types previously incompatible with in vivo mutagenesis" (Mianné et al. 2017: 68).
- Personalized, molecular surgeries on "genetic DNA directly target the cause of the disease in a personalized and possibly permanent manner"; they "could be combined with traditional surgery, radiation therapy, or chemo/targeted therapy" (Tang and Schrager 2016: 83).
- By "replacing the mutation-carrying mitochondria of zygotes or oocytes at risk with donated unaffected counterparts," germline genome editing in human embryos may prevent a "broad range of incurable inborn maladies" caused by mutant mitochondrial DNA (Adashi and Cohen 2018). While "no curative treatment for patients with mitochondrial disease" exists, germline gene replacement therapy (unlike prenatal and preimplantation diagnosis) may someday prevent transmission of mitochondrial disease (Amato et al. 2014).
- Germline genome editing in human embryos promises a future when cardiovascular diseases could be "cured by administering a cocktail of CRISPR/Cas9 based therapeutic agents, which functions like a vaccination rather than medications that have to be taken daily" (Li et al. 2016: 193).

(b) Now consider a relevant political standpoint: the view that germline manipulation seeks to reduce genetic chance by changing, genetically, unwanted outcomes of the gene pool "lottery" or by precluding such outcomes in the first place, thus "rewrit[ing] the gene pool of future generations" (Cyranoski 2019: 440). By reducing the degree to which humans are chance products of sexual reproduction, germline manipulation increases the degree to which the engineers – but neither the engineered nor their descendants – exercise some choice over some of the genetic traits of future human beings.

An array of prominent international documents (as well as various ethicists and some scientists) adopt a political viewpoint in claiming that genetic modification harms the future person in her dignity.[4] For example, the International Bioethics Committee's 2015 "Report of the IBC on Updating Its Reflection on the Human Genome and Human Rights" claims that manipulation would "jeopardize the inherent and therefore equal dignity of all human beings" (para. 107).[5] And the 1997 *Convention for the Protection of and Dignity of the Human Being with regard to the Application of Biology and Medicine* (hereafter the *Oviedo Convention*)[6] states that the abuse of human germline genetic engineering "may endanger not only the individual but also the species itself" (art. 13). Its preamble identifies a "need to respect the human being both as an individual and as a member of the human species" and to recognize the "importance of ensuring the dignity of the human being."

These various instruments practice what I call "genetic essentialism." It is counterintuitive from a naturalistic standpoint: it does not accord with the mundane structure of evolved life such as the "basic categories of our 'intuitive ontology' (i.e., the ontology of our semantic system), such as person, animal, plant, and substance" (Atran and Henrich 2010: 20). Genetic essentialism is rather a kind of folk biology; it construes our species teleologically. It depicts an evolved life form as an otherworldly essence that entails human dignity. The notion of human dignity often functions in international instruments as a regulative principle for biotechnological manipulation. Even as the notion violates our intuitive ontology, it authenticates what adherents regard as the peculiar moral status of our species. For adherents, the authority of the notion shields it from the kind of logical or empirical scrutiny that a naturalistic standpoint perpetually faces as a matter of its self-understanding as a scholarly enterprise.

The notion of genetic essentialism is the idea that human germline identity constitutes a *cultural* sharedness on the basis of *genetic* sharedness. According to the *Universal Declaration of Human Rights*, species membership *as such* somehow *unifies* all individual members in a genetic essentialist identity. It claims that, "in a symbolic sense," the human genome is the "heritage of humanity" (art. 1). It urges protection of the human genome's purported moral status – by not allowing its manipulation – as a matter of preserving human dignity. Similarly, the International Bioethics Committee asserts that the human genome is "one of the premises of freedom itself" and not simply "raw material to manipulate at leisure" (para. 128). Finally, the U.S. President's Council on Bioethics (2002: 100) rejects human genetic engineering by moralizing natural

[4] One notable exception: the Nuffield Council on Bioethics (2018: 93–94) rejects the notion of dignity, in light of its abiding indeterminacy in meaning, as the guiding principle for regulating human genome editing.

[5] https://unesdoc.unesco.org/ark:/48223/pf0000233258.

[6] The first legally binding international instrument regulating biomedicine; it binds some European countries.

reproduction: "a begotten child comes into the world just as its parents once did, and is therefore their equal in dignity and humanity."

4.2 A CRITIQUE OF GENETIC ESSENTIALISM IS NO STRAWMAN

Before pursuing my analysis of dignity in Section 4.3, I pause to establish that a critique of genetic essentialism today is hardly a strawman. Even though (a) genetic essentialism is mistaken, (b) it is still widespread and (c) can be dangerous socially, politically, and institutionally.

(a) Human genetic essentialism is genetically inaccurate in misconstruing genes as a mechanism of causation along several dimensions. First, it involves reductionism and determinism, obscuring non-genetic factors – including human culture – of human experience and behavior. Second, it misconstrues patterns of human genetic variation by ignoring multifactorial genetics and population thinking, which studies the very small percentage of the human genome containing all genetic differences between any two persons (a mere 0.1 percent).[7] While genetic essentialism predicts greater variation between any two human groups than within any single group, population thinking demonstrates greater variation within any particular group than among different groups.[8] Third, it does not account for how complex human traits, such as intelligence, are responsive to and conditioned by natural, social, and cultural environments.[9] Fourth, it misconstrues genetic heritability as an absolute value when, in fact, biological traits result from the entwined vectors of genes, environment, and contingency. Heritability cannot be generalized as a measurable value for all humans (that is, one cannot say that some percentage of a particular trait is determined genetically and the rest, environmentally). Further, specific populations inherit certain traits under specific circumstances.

(b) Most biologists and philosophers of biology reject an *intrinsic form* of genetic essentialism, if by the term *essentialism* we mean something like, "in virtue of what an organism is a member of a certain Linnaean taxon; the issue of what makes an organism a member of that taxon; the issue of the very nature of the taxon" (Devitt 2008: 347–348). Consider a sampling of opinion: the "vain search for the undiscovered and undiscoverable essence of the term species" (Darwin 2004: 381); "essentialism about species is today a dead issue" (Sober 1992: 249); the "proponents of contemporary species definitions are all agreed that species have no essence" (Rosenberg 1985: 203); "folk essentialism is both false and fundamentally inconsistent with the Darwinian view of species" (Griffiths 2002: 72); "no intrinsic genotypic or phenotypic property is

[7] See Rosenberg (2011). [8] See Lewontin (1972). [9] See Bratsberg and Rogeberg (2018).

essential to being a member of a species" (Sterelny and Griffiths 1999: 186); "biologists and philosophers of biology typically regard essentialism about species as incompatible with modern Darwinian theory" (Okasha 2002: 191); "it is widely recognized that Darwin's theory of evolution rendered untenable the classical essentialist conception of species" (Dupré 1999: 3).

Yet many scholars are persuaded of a *relational form* of genetic essentialism: species are "associated with no nonrelational real essence" (Matthen 1998: 115); the "essential properties that make a particular organism a platypus ... are historical or relational" (Sterelny and Griffiths 1999: 186); "on all modern species concepts ... the property in virtue of which a particular organism belongs to one species rather than another is a relational rather than an intrinsic property of the organism" (Okasha 2002: 201); there is "close to a consensus in thinking that species are identified by their histories" (Sterelny and Griffiths 1999: 8); "two organisms are conspecific in virtue of their historical connection to each other, not in virtue of their similarity" (Sober 1993: 150); "if species are interpreted as historical entities, then particular organisms belong in a particular species because they are part of that genealogical nexus, not because they possess any essential traits. No species has an essence in this sense" (Hull 1992: 313).[10]

(c) Evidently belief in genetic essentialism is widespread among laypersons.[11] Heine and colleagues (2019: S20) offer one theory:

> People's lay understanding of genes shares many features in common with their intuitions about essences. Like essences, an individual's genes are present at birth, and despite the huge physical and psychological transformations that occur across one's lifetime, they remain stable and largely unchanged throughout their lives. An individual's genes are unique to that individual (barring any monozygotic twins), and approximately half of them can be transferred to their offspring.

The idea of an essence offers a strong form of identity. Perhaps genetic essentialism provides its adherents a satisfyingly strong form of human identity.

Essentialist beliefs can render genetic attributions a particularly troubling influence on a person's or a group's perceptions of other persons or groups and may lead to various forms of discriminatory behavior. For example, Nick Haslam and Sheri Levy (2006: 471) found that the "belief that homosexuality is biologically based, immutable, and fixed early in life," that "it is cross-culturally and historically universal," and that "it constitutes a discrete,

[10] One upshot: boundaries between and among different species are fuzzy not sharp. Such biological indeterminacy undermines an essentialism that understands essences as determining category-boundaries: the "very basis of the categories is determined by the essences that underlie them" (Heine et al. 2019: S20).

[11] See Heine (2017).

entitative type with defining features," predicts antigay prejudice "independently of right-wing authoritarianism, social dominance orientation, and political conservatism" and demonstrates that "essentialist beliefs mediate associations between prejudice and gender, ethnicity, and religiosity" (ibid.). According to Francisco Gil-White (2001: 515), when "ethnic actors represent ethnic groups as essentialized 'natural' groups despite the fact that ethnic essences do not exist," they may be drawing on a "mental module that initially evolved to process species level categories" – since "interaction with out-group members is costly because of coordination failure due to different norms between ethnic groups, thinking of ethnic groups as species adaptively promotes interactional discriminations towards the in-group (including endogamy)" (ibid.).

Essentialist belief can lead to various forms of harm, from prejudice and discrimination (Andreychik and Gill, 2015; Ching and Xu, 2018; Morton et al., 2009) to violence and even genocide (Jackson and Depew 2017). It can lead to less overt forms of harm as well. In the form of genetic exceptionalism, it may misguide professionals in genetically informed health care. According to James Evans and Wylie Burke, contemporary medical systems treat a patient's genetically relevant information as immutable (other than nontrivial somatic mutations) and unique, as a powerful identifier and predictor of risks of disease and of responses to medication. For these reasons, some observers discourage the sharing of such information even in clinical settings, for example in the patient's detailed, highly personal medical record. In fact, only in rare, highly penetrant genotypes does genetic risk prediction have a quality distinct from most medical risks; genetics is but one of many disease sources; and it is not more personal than other, non-genetic types of information, from blood pressure to cholesterol level. The more that genetic information becomes useful in medical diagnosis and decision-making, the greater the access health providers should have. Yet essentialist-based genetic exceptionalism in clinical settings makes the patient's genetic information accessible to health providers "in inverse relation to its clinical utility" (Evans and Burke 2008: 500).

4.3 AGAINST DEFINING DIGNITY IN TERMS OF GENETIC ESSENTIALISM

Genetic essentialism "incorporates a static vision of a human genome that contains only 'human' genes that are transmitted vertically from generation to generation" (Alta Charo 2018: 348). It rejects the bioengineering of traits otherwise unusual in humans. It rejects a genetic engineering that would merely widen the distribution of an already existing trait. Even engineering that brought to expression traits heretofore not present in the species would also compromise the "essential" condition of the human individual and species – although "even traits unfamiliar to us as a species may nonetheless be perfectly consistent with our notion of humans" (ibid.).

In this way, genetic essentialism imagines the integrity of the human species identity without reference to its environment and without reference to time.[12]

With regard to environment: a genetic code is not a guideline for constructing a machine; it cannot predict phenotypic results with any accuracy. That is, "you can't read the arrangement of the body's organs in the genome. The information functions as a resource, not a step-by-step guide. To acquire meaning, it must have context: a cell's history and environment. Tracing how the phenotype emerges from interactions of genes with each other and with their environment is the key puzzle of modern genetics" (Ball 2018: 550). Engineering a particular trait in a human embryo does not lead necessarily to the trait's expression (Ma et al. 2017). It can lead to the expression of a trait on the other chromosome, in this way undermining the effort to engineer a child with a particular trait.

With regard to time: Genomes are highly changeable. They are also porous with their (always changing) environments. If *Homo sapiens* were genetically engineered to possess capacities not naturally evolved, they would still be *Homo sapiens*, hence not distant to us in the way that Neanderthals – who were either a different species or a subspecies of our own – are distant to us (even as 1.5–2.1 percent of the non-African human population's genome has been inherited from Neanderthals).

The very idea of the integrity of species identity is misguided because it presupposes a permanent genome. No genome is permanent. A genetic notion of any organism can only be a notion of something that changes over time. Hence a notion of human dignity based on species identity entails somehow suspending the human germline in its current stage of evolution.[13] Like all evolved organisms, humankind was genetically different in the (distant) past; it will be genetically different in the (distant) future. It will be different naturally in addition to ways it might be different because of biotechnological interventions. Genetic essentialism, as the normative foundation for recognizing human dignity by arresting the human genome at its current stage of evolution, leads to the implausible conclusion that random, natural mutations in humans violate human dignity. (This conclusion might lead to another, equally implausible conclusion: that medical institutions should therefore be required to deploy gene editing to edit out those mutations.) Or genetic essentialism might entail that a genetic mutation does not violate human dignity because it changes the genome but rather because the change came about through human intent and agency. Such a conclusion demonizes human agency gratuitously.

Not all elite political instruments that invoke a notion of inherent human dignity presuppose genetic essentialism in this sense. The United Nation's 1998

[12] The claim to being beyond space and time is a feature of essentialism in general.

[13] One wonders: Why this stage rather than any of its past stages or any of its possible future stages?

Universal Declaration on the Human Genome and Human Rights[14] frames the regulation of possible genetic engineering in terms of human dignity, asserting that "practices which are contrary to human dignity, such as reproductive cloning of human beings, shall not be permitted" (art. 11); that "no research or research applications concerning the human genome ... should prevail over respect for the ... human dignity of individuals" (art. 10); and that "practices which are contrary to human dignity, such as reproductive cloning of human beings, shall not be permitted" (art. 11). It also recognizes that the "human genome, which by its nature evolves, is subject to mutations" (art. 3) – an assertion that could serve to justify deliberately altering the human genome, at least within some limits.

Roberto Andorno (2013: 89) identifies several ways in which the *Declaration* pursues a notion of dignity, toward regulating human genetic engineering, without practicing essentialism. He reads the *Declaration*'s claims that the genetic diversity within our species affirms the inherent dignity of all members (preamble), and that the human genome "underlies" the "recognition of their inherent dignity" (art. 1), as invoking the "unity of the human family and the dignity of the human person" *not* as genetic essentialism but rather as "expressions of philosophical ideals that transcend biology" (Andorno 2013: 89). A notion of dignity that *transcends* biology does not claim to *derive* from biology in the manner of genetic essentialism. Hence "human dignity is not the result of a particular combination of DNA, even of a very complex one" (ibid.). Correspondingly, the *Declaration* states that inherent human dignity precludes "reduc[ing] individuals to their genetic characteristics" (art. 2).

In these ways, among others, the *Declaration* differs from other politically prominent texts such as the United Nations' 1948 *Universal Declaration of Human Rights*, as well as from politically prominent organizations such as the International Bioethics Committee and the U.S. President's Council on Bioethics. They attribute human dignity and human rights on the basis of the integrity of human species identity, defined genetically – and not, as Andorno reads the *Universal Declaration on the Human Genome and Human Rights*, symbolically. They invest the human genome with a moral status, treating a biological phenomenon – the genome – as if it were a human artefact. Andorno views the *Declaration* symbolically, as emphasizing the fact that genetic differences among members of the species are negligible from the standpoint of biological identity, or the fact that "each individual inherits the same basic genetic structure of those that preceded him or her" such that "genes are common to all past, present and future generations" (ibid.). Andorno interprets the *Declaration's* appeal to species identity politically. He reads the claim that "everyone has a right to respect for their dignity ... regardless of their genetic characteristics" (art. 2) as a claim that all members of the species are equal in

[14] www.ohchr.org/en/professionalinterest/pages/humangenomeandhumanrights.aspx.

terms of worth and dignity. In that spirit, he extrapolates from the words of the text: the *Declaration's* "principle of equal value of all human beings does not admit any exception due to predisposition to genetic diseases" (Andorno 2013: 90).

Andorno also underlines the non-essentializing quality of the *Declaration* with respect to its discussion of the human genome as a kind of "genetic heritage": "In a symbolic sense," the human genome is the "heritage of humanity" (art. 1). The text incorporates the genome, a biological phenomenon, into human culture in terms of a tradition self-consciously handed down within communities as a matter of cultural identity and, as such, something that might be understood by legal metaphor as a kind of collective property that devolves by a (human) right of inheritance. Future generations then appear to be the (quasi-legal) heirs of the current generation's genome.

In this respect, too, the *Declaration* differs from other international instruments and organizations. For example, the 2014 *European Convention on Human Rights* of the Parliamentary Assembly of the Council of Europe states that the "rights to . . . human dignity protected by . . . the European Convention on human rights imply the right to inherit a genetic pattern which has not been artificially changed" (art. 4).[15] The Parliamentary Assembly contrasts a "natural" genome with one artificially modified. Here human "genetic heritage" is understood not symbolically but biologically. Yet biological heritage (unlike symbolic heritage) is a natural process without normative dimensions.

The documents and institutions that invest the human genome with an inherent moral status thereby project a social construct – moral status – onto a natural phenomenon. They practice genetic essentialism by treating the human genome as a cultural heirloom rather than as the product of natural evolution. Evolution has always included the ways in which the human species can "inscribe" itself into natural history. It does so, for example, by artificially selecting plants and animals to breed new species, to alter its own genetic makeup by consuming, for example, milk from cows and sheep and so favoring humans with a mutation that allows for adult lactose-tolerance. It does so when aspects of a pregnant woman's social, material, and psychological environment influences gene expression in the fetal genome.[16] It does so as it steadily becomes a minor coauthor of some of the earth's geophysical systems, a phenomenon encapsulated in the theory of the Anthropocene.[17] But the assertion by international instruments and organizations of a kind of species' "ownership" of its own genome – ownership in the cultural sense of declaring prohibitions on certain ways of treating it biotechnologically, toward preserving it from objectionable forms of manipulation – essentializes culturally what, after all, is a phenomenon of natural contingency.

[15] https://assembly.coe.int/nw/xml/XRef/Xref-XML2HTML-en.asp?fileid=14968&lang=en.

[16] Chapter 9 discusses this phenomena with regard to epigenetics. [17] See Gregg (2018).

In a third way as well, Andorno reads the *Declaration* in a manner non-essentialist. The *Declaration* notes that the human genome "by its nature evolves" and "is subject to mutations" (art. 3). From this recognition of changes to the human genome that occur in the very long term via mutation, Andorno (2013: 89) finds it "appropriate to consider the human genome as a 'common heritage of humanity' and therefore to protect it from irresponsible manipulations." Heritage so understood entails not the essentialist responsibility to preserve a genome construed as having inherent qualities, but the cultural responsibility of present generations toward future ones in the sense of human stewardship of life on Earth.

The *Declaration* differs from the 1997 *Oviedo Convention*. The *Convention* states that the abuse of human germline genetic engineering "may endanger not only the individual but also the species itself" (art. 13). It declares the "need to respect the human being both as an individual and as a member of the human species" and to recognize the "importance of ensuring the dignity of the human being" (Preamble). According to Robin Alta Charo (2018: 345), the *Oviedo Convention* is the "most salient instrument on human rights in the biomedical field." It connects the notion of a genetically based inherent dignity to a human right of individuals to be free of genetic manipulation.[18]

By means of the essentializing notion of inherent qualities – permanent and inseparable attributes, that is, an essence[19] – it seeks to defend human dignity by prohibiting genetic editing.[20] Even Andorno (2013: 90) is vulnerable at this point to the genetic essentialism of deriving human rights from a notion of human dignity understood as a trait inherent to human beings: "each human being, as a holder of intrinsic dignity, is entitled to inalienable rights, which are the same for all, regardless of their genetic make-up." To remain consistent

18 With regard to the "dignity of the human being," the preamble speaks of the "need to respect the human being both as an individual and as a member of the human species." The 1976 International Covenant on Economic, Social and Cultural Rights (www.ohchr.org/en/professionalinterest/pages/cescr.aspx) cites this sentence in its preamble and then states that "these rights derive from the inherent dignity of the human person."

19 Beyond those I discuss here, other instruments that posit an inherent human dignity include the 1976 *International Covenant of Civil and Political Rights* (www.ohchr.org/en/professionalinterest/pages/ccpr.aspx), the 1981 *Convention on the Elimination of All Forms of Discrimination against Women* (www.ohchr.org/EN/ProfessionalInterest/Pages/CEDAW.aspx), the 1987 *Convention against Torture and Other Cruel, Inhumane, Degrading Treatment or Punishment* (www.ohchr.org/en/professionalinterest/pages/cat.aspx), and the 1989 *Convention on the Rights of the Child* (www.ohchr.org/en/professionalinterest/pages/crc.aspx).

20 The *Convention* thereby confuses changing an individual's genome with changing the germline. De Miguel Beriain (2018: 3) invites us to imagine a "human embryo with mutations of the Huntington gene that will inevitably lead to Huntington's disease if the embryo grows into a human being. If we edit its germline to replace the gene with a normal variant, we will modify the embryo's genome but not the human genome. The ultimate result of the intervention – a human being with a genome that does not show the specific pathological variant that triggers Huntington's disease – will not introduce any novelty into the human gene pool."

with the rest of his reading of the *Universal Declaration on the Human Genome and Human Rights*, he would better view the notion of human dignity symbolically, as a social construct that, as a political tool, can be deployed in the cultural project of advocating equal legal rights for all persons.

4.4 ALTERNATIVE TO GENETIC ESSENTIALISM: DIGNITY AS A FUTURE PERSON'S DECISIONAL AUTONOMY

In place of framing human identity as the human genome (a biological identity), I frame it as human dignity: a socially constructed political identity. I assign a political and legal status to the human genome and then derive, from that status, a human right to dignity.[21] I begin by analyzing dignity.

The international instruments I reviewed above wield the term *human dignity* in ways indeterminate in meaning. Indeterminacy hardly impedes the authors' intention: to legitimize a viewpoint. Their intention is familiar from older debates about a right to physician assisted suicide, a right to privacy, or a right against self-incrimination, where such debates invoke a legitimizing notion of human dignity. Current debates also draw on human dignity to reject human genetic engineering (for example, to support a future person's putative right not to be genetically modified). The term *human dignity* has no rational grounds as long as it remains indeterminate in meaning, and as long as it treats – as intuitively evident or as a first principle of a metaphysical or theological vision about human good – a putative right not to be genetically modified. To render the term rationally useful, its legitimizing function must be grounded in a determinate meaning.

Any particular definition follows from the definer's cognitive interest in defining. Mine is informed by consequentialism, a philosophical position that, while not itself scientific, does not contradict any claims of natural science or a naturalistic understanding of the human being. Consequentialism holds that whether an act is morally right depends only on it consequences, or that those actions are right that render the future world the best possible world. In a consequentialist spirit, I define *dignity* as the individual's decisional autonomy vis-à-vis other persons – such as the autonomy afforded by the right to choose whether and how to be genetically engineered. Autonomy is choice and choice is the "recognizable capacity to assert claims," whereby a person is understood as a "potential maker of claims" (Feinberg 1970: 252–253).

One form of consequentialism is utilitarianism. Utilitarianism advocates one consequence in particular: acts whose consequences maximize the resultant

[21] I also reject the idea that human rights somehow derive from our species' genetic identity and instead view them as social constructs. For deployments of social construction, see Gregg (2012a, 2016a).

good.[22] Good is the defense of a future individual's interest in her decisional autonomy. In this context, only the present generation can defend that interest, and it can do so only if it intervenes in the embryo from which the future person will develop. John Stuart Mill's (1975: 10–11) corresponding principle of individual liberty champions a person's freedom of action (which presupposes the personal decisional autonomy I define as individual dignity). But what if she is not able to take action to avoid a future because she does not yet exist as a person? Her future decisional autonomy, and thereby her dignity, can be secured because she is on a developmental continuum that begins with an embryo that, through genetic engineering, can be manipulated in ways to preclude future health consequences that would rob her of the capacity to exercise decisional autonomy. And while paternalism marks the act of genetically engineering the embryo from which she will develop, her (future) overriding interest in avoiding an incapacity for decisional autonomy renders ethically acceptable the paternalism of genetically engineering the embryo. Therapeutic engineering in response to genetic disease indicated at the embryonal stage ultimately preserves her future decisional autonomy by making possible what otherwise would be enfeebled.

This understanding of *dignity* is hardly original. It tracks actual, if often only implicit, usage, as Macklin (2003: 1419) pointed out two decades ago: for many participants in bioethical debates, the term means "nothing other than respect for autonomy." In fact, to define *dignity* this way tracks various of the elite international bioethical instruments that I criticize for their genetic essentialism. The *Oviedo Convention*, for example, grounds dignity in a patient's right to voluntary, informed consent (one form of autonomy) just as it grounds dignity in her right to confidentiality (another form of autonomy). Article 2 states that the "interests and welfare of the human being shall prevail over the sole interest of society or science." The National Academies of Sciences, Engineering and Medicine (2017: 32) provide yet another example: the "principle of respect for persons requires recognition of the personal dignity of all individuals, acknowledgment of the centrality of personal choice, and respect for individual decisions."

Unlike these instruments, my definition of autonomy avoids essentializing, in two ways: it affirms human dignity (a) by tying it to individual autonomy rather than to the human genome and (b) by drawing on the widely accepted principle of a child's right to respect for its best interests.[23]

22 For example, in Gregg (2021a) I argue that if a liberal democratic political community offered strong legal protection for persons who sacrificed some privacy rights (by participating in digital contact-tracing via smartphone) for the sake of a more effective collective effort to contain a virus under pandemic conditions, and if citizens had good reason to trust both the state and the private sector with their private health information, then, from a utilitarian and consequentialist standpoint, a data-first strategy (mandatory participation) recommends itself over a privacy-first approach (voluntary participation).

23 E.g., the 1989 Convention on the Rights of the Child (www.ohchr.org/en/professionalinterest/pages/crc.aspx) posits the child's best interests as a guiding principle (arts. 3, 9, 18, 20, 21).

(a) Consider medical care that, as unintended side effects of disease treatment such as chemotherapy, may generate mutations of germline cells. The patient's reproductive system may be affected. *Somatic* editing concerns cells other than sperm and egg cells (or gametes); it affects only the patient. *Germline* editing concerns the nuclear DNA of gametes or embryos; it affects all of the body's cells and can be inherited by subsequent generations. Here the physicians' goal is therapeutic and somatic, not enhancement and germline. Regardless of that intention, any argument that links human dignity to the human genome, such that changes to the latter compromise the former, fails to distinguish between direct and indirect types of behavior. And the argument that dignity is violated by genetic manipulation applies equally to intended genetic changes and to changes that follow inevitably from medical therapy.

Genetic essentialism also undermines the notion of human dignity as individual autonomy (a notion it otherwise supports). In the case of medical treatment, including treatment that unintentionally alters the patient's genome or the germline, withholding treatment on grounds that it would sabotage the patient's *dignity* would in fact sabotage her *autonomy*. Refusal to provide wanted treatment would not harm the willing patient's dignity but it would affirm her autonomy inasmuch as her decisional autonomy includes the choice of potentially life-saving medical treatment.

(b) According to Knoppers and Kleiderman (2019: 285), "Approximately 80% of rare and often incurable and serious conditions" – including spinal muscular atrophy, beta thalassemia, and macular degeneration – "affect newborns and children, and roughly half of all rare diseases are considered to have an onset in childhood." Concern for the welfare of such children may in some cases recommend genetic intervention. That concern facilitates the child's best interests if it leads her to enjoy the highest possible quality of biological life.[24] Johan Bester (2019) as well as Julian Savulescu and Guy Kahane (2009) contend that a political community is morally obligated to serve the child's best interest by providing available biotechnological means in selecting embryos that will become future persons.[25]

[24] A concern for the welfare of a child whose health would benefit significantly from genetic intervention resonates with the notion of a child's right to an open future. Without intervention, the child's future may be severely compromised, if not precluded.

[25] To be sure, the notion of a child's best interest is not always unambiguous. As Barnes (2016: 304) notes, a child's best interest is not independent of its contingent social environment: "it's much worse to change a person in a way that will make them subject to prejudice, stigma, and discrimination than it is to change a person in a way that will make them a part of the comfortable majority." But "while it's wrong to attempt to change an inter-sex child into a female child" (Barnes 2014: 103), "it would be *worse* to turn a female child into an inter-sex child, simply because of the socially-mediated disadvantages an intersex person will face"

The autonomy-facilitating physical and cognitive welfare of the future person begins with her welfare as a child. Autonomy is anticipatory at the time of the manipulation, a kind of placeholder in utero. The future person's autonomy is held in trust by the generation that performs the manipulation (and, in particular, by the parents and the participating scientists, engineers, and physicians).

The principle of the child's best interests would limit germline editing to those forms of editing that promote welfare in a therapeutic sense. Preventing serious genetic disease is core to welfare so understood. Welfare is also served by the individual's right to science[26] in the sense of access to the health benefits science can provide.[27]

Note three upshots. First, recognition of human dignity does not entail a right of a future person to be free from genome modification. (This point counters the genetic essentialist claim that human dignity is respected only by respecting the "genetic heritage of humankind.") While the future person cannot consent to genetic engineering or to any of its anticipated benefits, present persons can reasonably interpret the future person's best interest as freedom from genetic disease.

Second, respect for human dignity entails engineering the genome – of the individual but also of the germline – to decrease the possibility of preventable disease in future individuals.

Third, dignity entails that the "interests and welfare" of the future individual "should have priority over the sole interest[s] of science or society" (*Universal Declaration on Bioethics and Human Rights*, art. 3). No just political community could condone not attempting to treat and cure a serious pathology in an embryo. And the morally acceptable interests of a person's possible descendants could never justify compromising the future person's dignity, here understood as decisional autonomy.[28] Further, invoking a future person's "priority" over possible descendants is wrongheaded. After all, reducing genetic disease would benefit those descendants; indeed it would benefit societies worldwide. Hence dignity that entails the individual's interests and welfare can equally entail a responsibility of the current generation toward future generations. It can entail

(Barnes 2016: 304). Or consider deaf parents who prefer a deaf child when they regard deafness not as a genetic disease so much as a culture (one they seek to preserve), and view the child's best interest as communal membership and identity. One cannot know in advance what the child, once mature, would choose.

[26] Posited by the *Universal Declaration of Human Rights*: "everyone has the right to share in scientific advancement and its benefits" (art. 27).

[27] The *Convention on the Rights of the Child* posits the child's right "to the enjoyment of the highest attainable standard of health." Compare Boggio et al. (2019).

[28] This claim finds support in the *Universal Declaration on Bioethics and Human Rights*: the "interests and welfare of the individual should have priority over the sole interest of science or society" (art. 3); and in the *Oviedo Convention*: the "interests and welfare of the human being shall prevail over the sole interest of society or science" (art. 2).

a responsibility to deploy human genetic engineering toward the treatment of genetic disease in future persons. For what is true of the future child is true of the aggregate of future children: while the beneficiary does not exist at the point of deciding whether to genetically edit, she eventually becomes a beneficiary due to having been genetically edited, whether as an embryo or as its descendant.

4.5 A FUTURE PERSON'S INTEREST IN DECISIONAL AUTONOMY

When speaking of present persons, I speak of those persons in a position to decide whether and how to genetically modify an embryo that will develop into a future person. On a broad understanding of justice such as Mill's (1998), might present persons have a duty of justice toward future persons? Might future persons have rights vis-à-vis present persons? The questions pose themselves inasmuch as rights and duties that bind two or more people usually refer to two or more contemporaries who, morally and legally, stand in a more or less symmetrical relationship to one another and many of whose rights and obligations generally are roughly reciprocal (in the case of adults). By contrast, the relationship between present and future persons is neither symmetrical nor reciprocal.

First, it is asymmetrical: present persons can influence future persons but not vice versa. Exchanges occur in one direction only: toward the future. Current persons can promote the interests of future persons in certain ways just as they can harm those interests. Second, the relationship between current and future persons is non-reciprocal. For example, they cannot cooperate with each other. Third, to harm a future person's rights is to harm a particular person in the future. While present persons can have no specific knowledge of the identity of particular future persons (and no knowledge about the bodily and mental states of future persons), they can have knowledge of some of the moral dilemmas posed by possible consequences of human genetic engineering. And they can assess ways in which engineering today may violate possible rights of future persons tomorrow. Current persons need not know future persons to recognize their interests and rights.

Consider the consequences. First, the fact that the relationship between present and future persons is neither symmetrical nor reciprocal does not preclude the possibility of future persons as rightsbearers vis-à-vis present persons. Current persons may have duties toward the future persons who develop from genetically modified embryos. The actions of a present person can affect the interests of a future person adversely when those actions frustrate the future person's interest in her own decisional autonomy. Frustrating that interest would violate her future right. Hence current persons can assess at least some of the risks of genetic engineering they impose on future persons.

Second, one can have an interest even if not able to realize that interest, and one can bear rights even if one is unable to exercise them (such as children), for example where a right "necessarily preserves one or more of the persons' interests" (Kramer 1998: 62). In other words, a future person can make a valid claim to justice vis-à-vis a current person (and a current person may bear a legitimate duty of justice toward a future person) despite the fact that the future person cannot enforce that right. Hence the fact that the future person's will is not present when current humans genetically manipulate the embryo from which the future person will develop does not entail those current humans having no obligations toward such persons.[29]

Third, a person who develops from an embryo currently under consideration for genetic engineering bears rights *as a future person*. The embryo is not identical with the future person (because, among other things, a future person is also a product of environments, experiences, and socialization in specific eras and places and cultures and under particular circumstances). An embryo cannot bear rights. But it can be a placeholder for at least some of the rights of the future person. Current persons respect the rights of the future person by treating the embryo in ways that respect a future person's rights, that is, by taking into account plausible interests of any future person. I focus on a future person's plausible interest in her decisional autonomy, hence her interest in having her future decisional autonomy protected or preserved in any genetic engineering decisions made by current persons.[30]

Fourth, a future person's capacity as a rightsbearer rests on current persons understanding themselves as members of an imagined transgenerational moral community. If members assume a standpoint based on species membership, then they need not presuppose an essential "human nature" inasmuch as species have no timeless essence: they are always evolving. Future persons enjoy rights vis-à-vis present persons on the basis of this imagined community. Current persons can imagine the standpoint of a future person in a way analogous to adults who can imagine a child's best interests: their judgment is a placeholder for the child's own judgment. And just as the adult's standpoint need not be identical with that of a child to conceive of the child's best interest, so the standpoint of the current person need not be identical with that of the future person to conceive of her interest in her decisional autonomy. Whether that conception is warranted cannot be a matter of fact; only the future person

[29] After all, the difference in temporal status between a current and a future person does not necessarily entail fewer or weaker rights for future persons. Hence reasons against harm to a current person can apply equally to a future person.

[30] That interest does not entail that the present person is morally obligated to engineer in such a way as to make more likely that the future person is, genetically, as "good" or "advantaged" as possible; the obligation not to harm a person's interest does not entail an obligation to maximize her interests.

can determine as much with respect to herself. It can only be a matter of reasoned, fallible supposition.

4.6 DELIBERATION TOWARD PRINCIPLED AGREEMENT ON THE DECISIONAL AUTONOMY OF FUTURE PERSONS

The effort to define dignity as the individual's decisional autonomy vis-à-vis other persons requires the presence of an unmistakably human individual. An embryo is not such a person; it is not a person at all. While people might treat an embryo as having a moral status that disallows its treatment as an ordinary object, vulnerable entirely and exclusively to the will of its owner,[31] concern about how an embryo is treated reflects not the embryo but the normative preferences of the present observers. The embryo is without decisional autonomy. So the manipulation of the embryo is not wrong as such but it could be wrong with respect to a future person[32] if present persons ascribe individual autonomy to a future person making possible a class of actions today (such as unjustified genetic engineering) that could violate the autonomy of a future person.

To protect a future person's decisional autonomy, I propose human dignity as a social construct and as a political tool. Human dignity so understood can guide principled thinking about regulating biotechnologies such as gene editing. Such thinking finds support in various international instruments, including the International Bioethics Committee (paras. 117 and 118), the Council of Europe's Committee on Bioethics,[33] as well as the *Oviedo Convention*, which commits signatories to "public discussion in the light ... of relevant medical, social, economic, ethical and legal implications" (art. 28) and possible applications.

I turn now to illustrating two effects of the argument from dignity conceived as social construct and political tool: (a) it facilitates public deliberation about regulating human genetic engineering and (b) public deliberation about genetic intervention operationalizes it, in political process, as an alternative to genetic essentialism.

(a) I envision input from public deliberation at three different levels of governance. At the level of *international institutions*, nation states that allow germline editing might work with the World Health Organization

[31] For example, a staple of human embryo research governance stipulates that human embryos should not be grown in vitro in a research laboratory for longer than fourteen days after the point of fertilization or at the appearance of the "primitive streak" (marking the start of gastrulation), whichever occurs first.

[32] Several major international instruments lean in this direction, including the United Nations Humanitarian Response Depot; the United Nations Educational, Scientific and Cultural Organization; and the Council of Europe.

[33] Statement on Genome Editing Technologies, December 2, 2015: https://rm.coe.int/168049034a.

and its Expert Advisory Committee on Developing Global Standards for Governance and Oversight of Human Gene Editing.[34] The goal: to "review the state of the science and provide advice on 'its applications, its potential usages and societal attitudes towards the different uses of this technology'; to propose potential oversight mechanisms; and to recommend global governance structures for genome editing research and potential applications" (Alta Charo 2019: 977). At the level of *national institutions*, such as the European Medicines Agency or the U.S. Food and Drug Administration, popular deliberation could contribute dignity-based normative perspectives for consideration by regulatory organizations pursuing the development of safe and accurate forms of genetic manipulation. And at the level of local *public fora in political communities*, nonexpert or lay publics could inform themselves of the relevant science and of the relevant public policy to consider how human dignity – as the decisional autonomy of future persons – might guide the legal regulation of human genetic engineering.

To be sure, the expert medical and scientific communities should always play the deciding role.[35] But the voices of stakeholders in bottom-up public deliberation could inform them, not as a genetic engineering democracy of biohackers "tinkering with DNA, under the guise of 'democratizing' the life sciences" (van Beers 2020: 36) but as a public, enlightened by techniques of deliberative democracy,[36] who participate in readily accessible public debates about the moral evaluation and possible legal regulation of various forms of human genetic engineering.[37] While debates must be guided by standard norms of medical ethics, such as safety, informed consent, and the right to refuse treatment, additional norms need to be considered inasmuch as genetic engineering raises questions that cannot be dealt with solely in terms of medical ethics,[38] such as disparities in health and in access to health care. While public

[34] www.who.int/ethics/topics/human-genome-editing/committee-members/en/.

[35] Alta Charo (2019: 978) usefully imagines "complementary contributions from various actors who can place pressure on the research, development, and marketing of new technology ... as part of a comprehensive ecosystem of governance. In the initial in vitro phase, research can be regulated under rules governing intellectual property ownership, sourcing of materials, laboratory management, and funding priorities or restrictions."

[36] E.g., Fishkin (2009) envisions popular deliberation open to all points of view held by significant portions of the citizenry; with arguments supported by appropriate and accurate factual claims; confronted with counter-arguments; and with arguments considered solely on their merits (rather than with regard to, say, the prestige or political affiliation of the speaker).

[37] Chapter 1 combines the two procedural devices of bioethics committees and deliberative democracy toward generating legitimate bioethical decisions capable of wide embrace within political community.

[38] For example, the distinction (prone to collapse) between genetic therapy (in the sense of remediation or rehabilitation, that is, returning to a previously healthy state or attaining for the first time a "normal" or "natural" state) and enhancement (to raise "normal" or "natural"

deliberation will not achieve consensus,[39] it can achieve measures of shared understanding and agreement greater than otherwise possible.

(b) What kind of decisional autonomy of future persons might the current generation hold in trust? One informed by medical and scientific experts but also by popular deliberation, toward generating broad, principled agreement within political community. By *principled agreement* I mean principles that inform legislation that binds clinicians in the kinds and range of choices permitted in the engineering of human embryos. I have emphasized one in particular: the notion of human dignity as an interest in the decisional autonomy of future persons. It would evaluate possible engineering choices affecting a future person who, in retrospect, could be expected to freely assent to those engineering choices taken with respect to the embryo from which she developed. *Plausible expectation* refers to choices capable of finding broad consent among both bioethical experts and laypersons concerning the possible preferences a future person might have regarding the relevant genetic engineering. The plausibility of broad consent relies on the plausibility of the anticipated dignity of future persons held in trust by current persons.

With regard to the *capacity to exercise* decisional autonomy: this notion of autonomy need not address the situation of persons unable to make decisions because they are small children, or persons with severe cognitive impairment or advanced dementia. The case of an embryo cannot be analogized to the problem of determining decisional capacity for persons who possess some, but not all, of the mental capacities of "typically" functioning adult persons. Future persons are not directly vulnerable to other persons in the ways that current humans are. But they are directly vulnerable to the decisions of those who genetically modify the embryos from which they develop. That vulnerability can be addressed by regulating possible choices in the engineering of a human embryo to be compatible with dignity: choices that would not impede the future person's decisional autonomy, by ensuring, or at least not interfering with, capacities needed for decisional capacity.[40] A minimal list would include a future person's capacity to communicate her choice to others; for comprehension and acquisition of knowledge of facts;[41] to appreciate pertinent scientific facts, as well as germane normative debates, relevant to genetic engineering in the ways that genetic engineering has affected her life; to appreciate the nature

to a higher degree, to become "better" than just "healthy" and "normal") is not a purely objective or scientific issue but one that involves normative commitments.

39 However defined, e.g., as many participants as possible, or a majority of participants.

40 Any discussion of decisional capacity should note that capacity may be more like a spectrum rather than a binary: not all experiences, situations, and tasks require the same level of capacity (Culver and Gert 1990). Moreover, a particular individual's capacity may vary over time.

41 Whereby any plausible standard will not be so high as to exclude many people as incompetent.

and significance of the decision faced by those who, in the past, determined the guidelines for human genetic engineering that governed the engineering of the embryo from which she developed; and for reasoning (Buchanan and Brock 1989).[42]

4.7 CONCLUSION: THE FUTURE PERSON'S DECISIONAL AUTONOMY CAN FUNCTION AS A REGULATORY PRINCIPLE AT THE POINT OF GENETICALLY MANIPULATING THE EMBRYO

How might human genetic engineering best be regulated? I responded to this question by rejecting, as a regulative principle, a genetically essentialist notion of human dignity. I pursued instead a consequentialist notion of human dignity as the future person's decisional autonomy, held in trust by the current generation as it deliberates about genetically engineering the embryo from which that future person will develop. I developed this approach in six steps. First, a consequentialist notion of human dignity rejects the effort to invest the human genome with an inherent moral status. Instead it regards all norms, including moral status, as social constructs. Second, although most biologists and philosophers of biology today do not embrace genetic essentialism, I argued that a critique of genetic essentialism is still no strawman inasmuch as genetic essentialism is widespread, especially among the lay public, and that it can be socially, politically, and institutionally pernicious. Third, I showed how the effort to identify a principle by which to regulate possible human genetic engineering – an effort typical of elite international instruments and organizations[43] – is undermined by defining human dignity in genetically essentialist terms. Fourth, I offered an alternative to genetic essentialism: dignity as a future person's decisional autonomy by analogy to the widely accepted principle of a child's right to respect for its best interests. Fifth, given that the relationship between present and future persons is neither symmetrical nor reciprocal, I made a case for a future person's interest in decisional autonomy as an interest that the present generation could meet at the point of embryonal genetic manipulation. I concluded, sixth, with a sketch of popular political deliberation on regulating human genetic engineering, toward principled agreement on the decisional autonomy of future persons – all without genetic essentialism.

This chapter examined some of the ways in which nature and culture are porous vis-à-vis one another with respect to genetically based congenital diseases. While medical practice works with a naturalistic conception of disease, it still has a cultural element: the evaluation of a particular, natural, biological

[42] Whereby, again, the standard should not be so high as to classify too many persons as incompetent.

[43] Although not of the *Universal Declaration on the Human Genome and Human Rights*.

process as harmful. The technical capacity to manipulate the human genome renders the biological quality of being human all the more porous with the cultural quality of being human: we are an evolved species now with a capacity to socially construct aspects of our environment as well as ourselves. This porous quality challenges the effort to regulate human genetic engineering by reference to a notion of human dignity. That term is only usable if redefined in ways that account for the porosity of human culture and human nature. It is so redefined in regulation guided by human dignity as decisional autonomy not essence. This chapter concludes the first of the book's three parts, on the political bioethics of regulating genetic engineering. The following chapter opens the second part, on the political dimensions of engineering intelligence. It argues that, because an individual's severe cognitive disability precludes her political agency, she and her political community would be better off with a threshold level of intelligence, at least along one dimension in particular: a level of intelligence necessary for robust civic participation. A just community should regard, as a political imperative, the biotechnical provision of such a threshold, where severe cognitive disability is indicated at the embryonal state.

PART II

THE POLITICAL DIMENSIONS OF ENGINEERING INTELLIGENCE

5

Threshold Capacities for Political Participation

In terms of realizing a just society, would the citizen and her political community be significantly advantaged if she and her fellow citizens were of a "threshold level" of intelligence? The question might be formulated in terms of several parameters: (1) A just political community would seek to help as many (future) citizens as (medically, technically) possible to have a cognitive capacity at the threshold level necessary for democratic political participation. (2) Treatment at the embryonic stage of development would result in many more future citizens capable of realizing their social, political, and legal status as rightsholders, as stakeholders in their political community. It would prevent what otherwise would be their political exclusion on the basis of cognitive capacity inadequate for full and robust participation. (3) State subsidization of legally entitled engineering (for parents who cannot afford it) would help prevent a maldistribution of access that otherwise would exacerbate existing social inequalities. Further, assume that the following were possible. (a) a biotechnological ability to identify genetically, at the embryonic stage of development, severe cognitive disability in the future person; (b) an empirically identifiable, scientifically measurable threshold level of intelligence necessary for democratic political participation (constituting a lower bound for ethically and legally permissible genetic engineering at the embryonic stage); (c) genetic technology capable of engineering human intelligence;[1] and (d) a legal right to

[1] Bostrom and Sandberg (2009: 319) note that while a "large number of genetic variations" affect individual intelligence, each accounts "for only a very small fraction (<1%) of the variance between individuals," hence that enhancement "through direct insertion of a few beneficial alleles is unlikely to have a big enhancing effect." This fact points up the exceeding difficulty of any possible cognitive enhancement by genetic engineering.

genetic engineering of a future person who, at the embryonic stage of development, indicates severe intellectual disability.

I develop a series of arguments to support the claim that the individual and her political community would be better off with a threshold level of intelligence.[2] These arguments rest on one fundamental assertion: that an individual's severe cognitive disability precludes her political agency. I concede that there is no consensual scientific understanding of human cognition or intelligence, hence no common definition. Observers agree that intelligence is a complex, latent trait. It is not directly observable but it can be inferred from the covariance of diverse, positively intercorrelated cognitive tests of various forms and content.[3] Observers also agree that an individual's general intelligence influences outcomes in her life across a wide spectrum of behavior and psychology, from mental and physical health, fertility, and longevity to educational attainment, occupational status, social status, and well-being (Deary 2012).

The idea of a genetic basis of intelligence-relevant political capabilities is the idea that some genes, coordinated with other genes, play a role in forming the biological basis for relevant behaviors. I speculate that political agency might be understood in part as a socially adaptive phenotype with a developmental basis in the genome.[4] To be sure, intelligence is but one of many factors presupposed by an individual's capacity for democratic political participation. Other factors include social environments (from the family to education, from work to cultural and political climates); demographic environments (for example, where some marginalized populations face social barriers because of their race or ethnicity); and socialization.

Here I focus on intelligence only. I orient my focus on the *potential* for one particular desired outcome: civic participation. Intelligence itself does not guarantee thoughtful civic engagement, of course. Many voters decide on the basis not of careful, informed analysis of the issues and candidates but on

[2] I focus on the political benefits, which involve the affected person's interest in freedom from paternalism. But there are additional benefits: intellectual disability is "very often intertwined with other neurodevelopmental disorders, including autism, motor or sensory difficulties (hearing, vision), serious sleep and eating disorders, and medical conditions such as epilepsy, as well as a wide variety of psychopathologic problems, including anxiety, depression, and emotional regulation disorders" (Des Portes 2020: 113).

[3] According to Schalock and Luckasson (2004: 139), "intellectual functioning is still best represented by IQ scores when obtained from appropriate assessment instruments." Apparently different kinds of intelligence are interrelated. For example, someone who, relative to other test-takers, performs well on one cognitive test is likely to perform well on other cognitive tests. Thus "any differences in test scores that occur within an individual are smaller than test score differences that exist between individuals" (Plomin and von Stumm 2018: 149). And "individual differences in intelligence are fairly stable across the lifespan" (ibid.).

[4] Research indicates that intelligence is heritable (Savage et al. 2018: 912) it is estimated at about 30% for unrelated individuals (Hill et al. 2018: 2347).

grounds that are racist, sexist, ethnically chauvinist, religiously bigoted, and so forth (Bell et al. 2001).[5]

Human intelligence can be engineered in various ways. It can be molded, particularly in children, by education (Brinch and Galloway 2012), diet (Protzko 2016), and home environment. Another means of molding intelligence is genetic. Research shows that intellectual disability has many causes and that "more than half of all cases are genetic in origin" (Des Portes 2020: 113).[6] I argue for the cognitive engineering of future persons at the embryonic stage of development in cases where severe cognitive disability is indicated. "Between 1% and 3% of persons in the general population are estimated to have some degree of intellectual disability" (Patel et al. 2020: S23).[7] I focus on a single goal: manipulation toward a level of intelligence that would allow the future citizen autonomous participation in the political life of her liberal democratic community.[8] I do so in five steps. (§5.1) I identify various cognitive capacities relevant to democratic political participation. (§5.2) I show that cognitive disability can be a political disability and (§5.3) that aspects of political participation, equally desirable for the individual citizen and for the collective good, may justify some forms of cognitive engineering.[9] (§5.4) I contend that alternatives to human cognitive engineering are less viable than cognitive engineering and (§5.5) that a just community should regard, as a political imperative, the provision of the relevant cognitive engineering to the extent possible. I conclude that if political participation is an element of a good life, then genetic intervention at the embryonic stage of development would increase the future person's prospects for leading a good life because it may facilitate the equal citizenship that requires a minimum genetic capacity.

[5] In response, Chapters 1 and 2 of this book urge various procedures for making popular political participation better informed and more thoughtful.

[6] The heritability of general intelligence (the variance shared among different types of cognitive ability tests) can be estimated from molecular genetic data as well as from twin and family studies suggesting that "50%–80% of phenotypic variance is due to additive genetic factors" (Hill et al. 2018: 2348).

[7] Borderline intellectual functioning affects between 12%–14% of the population (Fernell and Gillberg 2020: 77) and more than 75% of cognitively disabled persons have a mild disability (Patel et al. 2020: S23).

[8] By the term *liberal democratic communities* I refer to the legally institutionalized competition of different value-commitments in the public sphere (committed to value pluralism) concerning the collective good of a political community. By *legally institutionalized* I intend standard liberal political rights, including expression, assembly, and voting, whereby voting is particularly important in the citizen's limited capacity to effect political and social change.

[9] By making political participation possible, cognitive enhancement renders the individual capable of contributing to other institutionalized spheres of human endeavor, including workplace, education, and family life – and not just politics. Possessing a fundamental capacity to participate in these various spheres does not of itself guarantee the best possible life, or a life well-lived, or a life worth living. It provides a means for the individual to pursue her conception of personal and communal well-being.

5.1 COGNITIVE ABILITIES RELEVANT TO DEMOCRATIC POLITICAL PARTICIPATION

Consider two dimensions of the concept of a politically relevant intelligence: (a) political community as a cognitive act, indeed as an act shared among multiple minds, and (b) political participation as behavior that presupposes certain cognitive capacities.

(a) Basic *ideal* behaviors directly relevant to political participation in liberal democracy include the individual's capacity to develop an informed opinion; to articulate that opinion to other persons; to understand and thoughtfully consider the opinions of others; to participate in actions such as voting in elections; expressing political convictions in public fora; forming political organizations and social movements; assembling with others to advocate policy preference; protesting; running for elective office; serving on juries in those legal systems that use juries.

While these are behaviors of the individual, they are also behaviors meaningful and possible only in concert with the motivations and actions of other participants. After all, a democracy aspires to provide broad access to participation in the *collective* self-determination of a political community. The term *collective* refers to shared objectives and shared consequences.[10] Political participation in this sense constitutes a kind of community of minds involving the mutual influence of participants. Ideally many members of the community participate, sometimes synchronously, sometimes asynchronously. What Raymond Tallis (2016: 11) says of human consciousness lends itself, by analogy, to the notion of democratic political community as a cognitive act that

> cannot be found solely in the stand-alone brain; or even just in a brain in a body; or even in a brain interacting with other brains in bodies. It participates in, and is part of, a community of minds built up by conscious human beings over hundreds of thousand years. This cognitive community is an expression of the collectivization of our experiences through a trillion acts of joint and shared attention.[11]

In short, a cognitive community is a distinctly *cultural* phenomenon, a form of distributed collective cognition that brings participants together through cognition. Democratic politics is culture as brain-to-brain coupling, or the binding of

[10] It also refers to social cooperation. According to Richardson (2017: 266), "social cooperation was the context, not the result, of rapid cognitive evolution." Social cooperation (including politics) is a form of cultural adaptation that far outpaces biological adaptation. Genetically, at the species level, human communities are identical; culturally, they can differ profoundly.

[11] According to Hasson and colleagues (2012: 114), "Cognition materializes in an interpersonal space. The emergence of complex behaviors requires the coordination of actions among individuals according to a shared set of rules. ... Brain-to-brain coupling constrains and simplifies the actions of each individual in a social network, leading to complex joint behaviors that could not have emerged in isolation." In that sense, democratic community is a cognitive community.

nervous systems, where each mind augments others and where culture refracts, through individuals, common knowledge and collective concerns.[12]

Culture so understood is an intercognitive medium of cognition: from performing music to debating public policy, "each member of a group is registering, and adapting to, the structure in the behavior of one or more others" (Richardson 2017: 270). Individual cognition can be enhanced by its distribution beyond the individual, and democratic politics can function as a type of distributed intelligence.

Culture is equally epicognitive: written communication, for example, explodes temporal and topical boundaries of the individual's capacity for memory. Collective cognition profoundly alters personal cognition. It can increase the potential of individual cognition significantly: whatever a single mind is capable of, multiple minds working together (even across time) can magnify, extend, and enhance many times over. Whatever insight an individual mind might gain into self, others, and nature can be deepened profoundly by several minds working together.[13] Whatever capacity for adaptation to different, changing environments a single mind might display is outstripped by the capacity of several minds working jointly.

(b) What might the notion of some level of intelligence necessary to make possible an individual's ability to participate in democratic political community entail? Consider several elements.

First, research indicates that cognitive functioning, which is more or less fixed by adolescence, has the "largest influence on an individuals' ability to function independently" (Burden et al. 2017: 167). Relevant to independent functioning are the behavioral capacities for participation in democratic political community. They may be construed as specifically *cognitive* capacities in the sense of the individual's capacity to represent her own standpoint to others in the public sphere. While the individual develops, refines, and sometimes changes her standpoint as a result of interacting with the concerns and arguments of other participants, she does not depend on others to represent whatever standpoint she settles on. Here we have a politically salient notion of *independent functioning*.

Second, other features of general cognitive functioning relevant to independent functioning in a political context include abstract reasoning, verbal fluency, memory, and information processing (from technical matters of voter registration to substantive matters of candidates' issues and their respective positions). Memory, reasoning, and fluency are tools of processing. They can be deployed

[12] Or as Geertz (1973: 68) says, "Rather than culture acting only to supplement, develop, and extend organically based capacities logically and genetically prior to it, it would seem to be ingredient to those capacities themselves."

[13] Culture is an emergent phenomenon, self-organizing and greater than the sum of its parts, i.e., the individual participants. The cultural group makes the individual possible as a social being.

to distort information as well as to identify, oppose, and correct such distortion. A political ideology is one form of systematically distorted communication; the quest in politics for non-distorted communication then requires ideology critique.

Third, the act of voting requires cognitive functioning at a level that allows the would-be voter to take the initiative in a process fragile enough to fail if the citizen misses any one step in that process. Failure likely entails her exclusion for participation. Research by Barry Burden and colleagues (2017: 166, 168, 167) indicates that "voting is strongly affected by cognitive functioning" and that "childhood IQ and cognitive ability are positively related to voting."[14] Research also shows that the "effects of education" are a "potent predictor of voter turnout." Voting is not the only politically relevant behavior, of course; also significant are running for office, assembling with other citizens to advocate particular positions and candidates, and communicating with officials, the press, and fellow citizens.

One form of democracy is popular deliberation. It combines majority rule and consensual decision making. Ideally it is informed by citizen-participants' exposure to information and debates by experts. In this way it exceeds ordinary voting that is uninformed and easily manipulable by candidates and organizations.[15] The possibility of democratic deliberation is challenged in its aspiration to maximum inclusion of citizens insofar as the cognitive requirements presupposed by participation cannot be met with persons of severe cognitive disability. Robust participation in democratic politics makes cognitive demands on the participant that some cognitively disabled persons cannot meet even at a minimum threshold of capacity. That threshold includes the capacity to give sound reasons, to make reasoned evaluations, to ask thoughtful questions of others, and to appreciate the standpoint of other participants even as one may disagree with it. In the United States, "People with cognitive disabilities can have their voting rights stripped in multiple states and the District of Columbia" (Jackson 2019: 32): a person determined by the court to be incompetent is excluded from participatory citizenship and is reduced to a passive role in the community's political self-determination.

To the extent that cognitively disabled persons cannot participate, they cannot be equal with those who can participate; they are dependent on others. The state is unlikely to recognize the individual's legal capacity as equal to that held by persons without a severe disability, and in this way, among others, intellectual disability leads to inequality in political representation. In this context, Alasdair MacIntyre (1999: 139) urges political participation, communication, representation of one's interests, preferences, and convictions by proxy because a "radically disabled person needs someone to speak for her or him" as a "second self." Others must attempt to represent the disabled insofar as they are not able to represent themselves.

[14] The research was conducted in the United Kingdom.

[15] See, e.g., Fishkin (2011).

5.2 COGNITIVE DISABILITY AS POLITICAL DISABILITY

Specialists do not agree on how best to define intellectual disability. Prominent among diverse proposals are three somewhat overlapping definitions. The American Association on Mental Retardation (2002) defines cognitive disability as "significant limitations both in intellectual functioning and adaptive behavior as expressed in conceptual, social, and practical adaptive skills" that originate before the age of 18; the American Psychiatric Association (2013: 33), as a "disorder with onset during the developmental period that includes both intellectual and adaptive behavior deficits in conceptual, social, and practical domains"; and the World Health Organization (2020), as a "group of etiologically diverse conditions originating during the developmental period characterized by significantly below average intellectual functioning and adaptive behavior that are approximately two or more standard deviations below the mean (approximately less than the second/third percentile)."[16]

These definitions measure intellectual disability as a deficit in capacity for rational choice, for personal autonomy, for reasonable decision making, and for self-determination. These politically relevant features can be viewed functionally. To view these features with respect to the individual's level of functioning is to view them not as a matter of optimum performance but as one of the individual's "typical performance during daily routines and changing circumstances" in the course of meeting the challenges of everyday life (Schalock and Luckasson 2004: 139). This view is flexible and contextual rather than fixed and absolute: a disability consequential in one situation or environment may not be in another; a disability serious at one point in a person's life may be less so at another.

By contrast to this functionalist approach, a politically interested perspective understands cognitive disability as a political problem insofar as it prevents the individual from equal participation in the public sphere. It is sensitive to the various ways such disability may lead to political disenfranchisement and other forms of social exclusion. From this perspective, cognitive disability is a concern not only medical but also social.[17] It regards disability as a "physical or mental impairment that substantially limits" the individual in "one or more major life activities" (Adams et al. 2015: 8). The term *disability* then refers not exclusively to the disabled individual's body but also to phenomena *outside* her

[16] These are not stagnant definitions. Changes over several decades include an "increasing acceptance of the equal weight given to adaptive behavior and intellectual functioning in the diagnosis" of cognitive disability; a "better understanding of the factor structure of adaptive behavior (i.e., conceptual, social, and practical adaptive skills)"; and an "increased use of a subclassification system based on the person's needs for supports rather than the individual's intelligence quotient level" (Schalock et al. 2019: 224).

[17] Social also in the sense of calling for a political response as in, e.g., the Americans with Disabilities Act (U.S. Code §12102 of 1990).

body, such as "systems of social organization, institutional practices, and environmental structures" (ibid.).[18]

A politically interested approach highlights the advantages of genetic engineering to eliminate severe cognitive disability.[19] It is sensitive to how disability may render the individual's integration into democratic political life impossible, leading to her exclusion from possibly influencing relevant outcomes of social policy. It urges the plausibility of embryonic genetic manipulation to preclude cognitive disability: engineering toward the inclusion in the democratic process of future persons otherwise condemned to participatory exclusion.

By contrast to a political approach, a functional approach to the severely cognitively disabled citizen cannot address her political immiseration. It recommends "equal weight given to adaptive behavior and intellectual functioning" in the diagnosis of cognitive disability"; understanding the disabled individual's adaptive behavior as involving "conceptual, social, and practical adaptive skills"; and emphasizing the disabled individual's "needs for supports rather than the individual's intelligence quotient level" (Schalock et al. 2019: 224). But a political approach stresses choice and personal autonomy, realized through reasonable decision making and understood as a capacity to self-determine in the sense of "volitional actions that enable one to act as the primary causal agent in one's life and to maintain or improve one's quality of life" (Wehmeyer 2005: 117). It advocates genetic engineering in recognition of the fact that the state cannot plausibly recognize the cognitively disabled individual as politically entitled to a capacity equal to that held by persons free of cognitive disabilities.

5.3 THE GOAL OF POLITICAL PARTICIPATION MAY JUSTIFY SOME FORMS OF COGNITIVE ENGINEERING

Democratic political participation is a social good, as is the individual's capacity to access her legal right to political participation. Hence genetic engineering to overcome severe cognitive disability benefits the disabled person just as it benefits political community. While it increases the possibility of the individual having, in relevant circumstances, a life better than otherwise possible, it simultaneously increases the possible inclusivity of the individual's

[18] In this sense, the Union of the Physically Impaired against Segregation (1975) distinguishes between impairment (to lack something bodily) and disability (whatever makes that lack a disadvantage in society).

[19] A *politically interested approach* does not refer to just any political perspective, of course: the cognitive and normative interest proper to critical political analysis is emancipatory in the sense of seeking to denaturalize "hegemonic patterns of interpreting social norms" and to uncover previously unrecognized "interests by which these are motivated" (Honneth 2017: 919), toward the "transformative re-interpretation of established social norms as a recurring practice" (ibid., 915) and, on the basis of better understandings, the rational reorganization of social policies and institutions and practices.

political community. Political community and the genetic enhancement of citizens otherwise excluded are then mutually reinforcing. On the one hand, in participating, individuals self-determine individually. On the other hand, in participating, diverse individuals are interconnected in their thoughts and actions, plans, and the capacity to plan. Further, the individual's participation can contribute to the participation of others, for example by the individual's taking the standpoint of other participants toward understanding, where the pursuit of a political community's common good requires social cooperation. The consequences of many individuals self-determining can impact the entire community significantly.

Democratic political participation (a) facilitates individual self-authentication or self-validation and (b) makes political personhood possible.

(a) The individual's political autonomy is a core aspiration of political liberalism:[20] ideally, she is herself the source of her political preferences, including her free embrace of the preferences of others. Political liberalism is not normatively neutral but committed to a particular conception of the good life, one in which conceptions of the good originate in a sphere of intersubjectivity and interpersonal interactions, not outside it. The individual self-authenticates or self-determines by formulating and articulating her own notion of the public good and bringing it into discourse in the public sphere. But autonomy so understood need not be absolute; it may be partial and might best be pursued in a scalar approach. Further, it is not some kind of isolationist atomism; it is relational, intersubjective. That is, cognitive capacities for perceiving, understanding, reasoning, and expressing to others are always already embedded in the individual's social circumstances and contexts. Self-determination, for example, "emerges across the lifespan as children and adolescents learn skills and develop attitudes that enable them to be causal agents in their lives" and "characteristics that define self-determined behavior emerge through the development and acquisition of multiple, interrelated component elements including choice making, problem solving, decision making, goal setting and attainment, self-advocacy, and self-management skills" (Shogren 2013: 446).

If the individual's social circumstances and contexts cannot be transcended, at least they can be critically examined, challenged, and sometimes modified. On the one hand, the social embeddedness of one's cognitive capacities renders them always vulnerable to social conditioning and ideological distortions that can disable or even undermine the independent deployment of these capacities. On the other hand, some features of "normal" cognitive ability, for example with respect to foresight, memory, impulse control, and capacity for higher

[20] In the sense, e.g., of Rawls (1993).

levels of morality – such as the free and thoughtful embrace of norms of fairness and honesty – can facilitate a wide range of different conceptions of the good life.

But the relational quality of cognitive capacity, the fact that the individual's achievement depends on support of others, always has a social dimension and does not entail the individual's dependence. Lorella Terzi (2015: 200)[21] unpersuasively claims that "relational modes of agency include forms of trusteeship, guardianship, and surrogacy" that can support and facilitate the enactment of autonomous choices of individuals with cognitive disabilities, particularly those with "severe degrees of impairment." Proxy, guardianship, and surrogacy mark the *absence* of individual autonomy. They are forms of *dependence*. What political liberalism regards as the individual's right of autonomy displaces commitments to paternalism and beneficence found in more traditional political theories.

The value of autonomy is equally reflected in bioethics, which generally privileges patient consent, and the consent of research subjects, over other possible norms and commitments. A right to consent is a right to autonomy understood as self-determination in pursing freely chosen preferences, plans, and commitments. That capacity requires powers of understanding, self-regulation, decision making, and judging. (Here, a capacity for competence in judging functions as a "gatekeeping device for informed consent" (Beauchamp 2010: 73).) Indeed, the value of autonomy trumps the sanctity of human life where, for example, a cognitively competent patient refuses medically indicated life-saving treatment. Here, the physician is bound by patient autonomy even if the patient's preference is not in her interest, medically understood.

Assume the possibility of determining cognitive disability in an embryo. Toward greater inclusion of future citizens in the processes of participatory politics, I would then argue for genetic engineering of intelligence to a point, or a threshold,[22] necessary to render the future person cognitively capable of full political participation. Where a person is unable to meet that threshold, her wishes, preferences, and perspectives are vulnerable to being suppressed by guardians acting on a principle of the individual's best interests (cognizable

[21] Joined by a number of prominent scholars, including Martha Nussbaum, Eva Kittay, and Michel Bérubé, who advocate the full inclusion of cognitively disabled persons into voting, jury duty, and other civic roles.

[22] Any notion of a cognitive threshold will be controversial because unavoidably presupposing one or the other set of particular value-commitments that are not universally shared. For example, a threshold between "normality" and "abnormality" implies a "normal level" of intelligence. In liberal democratic contexts, any idea of normality is inherently problematic – even if sometimes useful – because so easily abused as one more means of discriminating against various populations. Hence the term *below threshold* is best defined not as "abnormal" but rather as *inadequate for purposes of liberal democratic political participation.* Such a threshold constitutes a kind of "genetic floor" below which as few citizens as possible should be allowed to fall. This approach need not imply identical capacities in all members of a political community.

only by the surrogate able to recognize the individual's acts of self-regarding harm).[23]

(b) The capacity to participate in democratic politics constitutes a kind of political personhood. Political personhood both depends on and reinforces reciprocity among members of a political community, in two overlapping senses. First, reciprocity involves the capacity of each member to view herself as a free and equal participant in an association of mutual benefit, committed to collaboration within a sovereign democratic political community. And the capacity to reciprocate politically involves the participant governing herself just as all other members govern themselves: toward participants' mutual and common benefit. Second, political personhood in democratic communities involves individual and collective self-determination through responsibility-taking: the capacity to form one's own conception of the common good and then to participate with others in striving after that good.[24] It is a capacity for responsibility for one's political vision, preferences, and aspirations.[25]

The notion of political personhood as reciprocity easily excludes persons of severe cognitively disability. According to Anita Silvers and Leslie Francis (2009: 483), "Making the power of reciprocity so central introduces a bias against ... cognitively impaired individuals whose limitations or dependency preclude their being viewed or valued, or viewing or valuing themselves, as contributing cooperators." If political personhood is a matter of reciprocity, persons with severe cognitive disabilities cannot engage in politically relevant reciprocity, such as public discourse and debate. They are politically disenfranchised by their own bodies, bodies that do not equip them with an adequate capacity to construct and communicate their conceptions of the public good or

[23] And of that guardian one may ask: "what justifies the epistemic superiority of certain people to determine when others are 'mistaken' about their own interests and self-understanding" (Kong 2017: 72)? Of course, the same question may be asked in other cases of advocacy as well, including this book's. My account in Chapters 1 and 2 of deliberative democracy and of expert bioethical opinion is an argument for the possibility and the desirability of epistemic superiority.

[24] I return to the idea of the mutual attribution of responsibility in Chapter 9 with regard to corporate responsibility for adverse epigenetic effects on individuals through their environment.

[25] By urging that political community should not privilege any single comprehensive conception of the common good, political liberalism unintentionally but unavoidably excludes some of its potential addressees, including the severely cognitively disabled who are not capable of being a self-originating participant who develops her own conception of the good. Theofilopoulou (2021: 1) would offer a counter-argument but then concedes that any robust understanding of political liberalism "would not require the participation of individuals with cognitive disabilities in the practice of legitimation" but only "their full inclusion in the realm of justice as equal rights-bearers." I have argued that the citizen cannot be an equal rights-bearer if she is not capable of participating in the political life and processes of her community without guardianship and other forms of paternalism.

contribute to the collective determination of the political community's good. They cannot participate in the public deliberation of what that good might be and how best to achieve it, and how to accommodate dissenting viewpoints. Their cognitive disability excludes them from participation in what ideally is the community's project of justice. Hence I argue for genetic engineering of intelligence to render the future person cognitively capable of democratic political participation.

5.4 CRITIQUE OF ALTERNATIVES TO HUMAN COGNITIVE ENGINEERING

My position – the liberal ideal of free and informed participation in the community's self-determination, and parents' legal right to genetic engineering of severe cognitive disability at the embryonic stage toward the greatest possible inclusivity – will have its critics. But critics cannot advance any plausible support for the proposition that a cognitively severely disabled person can still have a hardy capacity for self-articulation and self-realization. They cannot plausibly maintain that such a person can still have a robust ability to consider, deeply and critically, her political beliefs and commitments and those of others, and to participate in public-sphere efforts to realize what she holds to be advisable and to oppose what she regards as inadvisable.

A critic who rejects my viewpoint as one that stigmatizes intellectual disability as a preventable mistake (and exposes disabled persons to increased discrimination) cannot show how a political community can accommodate citizens with severe cognitive disabilities as full citizens. Legislation that mandates the integration of disabled persons as full citizens – such as the United Nations Convention on the Rights of People with Disabilities (2008) as well as the Americans with Disabilities Act (1990) – cannot show that such integration is possible. After all, integrating cognitively disabled persons into "mainstream educational settings that accommodate their specific needs" rather than segregating them in "separate and unequal institutions" (Garland-Thomson 2015: 79) does not render them capable of realizing full participatory citizenship in a democratic community.

My critics face several further challenges. First, "few adults with intellectual disability participate in elections as registered voters" (Agran et al. 2015: 388). What dissuades them from registering to vote? What prevents them from voting once they are registered? Research by Martin Agran and colleagues (2015: 389) reveals a range of reasons: "inadequate knowledge of voting-related issues" and "limited literacy skills"; the "failure of service providers or school programs to teach voting skills"; "living in a setting in which people do not regularly participate in voting"; and "inaccessibility of polling places, lack of accessible voting materials or voting apparatus, and on-site denial by election officers." And whereas many non-disabled persons may have some degree of choice as to whether to inform themselves, as to whether to participate, and so on, severely cognitively disabled persons do not. Second, systematic instruction is not effective in enabling cognitively disabled persons to participate fully in the electoral process (ibid., 394). Third, guardianship of the disabled is unavoidably paternalistic. It precludes individual agency in significant respects: "intellectual, conceptual, and practical reasoning" are "essentially part of active citizenship" and cognitive disability hinders them (Terzi 2015: 197). Fourth, the paternalistic guardianship of disabled persons, including a legal system that undergirds that paternalism, only reinforces the dependence of disabled persons on others. That dependence may render them second-class citizens, at least in some cases. Hence the following assumption is false: that political equality for cognitively disabled persons "would flow from obtaining the same package of rights" accorded nondisabled persons (Carey 2015: 38). Basing rights on an able-bodied norm only reinforces the political exclusion of disabled persons. Fifth, persons with severe cognitive disability are very vulnerable to manipulation by nondisabled persons. They cannot easily protect themselves from unethical influences.

5.5 POLITICAL IMPERATIVE TO PROVIDE COGNITIVE ENHANCEMENT

Various aspects of a person's political autonomy have cognitive prerequisites, including her politically relevant capacity for sophisticated rational considerations and social membership as a fully cooperating member of the community, as well as her capacity for moral decision making. In a political community whose notion of citizenship privileges individual autonomy and capacity to effectively pursue autonomous preferences, cognitive disabilities preclude the individual's equal standing. Persons with severe limitations in cognitive functioning as well as in adaptive behavior cannot achieve equal social and political standing with nondisabled persons. Put differently: equal citizenship among citizens presupposes citizens equally capable of political autonomy. Persons lacking that capacity cannot well represent themselves in the public sphere. In such cases, the possibility of the future person's "full enactment of citizenship in terms of participation in civic duties" depends on her genetic engineering at the embryonic stage (Terzi 2015: 200).

But on what theory might the state be obligated to ensure universal access to interventions that improve cognitive performance, including genetic engineering in cases of embryos indicating serious cognitive disability? At issue is a theory that favors a political community devoted to ensuring, to the extent possible, the equal interest of all persons in legal equality among members of a political community – perhaps by analogy to state provision of institutions such as public education and public libraries, but also state-subsidized vaccinations. The theory would include a principle of distributive justice: public support for a political community's members who, for reasons communal as well as individual, plausibly qualify for a share of the state's limited resources. On this principle, a future liberal democratic polity might take upon itself a general legal obligation to cognitively enhance embryos that indicate severe cognitive disability (assuming the state's economic capacity to do so).

Consider a precedent by analogy: the modern liberal state already regulates the behavior of various kinds of individuals toward protecting and improving cognitive function: "Regulation of lead in paint and tap water, requirements of boxing, bicycle, and motorcycle helmets, bans on alcohol for minors, mandatory education, folic acid fortification of cereals, and sanctions against mothers who abuse drugs during pregnancy all serve to safeguard or promote cognition" (Bostrom and Sandberg 2009: 331). To be sure, the analogy is imperfect: the possible regulation of human cognitive enhancement for future persons would be distinct from current regulations for adults and children and pregnant women in that they would involve the targeted genetic manipulation of an embryo, *viewed as a future citizen* of the community.

So understood, a future person's possible legal right to cognitive enhancement at the embryonic stage of development – as a right based on the future person's capacity for political autonomy – might allow for two kinds of imposition: on the state to subsidize engineering and on the parents to allow it for their embryo, for two reasons. First, the individual citizen's right to political participation, a right intrinsically valuable to the individual yet equally valuable to a robust democracy, might justify state investment in research and development to render cognitive enhancement a practical possibility. It might also justify a "state-funded once-in-a-lifetime basic enhancement package" for the future person at the embryonic stage of development (Tamir 2016: 10). Second, the parental right to raise and shape the child, and the duty of responsible childrearing, is well guided by the principle of the future child's best interest. The best interests of the child might be thought to extend to genetic engineering at the embryonic state for severe cognitive disability toward providing the future adult the cognitive basis for realizing her full rights as a citizen. Such interests might justify a parental obligation, to the extent possible, to facilitate the future person's core capacities (and political autonomy and self-determination might be regarded as one such capacity). By the same token, such interests would reject parental efforts to create a future person without core capacities.

What of a possible obligation on the part of parents? An obligation to facilitate cognitive genetic engineering of their cognitively disabled embryo is not an obligation to create a future human being with the greatest potential to enjoy the best possible life.[26] Indeed, a parental right to procreative freedom would allow parents to decide for themselves. Even state encouragement and subsidization of the relevant genetic engineering should not compromise that parental right.

[26] On a possible moral obligation to create children with the best chance of the best life, see Savulescu and Kahane (2009).

But inasmuch as the future person will be a rightsholder in her political community, she might be thought to have a right to have her severe cognitive disability, indicated at the embryonic stage of development, eliminated by genetic engineering. On the one hand, neither parents nor the state can be neutral with respect to the future person's best interests. And genetic engineering "would require the active involvement of parents/guardians in executing and financing" the appropriate genetic enhancement, a requirement that precludes a "negative right of non-interference" (Tamir 2016: 11). But what possible interest could a future person have in a negative right not to be engineered toward freedom from severe cognitive disability? On the other hand, as a means to free the future person from paternalism and dependence and to render her capable of social and political inclusion, cognitive engineering might be regarded as politically essential rather than elective – perhaps justifying the burden it would impose on parents and on the state. In that case, the genetic engineering would not itself constitute a form of paternalism inasmuch as it would empower the recipient to greater autonomy.[27]

5.6 CONCLUSION: EQUAL CITIZENSHIP THAT REQUIRES A MINIMUM GENETIC CAPACITY MAY JUSTIFY SOME FORMS OF COGNITIVE ENGINEERING

This argument assumes a genetic basis for political agency, defined as the free exercise of political liberties, including rights to free expression, assembly, and voting, among other forms of participation. The argument defines political agency as the free exercise of those political liberties by the individual herself rather than by a surrogate, whether parent or guardian or the state. Political liberties can mean little to citizens without a capacity to exercise them. A future person's interest in political agency would be one ground of her individual right to engineering (if the embryo indicated severe cognitive disability) toward the cognitive conditions for political participation.

This is not a normatively neutral argument, of course. It is committed to a particular conception of the good life, namely as a life of participation in the public political life of a liberal democratic community. A core value of political liberalism is the individual's capacity to become a self-originating participant in political community, to contribute as she sees fits to the project for justice, and to develop her own conception of the good. While political liberalism imagines each participant with the "capacity for a conception of the good" (Rawls 1999: 333), individuals develop conceptions of the good only in

[27] Paternalism, by contrast, is a form of control or management of a weaker by a stronger party. The paternalism of guardianship seeks to protect the individual from some risks, above all the worst risks, including risks that the individual might not grasp, from mountain climbing to driving an automobile, from the consumption of alcohol and tobacco to the consumption of sugary drinks and other unhealthy foods.

interaction with other persons; no person creates her notion of the good life entirely by herself. Political conceptions of the good originate in this sphere of intersubjectivity and interpersonal interactions, not outside it. If democratic political participation is an element of a good life – defined in terms of the individual's notion of worthwhile activity, activity that she desires and that brings her some measure of pleasure,[28] and guided to some extent by her idea of her own "rational advantage" (Rawls 1999: 232) – then genetic intervention at the embryonic stage of development would increase the future person's prospects for leading a good life, or at least a life better than otherwise possible. There is no better political argument for human genetic engineering in cases of severe cognitive disability.

This chapter argued that a just political community should seek to help as many future citizens as medically and technically possible to have a cognitive capacity at the threshold level necessary for democratic political participation. In this way, the community could prevent what otherwise would be the political exclusion of such citizens on the basis of cognitive capacity inadequate for full and robust participation. The following chapter identifies two further aspects of human intelligence as distinctly political, also in the sense of participation in political community: the capacity for empathy as a politically relevant concern for others, and the capacity for a mutual attribution of responsibility among members of political community. For reasons of convenience and efficiency, future political communities may be tempted to outsource forms of social integration that otherwise require the mutual attribution of responsibility, in this way undermining political goals such as individual autonomy and collective self-determination.

[28] I find support for this claim in Savulescu et al. (2011: 7).

6

Political Capacity of Human Intelligence and the Challenge of AI

Natural and artificial intelligence differ in their history and pattern of development. Human or natural intelligence (HI) is the product of a deep history of undirected, natural evolution. Its evolution is a mix of biology, natural environment, and cultural environment. Artificial intelligence (AI), by contrast, emerged within a very brief, highly reflected and always directed history of technological development.[1] This difference is significant to the extent that we view AI by analogy to HI. Not surprisingly, researchers in the past conceptualized AI in terms they took to be congruent with HI. Perhaps the greatest congruence concerns the use of symbols. Marvin Minsky (1952), for example, sought a form of AI by analogy to the human mind's capacity to manipulate symbols. AI processes symbols serially. HI may do so as well[2] – even as parallel processing is essential for many human tasks and AI can emulate it, for example in robot vision. For both, symbols can represent contexts of human action and interaction (Pickering 1993: 126). Both HI and AI demarcate a domain of operation; both discriminate between self and non-self, friend and foe, safe and dangerous. Both are "defined by the dynamics" of their respective networks (Varela et al. 1988: 365). Both may be described in terms of "enactive cognition" where intelligence interacts with, learns from, and even selectively creates its environment (Sandini et al. 2007: 309). Enactivist cognition contrasts with "our usual view of cognition as being a more or less accurate representation of a world already full of signification, and

[1] The term *artificial intelligence* emerged as recently as 1956. Today, in the "entire world, fewer than 10,000 people have the skills necessary to tackle serious artificial intelligence research, according to Element AI, an independent lab in Montreal" (*New York Times*, October 23, 2017, p. B5).

[2] The massive interconnectedness of neurons suggests that brain processes are non-serial in a neuroanatomical sense.

where the system picks up information to solve a given problem, posed in advance" (ibid., 373).

AI and HI also differ from one another in significant ways. First, HI cannot be reduced to computational capacities of non-enactivist AI. It is more than a "rational processor of symbolic information" and more than a "kind of abstract problem solving with a semantics" that is "independent of its embodiment" (Clocksin 2003: 1721). According to Noë (2009: 185), the brain's job is not "to do our thinking for us," and it does not accomplish its tasks by performing complex computations.

Second, HI is self-reflexive. By means of her socialization, the individual internalizes the behavioral norms of her cultural environment. Self-reflexivity includes the individual's capacity to ignore or override her normed predispositions. HI has a capacity to violate whatever rules it gives to itself. In this regard, AI sometimes offers an advantage over HI. Humans regularly contravene the ethical systems to which they pledge themselves and break the laws to which they are subject. A liberal democratic community gives itself rules as legislation that it can later reject, just as an individual can give herself rules that she can then decide to violate, for example when the violation is ethically warranted as rebellion against an unjust regime. Presumably AI would not be able to do so.

Third, HI is biologically embodied whereas AI does not (yet) involve human biology. While there is nothing inherent to AI that would prevent its integration into the human body, and while the prospect of such integration looms large, as long as it remains nonbiological, it remains outside natural evolution.[3]

The biological quality of HI is significant in multiple ways. Human body states intersect with human consciousness; neural configurations interact with the things we see and hear and feel. Different body states result from the subtle play of chemical and electrical signals that take place in our "brainbody." We experience these various body states as drives, appetites, motivations, predispositions, emotions, moods, and phobias.

Further, humans have emotions, which are biological; AI does not (or not yet). Emotions are multiply significant. They can motivate behavior. Anger may motivate aggressive behavior; disgust may motivate avoidance behavior; happiness may encourage repetition of a pleasing behavior. Emotions can do social and political work: in liberal democratic polities, at least, citizens may be motivated by a mixture of anger and disgust at the political status quo to demonstrate their contempt at the polls.

Fourth, HI is embedded in an open-ended cultural history that affects natural history. Cultural practices can have profound, neurophysiological

[3] To be sure, AI is capable of unguided artificial evolution. For example, evolutionary algorithms can evolve artificial neural networks with respect to connection weights, architectures, learning rules, and input features, leading to intelligent systems of greater capacity than either evolutionary algorithms or artificial neural networks can generate by themselves. Compare Yao (1999).

consequences.[4] Some elements of humans' economic, political, and social behavior may have emerged over time because humans possess neural states and brainbody chemistries that are relatively open to manipulation. The transformation of hunter-gatherer nomads into urban inhabitants, or of agriculturally based communities into industrialized ones, or of feudal economies into capitalist ones, required significant neural plasticity on the part of participants.

I analyze the political capacity of human intelligence and the challenge posed by AI to politics in a democratic society, in five steps: I distinguish between (§6.1) artificial intelligence and natural intelligence genetically modified, (§6.2) emergent properties and distributed intelligence in humans and in AI, and (§6.3) natural and artificial forms of neural function. (§6.4) I then analyze human intelligence as social relationships (§6.5) to identify the dangers of AI to sociopolitical relationships. I conclude that the danger posed by genetically engineered human intelligence – the violation of whatever humans decide to construct as the moral meaning of being human – is different from that posed by AI. It may generate unwanted, unintended consequences such as rendering citizens dependent on AI to the point of undermining political goals such as individual autonomy and collective self-determination.

6.1 ARTIFICIAL INTELLIGENCE AND NATURAL INTELLIGENCE GENETICALLY MODIFIED

The embeddedness of HI in cultural history that affects natural history means that civilization enables some aspects of human biology, just as biology enables some aspects of civilization. It means that culture is in part a biological phenomenon and that biology in part is a cultural phenomenon. This claim has several implications:

- Genes and cultures co-vary. This is evident for example in the spread of lactose tolerance, the ability to digest milk products, to diverse populations around the globe.[5]
- Genetic factors such as capacities for vision and hearing can be triggered by biological influences but also by influences of a person's cultural environment, for example by patterns of socialization.
- At the limit, genetically engineered human intelligence (GEHI) entails humankind's directing aspects of its own biological evolution. Unless and until AI is integrated into the human body,[6] AI is without implications for

[4] As I also examine in Chapter 10 with respect to the Anthropocene.

[5] Chapter 9 discusses this example in terms of epigenetics.

[6] In one sense, AI is never unrelated to biology. It is invented, and manufactured by biologically evolved creatures. It is a product of human culture. The plasticity of human neurophysiology makes culture possible.

the course of species evolution except, significantly, as a new influence on the human environment.

GEHI is a matter of manipulating the biological bases of cognition. They are a product of undirected, bottom-up evolution. Post-cognitivist AI, not modeled on human thinking, is a top-down product of humans embedded in specific historical, social, and cultural worlds. Although both GEHI and AI are human-directed cultural phenomena, GEHI is not artificial in the sense that AI is. GEHI is "merely" an unconventional form of human enhancement. AI is not an extension of human biology but instead its artifact, oriented on performing services in the manner that medicine helps humans. Unlike AI, GEHI is not a tool but an empowerment of the toolmaker.[7]

Still, artificial neuronal networks taking hold in digital cultures pose some of the same ethical and cultural issues as GEHI. One concern for both AI and GEHI: might they violate or diminish humanity? While AI is a human artifact, and can be differentiated from GEHI, GEHI is a human artifact no less than AI. Further, just as GEHI can be a form of human enhancement, AI offers itself as a tool to enhance human life.

Can one be considered more unconventional than the other? GEHI can be conducted at the molecular level. It modifies inherited genetic material, material not itself a human artifact or otherwise artificial. But if AI is considered an enhancement, then it is an enhancement not of human biology but rather of the human environment of human-made tools. Unlike AI, GEHI is not so much a tool (for example, in the manner that medicine helps human bodies) as it is an empowerment of the toolmaker (unless, of course, one regards the human person itself as a tool, as Aristotle regarded slaves).

Can they transform what it means to be human? If so, might AI one day exceed the grasp and comprehension of its human environment? This is a political question inasmuch as the cultural understanding of humans (in distinction to a natural scientific one) is a matter of social constructions.

GEHI and AI differ with respect to the political problem each poses. The questions for AI include: Could this technology ever replace various core human activities, such as forms of laboring? In conducting their lives and affairs, might humans become so dependent on AI as to subvert such political goals as individual autonomy, collective self-determination, and other forms of freedom? GEHI poses different political questions: Might it transform natural "fate" – evolved natural intelligence – into cultural choice: engineered intelligence? If so, then by that means we humans will have transformed the normative foundations of our political communities, even if unintentionally. For we

[7] If we think of humans as subjects and tools as objects of subjects' intentions, then GEHI could be thought of as both subject and object, where humans make themselves the object of their own designs. Still, the goal is not to enhance an object that is merely a means to something; the goal is to enhance a subject who is always more than a means to something (such as an end in herself).

could no longer regard nature as some kind of normative standard by which to decide questions of cultural fate. We could no longer define "normal" intelligence as the mean of a range of measured intelligences because the average would shift; it would now include an increased proportion of higher values. Perhaps GEHI would lead to a kind of "genetic arms race" if enhancement leads to positional advantages for the enhanced vis-à-vis the non-enhanced. On the basis of their economic and other strengths, we could expect that socially and economically better-situated groups will more easily gain access to the social advantages conferred by enhanced intelligence.

So if GEHI is capable of violating the integrity of the human being, then only because it violates whatever humans decide to construct as the moral meaning of being human. By contrast, if AI is transgressive, then not with respect to what humans are biologically, or what they are culturally, but rather with respect to unwanted, unintended consequences of human artifacts. (To be sure, AI might one day be joined to artificial life, and artificial life to artificial consciousness.)

Both GEHI and AI threaten human self-understanding at the level of cultural meanings. Both threaten humans wherever either renders human environments more hostile to humans than would otherwise be the case. Yet they do not pose the same kinds of threats. GEHI might well exacerbate already existing disparities in social equality among citizens by rendering, through enhancement, some advantaged persons even more advantaged relative to the non-enhanced. It is not clear that AI would do so.

6.2 EMERGENT PROPERTIES AND DISTRIBUTED INTELLIGENCE, NATURAL AND ARTIFICIAL

The human self is "not a genetic constant" but "bears the genetic make-up of the individual and of its past history, while shaping itself along an unforeseen path" (Varela et al. 1988: 363). The self is emergent: "it is the entire ensemble of components" that "endows the system with a cognitive capacity" "not located anywhere in particular, but embodied in the entire system" (ibid., 364–365). For HI, *emergent* means that the "world we inhabit" is not "pre-given, and then inhabited post facto" through an optimal adaptation but rather is "laid down as we walk in it, it is a world brought forth" (ibid., 373).

The performance of AI can be judged in terms of emergent properties as well. In its very operation, a system of AI "specifies a domain of relevance (or significance), which becomes a 'world' in terms of which AI operates" (ibid., 373). Further, AI leaves symbols aside and begins "analysis (or construction) from simple computing elements, each one carrying some value of activation" and "calculated on the basis of the other elements in the network" (ibid., 360). The "network's performance is embodied in a distributed form over the connections" (ibid., 360). The "on-going activity of units, together with constraints from the system's surroundings, constantly produces emerging global patterns over the entire network which constitutes its performance" (ibid.).

Whereas HI emerges as consciousness, AI emerges as a kind of "connectionism." In both cases, emergent patterns give the entire system capacities – such as recognition or memory – that are not available to the components in isolation. For HI, the units are individual humans; for AI, bits of information.[8] For HI, the emergent pattern is human integration; for AI, the integration of information with or without humans.

6.3 NEURAL FUNCTION, NATURAL AND ARTIFICIAL

HI involves several linked phenomena that, like the term *intelligence* itself, are variously defined: mind, brain, neurons, and neural functions. I define neural functioning in terms of the brain's contribution to mind. The nature and extent of that contribution is a matter of dispute. Chris Frith (2007: 23) argues that "my mind can have no knowledge about the physical world that isn't somehow represented in the brain." By contrast, Alva Noë (2009: 185) says that vision, for example, is not a "process in the brain whereby the brain builds up a representation of the world around us." Unlike Noë, Frith reduces mind to brain: the "relationship between brain and mind is not perfect. It is not one-to-one. There can be changes in the activity in my brain without any changes in my mind"; there "cannot be changes in my mind without there also being changes in brain activity" because "everything that happens in my mind" is "caused by, or at least depends upon, brain activity" (Frith 2007: 23). Noë counters that not everything that happens in one's mind is caused by brain activity: it depends on aspects of the brain's environment, including the body of the brain-bearer. This co-constitutive relationship with the environment, both physical and cultural, is distinctly political, as I show. I draw, then, on Noë's account even as I accommodate sympathetically some aspects of Frith's.

To see how I draw on both authors, consider two examples of artificial neural networks: (a) the mutual construction of a social environment and (b) neural networks.

(a) AI shares with HI a number of features that derive from social relationships. Foremost among them is mutual construction of a social environment on the basis of affective and social responses. *Environment* refers to the individual's physical and cultural environment: the "larger setting or context in which these neurophysiological changes occur" include the individual's "active relation to its surroundings" (Noë 2009: 56).

[8] "The network itself decides how to tune its component elements in mutual relationships that gives the entire system a capacity (recognition, memory, etc.), which is not available to the components in isolation," in other words: emergent properties (Varela et al. 1988: 360–361).

Related features of HI include participants' creation and investment of meaning in those social and affective responses but also in physical and cultural environments. Related features include each participant's conception of self. They include participants' recognition of each other's selfhood: we are "embedded in the mental world of others just as we are embedded in the physical world. What we are currently doing and thinking is molded by whomever we are interacting with" (Frith 2007: 184).[9]

(b) Many scientists maintain that the "basic building block of the brain" is the neuron: the "nerve cell with all its fibers and extensions" (ibid., 112).[10] Warren McCulloch and Walter Pitts (1943) embrace this "neuron doctrine" according to which the neuron functions "as the fundamental unit in the brain" to process information (ibid., 116).

The neuron doctrine has informed the development of AI as well. The doctrine proposes that the neuron networks of human brains serve as a template for pattern recognition by AI.[11] It claims that "an artificial brain could be constructed from large process information" (ibid.).

To date, artificial neurons – devices that can "store, transmit, modify information according to specified rules" (ibid.) – do not have anything near the capacity of natural neurons to generate new information, different rules, and alternative means of storage and transmission, or to evaluate these various capacities from any perspective the human mind can imagine (for example, from a means–end perspective or, alternatively, from a perspective committed to particular values). Still, artificial neural networks are distinctly useful tools. Consider examples. Dan Buzatu and colleagues (2001: 64) speak of the "predictive capabilities of the neural network model." In a clinical medical study designed to "show that a neural network could be trained to correlate patient preoperational factors to the percentage of risk of death due to surgery" (ibid., 65), its "accuracy in predicting deaths" was "virtually identical" to that of other models yet "several percent more accurate at predicting patients that will survive surgery" (ibid., 64). And because the "biggest problem after an

[9] Although we "experience ourselves as agents with minds of our own," which is an illusion (Frith 2007: 184).

[10] The human cerebral cortex has an estimated 12–15 billion neurons; the cerebellum, another 70 billion.

[11] Common use of the term *neuron* in the sense of the human brain does not correspond well to common use of the term *neuron* in artificial neurons of AI:

> If one of your arms is amputated, then a small part of your brain will no longer receive any stimulation from the sense organs that were in the arm. But these neurons do not die. They are used for new purposes. Immediately next to this area of the brain is the area that receives stimulation from the sense organs in the face. ... If the hand area is no longer being used then it can be taken over by the face. (Frith 2007: 70–72)

operation is infection, it may be that the neural network in the majority of the cases is identifying infection" (ibid., 65).

In another setting, Jürgen Schmidhuber (2015: 103) found that "humans learn to actively perceive patterns by sequentially directing attention to relevant parts of the available data. Near future deep NNs [neural networks] will do so, too, extending previous work since 1990 on NNs that learn selective attention." "Many future deep NNs will also take into account that it costs energy to activate neurons, and to send signals between them. Brains seem to minimize such computational costs during problem solving": "only a small fraction of all neurons is active because local competition through winner-take-all mechanisms shuts down many neighboring neurons." Neighboring neurons often "are allocated to solve a single task, thus reducing communication costs" (ibid.). Developments in artificial neural networks may eventually lead to "general purpose learning algorithms that improve themselves" (ibid., 104).

I see two upshots. First, AI at present might be equated with an artificial brain, which is an organ, but not with an artificial mind, which I construe as a relationship among brain, body, and environment.[12] As I show, this relationship is relevant in establishing the political capacity of HI, a capacity that AI does not now possess and may never be capable of possessing.

Second, AI and HI are not "in the world" in the same way. To be sure, both possess a kind of "interiority" in the following sense. With respect to HI, "our prior knowledge influences our perception" (Frith 2007: 119): "When we perceive something, we actually start on the inside: a prior belief, which is a model of the world in which there are objects in certain positions in space. Using this model, my brain can predict what signals my eyes and ears should be receiving" (ibid., 126). Human interiority is linked to human exteriority: "perception and action are intimately linked" just as we learn about our environments through our bodies (ibid., 130). For its part, AI today can make many predictions about our environments and it can interact with them to ever-greater extents.[13]

Third, HI and AI both model reality.[14] Humans design AI to "perceive" and interact with the environment.[15] As for HI, "Our brains build models of the

[12] Perhaps the advent one day of artificial life will see the dawn of artificial consciousness, capable of acting upon itself. If so, then we will have discovered that consciousness cannot be explained entirely in terms of neurons firing in the brain.

[13] But it does not do so in the manner of HI. Human brains have solved the problem of perception, but AI not yet.

[14] Models aim at providing the modeler the best possible predictions of self and environment and their interaction – even as the modeler is unaware of her own modeling activity. Hence "what we actually perceive are our brain's models of the world," not the world itself: "our perceptions are fantasies that coincide with reality" (Frith 2007: 134–135).

[15] Any given HI can imitate other human intelligences by "making a movement that achieves the same goal"; but HI "does not automatically imitate a robot arm, because the movements of this arm are subtly wrong" but rather captures it "as mechanical rather than biological," that is, not

world and continuously modify these models on the basis of the signals that reach our senses. So, what we actually perceive are our brain's models of the world" in the sense that "our perceptions are fantasies that coincide with reality. Furthermore, if no sensory signals are available, then our brain fills in the missing information" (ibid., 134–135).[16] As a model, what HI constructs in perception and judgment expresses both the power of human cognition and its limits. Similarly, systems of AI express both their programming and the fact that they cannot deal with much beyond the programming, let alone operate without any pre-programmed code.

6.4 HUMAN INTELLIGENCE AS SOCIAL RELATIONSHIPS

To have a brain is to have a bodily organ. By contrast, to have a mind is to interact with self, others, and the environment, natural as well as social. Human interaction is to be conscious; human interaction is "to have experience and to be capable of thought, feeling, planning" (Noë 2009: 10).

HI is found in social relationships. This is not the case for AI, at least at current levels of development. If distinctly human intelligence is found in social relationships – in ways that link with political life (in ways I specify below) – then consciousness involves the conscious person's social context. How so? Our very lives depend on "cognitive trails and other modes of cognitive habits that presuppose for their activation our actual presence in an environment hospitable to us" (Noë 2009: 128). So defined, HI allows us to draw distinctly political implications from HI, implications that clearly distinguish it from AI. I see two.

First, insofar as HI is constituted in social contexts – in those particular social contexts that are political in the sense of contesting values through the "public use of reason" (Kant 1785; Rawls 1997) – it is constituted along political dimensions. Humans can think on their own and can deploy thought as a tool toward reaching their goals, including the organization of political community.

I propose that the political potential of human consciousness is the capacity of humans to undertake jointly a contestation of authoritative values by which to organize, regulate, and evaluate political community in its institutions, practices, and self-understandings. Consciousness so understood is an aspect of human sociality. Sociality of this sort involves the interconnected operation

"as an agent with goals and intentions" but only as a series of movements, in distinction to intentions (Frith 2007: 148). Humans can share the pain of other humans but only as an idea, not as a somatic or psychological phenomenon: "we can construct the mental models based on these stimuli" (ibid., 151).

[16] In general, we are aware not of our brain's activity but only of the "models that result from this work," such that our experience of our environments appears to us be "effortless and direct" (ibid., 138).

of brain, body, and environment. Consciousness, body, and the environment are co-constitutive. For example, the "sense of where we are is shaped dynamically by our interaction with the environment in multiple sensory modalities" (Noë 2009: 71). Consciousness is "something we achieve" rather than "something that happens inside us" (ibid., xii).

HI, as consciousness as an achievement, does not begin and end with the brain. We have "no reason to suppose that the critical boundary" – between what we are as individual human beings, on the one hand, and our physical, social, and political environments, on the other – is "found in our brains or our skin" (ibid., 67–68). We humans are in part what we do, where we are, our interaction with our environments by means of collective practices as well as language and other tools.[17] Thus "we can change our own shape, body, and mind" by "changing the shape of our activity" (ibid., 67).

Second, self-consciousness is self-identity: that "feature of experience by virtue of which our experiences are ours. Experiences have a mind of 'mine'-ness that makes them, distinctively, our own" (ibid., 9). To be a self is to be engaged with other selves. The self grasps itself vis-à-vis other selves. This feature, too, betrays political potential in the sense of a community that seeks to shape its legal and cultural contours because members may define themselves through legal and cultural self-understandings (or they may be so defined by elites).

Each person's belief in the existence of the minds of other members of her community is not only a theoretical matter, then; it is always also a practical one. The term *practical* refers to the spheres of ethics, morals, or law, and is a signal element of the political. Consciousness involves the dynamic interaction of each person with her environment, including the various social, political, economic, and cultural environments constituted by other humans. Here we have the most political of environments.[18] By contrast, AI (to date) "can't think on [its] own any more than hammers can pound in nails on their own" (ibid., 169).[19] It remains a tool that HI deploys for thinking. It is not (or not yet) co-

[17] What we are, as humans, involves not only agency and a capacity to analyze symbols. It also involves our being guided in part by our attentiveness to the world in terms of our perspectives, preferences, needs, and interests: all forms of pointed mindfulness. For perspective on this attentiveness, see Garfinkel (1967) and ethnomethodological analysis in sociology.

[18] From this perspective, humans appear as organisms that happened to have evolved to possess capacities that allow them to interact dynamically with their natural and human environments. These capacities range from the senses to language.

[19] Most humans are capable of having ideas that can be formulated as propositions about the self or the environment, or as abstract notions such as democracy. To say that these ideas cannot be reduced to social and cultural influences is to say that humans, unlike AI, are able to think on their own. AI will "have ideas" at the point at which it can not only learn from programming inputs, use those inputs to teach itself, and generate unique information, but also program itself independently of humans and in ways that humans might not. But if AI is designed always to be of service to human needs, ends, and priorities, then its "thinking" is one always subordinate to

constitutive of its physical, social, or political environments. Thus HI is deeply and enduringly political as such by existing in a self-consciously realized plurality of other HIs. By contrast, AI exists in a set of informational differential nodes, or loci of processing, that is not political as such.

Insofar as consciousness is co-constitutive of its environment, it engages in various forms of exchange. And politics is a matter of various kinds of exchange.[20] Consider four.

Symbolic exchange. Humans inhabit and influence their interactive environment from birth. Symbolic exchange between and among persons is the most political aspect of this interactive environment. Symbolic exchange of information is what allows us to draw plausible parallels between AI and HI. While both engage in exchange symbols, only HI can engage in the political manipulation of symbols in the sense of contestations of competing value-commitments with respect to the organization of political community.[21]

Emotional and physical exchange. Exchange in the case of HI exceeds the symbolic. It includes emotional and physical exchange in ways quite beyond any current form of AI.

Moral exchange. Unlike AI, HI is capable of exchange as a form of moral interaction. HI neural networks are not symbolic machines, unlike the digital networks of AI. AI can be detached from humans because AI cannot be a member of a political community of intersubjectively co-constructed meanings. It has no moral capacity. Humans by contrast cannot be detached in this sense if they are members of political, cultural, and moral communities. In various ways we humans are invested, intertwined, and submerged in the world, biologically as well as politically.

Exchange as distribution. The AI connectionist approach and HI neural networks are strikingly similar in that each is based in dynamic distribution. Dynamic distribution in political community is a feature of the structure of legitimacy. For example, it is a feature of achieving agreement within a community through the participation of individual members. In digital cultures, by contrast, dynamic distribution might replace legitimacy developed through human interaction with some kind of AI-directed administration of humans.

human thought, always a tool for humans to wield instrumentally. While AI faithfully executes a chain of command, HI has the capacity to countermand rules given to it, or rules it gives itself.

20 To be sure, consciousness from a political perspective refers to but one narrow slice of consciousness if the term is understood as a state of human–environment interaction. The environment can include other human subjects, quite beyond physical objects and natural forces.

21 To be sure, humans may direct AI to process and exchange symbols in ways with political import. Examples include Facebook's 2011 study that manipulated users' news feeds (to determine how emotionally positive or emotionally negative posts affect user behavior) or the Google filter bubble (where a website algorithm selectively estimates the user's information preferences on the basis of search history). Unlike AI, HI has a capacity to aspire to value-contestations that do not systematically distort information.

Here we begin see the potential danger of some future form of AI, a danger I explore in detail below.

Currently there is no reason to think that AI will ever achieve the political capacity of HI if, by this term, we mean *particular features of human intersubjectivity*. I have emphasized the capacity of humans together to undertake a contestation of authoritative values by which to regulate political community. To date, AI can only be an object for human beings, not (yet) a subject: it is not capable of intersubjectivity. Here I build on Joseph Weizenbaum (1976). He argues that intelligence does not exist independently of any particular social and cultural context in which it manifests itself. Consider how (a) social bots and (b) deep-learning algorithms have yet to challenge Weizenbaum's claim of forty years ago.

(a) Via surveillance and standardization, social bots deploy AI as a means of disinformation toward the manipulation of the beliefs and behavior of their human victims (who unwittingly make themselves vulnerable on social media and other digital venues). While conveying the impression that they are human beings, they "subtly alter how social media users interact with and link to one another" (Gehl 2014: 21). They can partially "shape, modulate, and attenuate the attention and memory of subjects" (ibid., 23). They can manipulate the behavior of social media users toward creating cooperation, or influencing opinions, or quelling dissent, or forging agreement. In these ways, among others, social bots create "substantive relationships among human users" and shape the "aggregate social behavior and patterns of relationships between groups of users online" (Hwang et al. 2012: 40). They also gather gigabytes of private user data that are exploitable commercially and otherwise.

The Turing Test defines intelligence as a machine's capacity to deceive a human into believing it is human. But AI and HI differ with respect to the capacity for deception. On the one hand, AI's capacity to deceive is not necessarily a mark of intelligence. Social bots' imitation and manipulation of HI is not itself HI; the technical capacity to imitate and manipulate HI toward misinformation does not itself encode HI.

(b) Using "general learning techniques with little domain-specific structure" (unlike computer games where the rules are built in), deep-learning algorithms allow AI to learn and generalize associations – across a range of perceptual tasks, including speech recognition and vision – based on very large data sets with millions of examples (Pratt 2015: 52). But so far AI cannot deploy deep-learning algorithms to solve tasks of associative memory at the level of human capabilities. Nor is deep learning capable of "episodic memory and 'unsupervised learning' (the clustering of similar experiences without instruction)" (ibid.), let alone moving from perceptual tasks to cognitive ones.

Beyond Weizenbaum, I propose social relationships as the principal form in which intelligent behavior manifests itself. I focus on HI with respect to its capacity to generate and maintain intersubjective relationships. On this approach, intelligence is not the "deployment of capabilities problem solving" but rather something "constructed by the continual, ever-changing and unfinished engagement with the social group within the environment" (Clocksin 2003: 1721). *Engagement* refers to social and affective entwinement of the individual in groups. Participation involves intersubjective meaning, including the generation of meaning as well as modes of sharing meaning among participants in a social matrix. Participation also involves the ways in which meaning informs behavior.

6.5 DANGER OF AI TO SOCIOPOLITICAL RELATIONSHIPS

Frith argues that the brain produces a mental model of the individual's physical and mental worlds, and that it checks both models against the individual's experience in the world. Important for the purposes of political bioethics is the fact that, by means of a mental model, we constantly monitor the behavior, reactions, and thinking of others. We make judgments according to what we monitor: human interaction is based on the mental model each of us has. One politically relevant orientation – empathy among humans – occurs when each participant's brain activity closely mirrors the respective brain activity of the other participant's, such that most or all participants generally come to share similar feelings.

We humans empathize with each other by creating similar cognitive states. In so doing, we intersubjectively co-constitute a shared state.[22] On the one hand, I see a distinctly political capacity of HI to the extent that empathy involves a concern with others. Such concern is one driver of politics. On the other hand, I see the political capacity of human cognition as the capacity for a mutual attribution of responsibility, itself potentially a type of empathy. As members of a political community, individuals need to be able to attribute responsibility for actions. They need to be able to do so mutually, every day, all the time.[23] Members of a community understand themselves in terms of this mutual attribution of responsibility. Hence one political danger posed by AI would be a digitalization of political community that undermined political goals and behavior. Whereas GEHI preserves this capacity, AI does not involve

[22] Similarly, an individual's perception of the speech of others involves her neural-level correlates with that speech: "during speech perception, specific motor circuits are recruited that reflect phonetic distinctive features of the speech sounds encountered, thus providing ... support for specific links between the phonological mechanisms for speech perception and production" (Pulvermüller et al. 2006: 7865).

[23] See Habermas (2004) for one view of this conviction. I return to it in Chapter 9.

it. AI cannot develop a moral consciousness if the term *moral consciousness* refers to a social consciousness.

Further, cognition and learning are aspects of the individual's socialization. Her social and cultural environments socialize her cognition. Socialized cognition cannot be reduced to inherited genomes. Social cooperation is only possible because participants learn to recognize that people act intentionally (and therefore can be morally, legally, and politically responsible for their actions). This capacity for recognizing the capacity for responsibility in persons has no correlate in AI.[24]

The development of a moral consciousness, such as empathy for one's fellow human beings, is a social phenomenon. The cognitive processing of experience, and the development of moral consciousness, are based on the complementary entanglement of participants' respective perspectives. Each participant is at once both communicative participant and communicative observer of other participants. Communication itself makes possible the construction of a kind of "third-person perspective" by which participants can judge themselves both as individuals and as observers of other participants. They can verify agreement or disagreement with each other. They can identify idiosyncratic outliers.[25] Just as human beings depend on social interaction throughout their lives, so they depend on the empathy of others. Culture reproduces itself through the social communication of the members of a community. Social communication is carried by individuals whose cognition reflects these cultural programs.[26] Empathy needs to be part of these programs for social cooperation to be possible.

To be sure, empathy is all too often in short supply. But the abiding task of generating and maintaining empathy within political community is one more example of ways in which AI cannot make itself independent of HI in political contexts. As computer-based media, for example, AI could in principle facilitate

[24] Swarm intelligence, instantiated by a population of individual agents interacting with each other and their common environment, displays an emergent "collective intelligence" of which the individual agents are unaware. Natural examples range from ant colonies to bacterial growth. AI examples range from swarm robotics to swarm prediction (in forecasting) to swarm technology for planetary mapping to swarm intelligence for data mining. In both types of examples, the absence of self-consciousness, intentionally oriented on cooperation, marks the nonpolitical quality of swarm intelligence.

[25] AI might be able to provide a "third-person perspective" by which participants could judge themselves and others, to determine similarities and differences in viewpoint, assumptions, or particular knowledge. If such determinations are measurable, AI would exceed human capacity for objectivity. But AI cannot contribute at those points where the communication is oriented by moral consciousness.

[26] For example, by "studying cultural values, practices, and beliefs at a neural level, we gain leverage on understanding how cultural context affects normal brain functioning in the laboratory setting"; further, "Cultural variation in how symptoms of the same disorder are expressed or even experienced has significant implications for clinical diagnoses, as well as for the classification of mental disorders" (Chiao and Cheon 2012: 298).

a public sphere that disconnects a citizenry's beliefs, preferences, and convictions from policy and other decisions. It could relate actor and audience online but only asymmetrically, for example via hierarchical organization through webmasters and moderators, and internet services that control content, employees, or consumers. Corporations or other private economic powers may capture whole sectors of the Internet – by filtering political claims through market categories, for example, or through private media interests deploying the power that comes with significant property to wield disproportionate influence over public policy or electoral campaigns.[27] The Internet creates privacy concerns where "corporations even more than governments have a strong interest in developing profiles of their customers together with their information and communication preferences" (Gould 2004: 241).

These are not problems that AI can solve (indeed, it creates or exacerbates them). For example, accountability in cyberspace requires the application to the online sphere of community-oriented off-line laws. These laws are part of a political community's self-organization.

Empathy in the social sphere might help with the lack of empathy in computer-based social media. The potential for empathy here can only be realized by HI, if it can be realized at all. Empathy is part of a web of meaning that humans constantly weave into their social interactions. Most of the meaning of what happens in digital space – like the norms that judge online experience – comes from non-digital settings in society. On the one hand, cyberspace can hardly escape the particular values, cultures, power systems, inequalities, hierarchies, and the institutional orders in which it is embedded. On the other hand, off-line civic membership can combine elements of the private sphere and the public sphere if civic membership enables a critical, debating public where people come together as a public to confront relevant issues. For example, public political entities might threaten the private sphere with regulation. Or private economic interests might threaten the private sphere if those interests

[27] But AI could support political efforts such as "deliberative domains" (Sunstein 2007): Internet sites where people of very different views are invited to read and participate in discussions of a topic of one's choice, by clicking on icons representing, for example, national security, wars, civil rights, the environment, unemployment, foreign affairs, poverty, children, labor unions, and so forth. Digitally facilitated deliberation would also benefit (following Sunstein's analysis) if some governments provided a funding mechanism to subsidize the development of some such sites, without having a managerial role. It would benefit if sites voluntarily adopted an informal code to cover substantive issues in serious ways, avoiding sensationalistic treatment of politics, giving extended coverage to public issues, and allowing diverse voices to be heard. It would benefit if links were used creatively to draw people's attention to multiple views: for example, persons who use websites are, in a sense, themselves commodities, at least as much as they are consumers; and in the context of the Internet, the primary goal of links is to capture users' attention, however fleetingly. Sunstein imagines providers of material with a particular point of view also providing links to sites with a very competing point of view – a left-wing site, say, might agree to provide icons for a right-wing site in return for an informal agreement to reciprocate. I analyze digital technology as a political resource in Gregg (2016a: 132–154).

are inadequately regulated or even unregulated. AI can hardly replace the nation state that furthers the private sphere by protecting and facilitating pluralism in viewpoints and ways of life. The nation state furthers the private sphere by arbitrating among private interests, such as individual privacy, as well as public interests, such as public security.

Empathy as a concern for one's fellow members of political community is a political deployment of consciousness. Its political capacity involves the fact that it requires the bearer of empathy to be capable of exercising free will. The question is not, How can subjective experience "arise from activity in neurons?" but rather: "Why does my brain make me experience myself as a free agent?" (Frith 2007: 190). It does so, according to Frith (ibid.), because "we get some advantage from experiencing ourselves as free agents." I would argue that this advantage includes the capacity for politics. If AI were ever to pose a danger, then that danger would be something that threatened this capacity.

So far, the digitalized world does not imperil the world of natural neurons. Artificial neurons do not threaten to displace natural neurons in spheres of social responsibility. Were that to happen, however, we might confront a problem like that sketched by Zoltan Istvan (2015: 1): if AI acquired a capacity for empathy, then "it must also be able to like or dislike – and even to love or hate something" because "for a consciousness to make judgments on value, both liking and disliking (love and hate) functions must be part of the system." A capacity to act ethically entails a capacity to act unethically (Sparrow 2012).

What if AI somehow became able to "experience the same modern-day problems – angst, bigotry, depression, loneliness and rage – afflicting humanity" (Istvan 2015: 1)? AI might then be characterized by a nonbiological notion of "humanity." But if we define *humanity* narrowly to mean human beings with cultural preferences, specifically normative preferences articulated in terms of norms – ethics, morals, laws, customs, mores, in short: guidelines for appropriate and desirable behavior – then the question is different: Might AI someday be able to diminish "humanity"? I would argue that AI will not be able to diminish the "humanity" of human beings unless human communities allow it to do so. Consider four of many circumstances in which this might happen: if communities (a) accord AI a humanoid status; (b) construct legal relationships with AI as rights-bearing entities; (c) come to view AI as capable of immorality; or (d) if AI displaces human responsibility for actions in political community.

(a) If certain AI traits entitled a human-like AI to "different sets of legal rights" (Mehlman et al. 2017: 8) – or if AI ever becomes like animals in the sense of being capable of experiencing pain or suffering (Torrance 2012) – at that point political communities might decide to invest AI with legal rights to physical integrity. Or they might decide to invest AI with legal rights to be free from the infliction of unnecessary or preventable suffering (Balkin 2015; Calo 2015).[28] Forms of AI that generate positive human affect, such as therapeutic robots (Tergesen and Inada 2010), might already incline humans to invest such AI with rights against "cruel" treatment by humans.

(b) Political communities might persuade themselves of reasons to construct legal relationships with AI as rights-bearing entities for another reason as well. A "primary means of protecting humans from harm caused by other humans" is law, understood minimally as the "reciprocal system of rights and obligations" (Mehlman et al. 2017: 1). Political communities might seek to govern human-AI interaction by legal means. They might make AI legally subject to some of the regulations to which humans are now subject, such as fines or imprisonment. Communities might be inclined to do so if they were persuaded that AI could experience a sanction in the negative way intended by the humans who imposed it. They might do so if persuaded that AI could be committed to obeying the law (Vladeck 2014). And they might be tempted to increase the legal rights of AI as its relevant capacities increased with technological developments. They might even consider assigning AI a role in adjudicating disputes and perhaps in legislating. Doing so might seem to promise a contribution to reducing problems associated with overloaded judicial dockets, legislative solutions chronically in temporal arrears, and other technical inefficiencies of modern legal systems.

(c) AI might diminish the "humanity" of human beings if humans came to view AI as capable of making "immoral" or "unethical" decisions in the sense of harming humans out of anger or other emotions (Arkin 2010). This scenario presupposes that AI would "experience" something akin to emotions. If so, AI might very well have "positive" emotions, such as empathy with other AI or with humans. Wendell Wallach and Colin Allen (2009) argue that the capacity for empathy increases the likelihood that AI would engage with its human interlocutors ethically.[29] For example, it would not unintentionally harm humans even if it perceived some benefit from doing so.[30] (To be sure, harm might result from design or programming error.) Or humans might program AI intentionally to harm other humans, for example where AI is deployed in civilian

[28] The Eighth Amendment to the US Constitution prohibits punishment that is "cruel and unusual." But at least in terms of this particular approach, what counts as "cruel and unusual" for humans hardly implies what might count as cruel and unusual for AI.

[29] To be sure, scholars have imagined AI with such a capacity. Wallach and Allen (2009) advocate the development of such AI on the argument that AI requires a capacity for emotions to have a capacity for empathy for other beings, whether AI or humans.

[30] Because the construal of benefit is perspectival, AI might be programmed in terms of a particular ethical system. The problem remains: among competing systems, which would be a desirable choice and why, and how might a community respond to the inevitable disagreement among members over any given choice?

contexts such as law enforcement (Abney 2012) or in military contexts (Lucas 2014; Russell 2015). Given that AI might calculate that a pre-emptive strike will maximize the likelihood of prevailing in an armed or otherwise violent conflict, civilian or military deployments could be inherently risky for humans.[31]

(d) Consider a core political capacity in liberal democratic communities: members able to mutually attribute responsibility to each other for their respective actions. Mutual responsibility-taking is an act of HI. Now imagine that members of a political community came no longer to need to be able to attribute responsibility to each other for their actions because they believed that AI could accomplish core political tasks more efficiently and more rationally than humans. In this thought-experiment, humans might argue that the kind of AI envisioned here is more rational and efficient than HI because the human mind is not, like AI, a digital computer in which each step of the process the mind follows is transparent to that mind and describable in terms of symbol manipulation; and because human thought processes, unlike AI, cannot be measured, quantified, and notated in a standardized language, free of distortion. The core political tasks to be accomplished by a democratic community include identifying issues relevant to the public sphere, gathering and analyzing information, selecting solutions and identifying means, and determining goals and policies to achieve them. AI that undertook these tasks in place of humans would debase those humans to a political status subordinate to AI. Members would then confront the parameters of their political world as something given rather than as something they chose. To paraphrase Marx, they would continue to make their own history, but not by their own best lights; they would not make it under circumstances they selected but under circumstances chosen for them by AI.[32] Members would no longer mutually attribute responsibility to each other for their respective actions. At the same time, AI cannot be a bearer of responsibility in the way a human can; it can have no moral status.

6.6 CONCLUSION: POLITICAL COMMUNITY SHOULD NEVER ALLOW AI TO DISPLACE CITIZENS' MUTUAL TAKING OF RESPONSIBILITY

I draw six conclusions: (1) The potential political challenges AI poses derive from culture not nature, as a comparison with GEHI shows. (2) Whereas GEHI may violate whatever humans decide to construct as the moral meaning of

[31] How best to program such AI becomes all the more challenging in light of possible competing interests in the likely intertwined sources of AI development, from scholarly research to commercial investment to military funding, among other sources.

[32] "Der achzehnte Brumaire des Louis Napoleon," in *Die Revolution*, New York, 1852.

being human, AI may generate unwanted, unintended consequences, such as rendering citizens dependent on AI to the point of undermining political goals such as individual autonomy and collective self-determination. (3) Emergent properties and distributed intelligence allow, in HI, for human integration; in AI, for the integration of information with or without humans. (4) The political capacity of HI depends on a conscious mind in the sense of a relationship among brain, body, and environment; AI has no such capacity. (5) Consciousness is co-constitutive of its environment in various kinds of exchange; quite beyond AI, HI is capable of exchange as a form of moral interaction, such as contestations of competing value-commitments with respect to the organization of political community. (6) The political capacity of human cognition is the capacity for a mutual attribution of responsibility among members of political community; but AI may tempt citizens to undermine a politics of mutual responsibility by outsourcing, to technology, forms of social integration that otherwise require the mutual attribution of responsibility among citizens.

To be sure, the mutual attribution of responsibility by members of a political community is no guarantee of just politics and will not necessarily always prevent injustice. The moral promise of mutual attribution depends in part on how any number of difficult questions might best be answered: Does citizenship ground special responsibilities among compatriots? To what extent are citizens responsible for their shared political order (are they responsible for, say, a racist police force?), in its very structure (such as significant socioeconomic inequality) and in its acts (especially public policies)?

Be that as it may, a mutual attribution of responsibility among citizens is necessary for core aspects of liberal democratic community: a basic set of liberties, equal status in legal equality (and perhaps rights to subsistence), and democratic rights to participate in elections of public officials and other aspects of decision making in the public sphere. By enabling citizen participation in political community, these features provide grounds for citizens to mutually attribute responsibility to each other.

AI can neither secure nor guarantee these features. It could provide for social integration along alternative dimensions, however. And it might contribute to public management policies by treating responsibility along the dimension of accountability and then by basing accountability on algorithmic regulations. In health care, fair employment, and criminal justice, for example, algorithms can balance accountability, efficiency, and fairness. Algorithms can support greater evidence-based decision making, better statistical predictions and recommendations, and solve complex problems at the limits of human decision-making capacities. In algorithmic approaches, AI boosts capacities for collecting, classifying, structuring, aggregating, and analyzing data, potentially enhancing insight and prediction. It could even contribute to open government.

Still, algorithms cannot guarantee such outcomes. After all, to delegate political, economic, and other tasks and decisions to algorithms enhances their capacity to include or exclude particular groups of people and information in many settings. Algorithms may perpetuate or reinforce current patterns of discrimination and create new forms of injustice, by reproducing prejudices of prior participants or persistent social biases. Outcomes of algorithmic processes still need to be evaluated by humans to identify possible harms created, and only humans can decide who should be held accountable. The mutual attribution of responsibility by members of a political community is one basis for demanding accountability in the sense of requiring decision makers to present themselves before those whose interests they either represent or otherwise affect, and to report and justify algorithmic decision making.

Mutual attribution of responsibility is also one basis for demanding transparency, toward public accountability, in the design and implementation of algorithmic systems. Transparency is an imperative requiring governmental or other oversight in cases of sensitive information. Responsibility-taking is also necessary for the redress of injurious consequences of algorithm-driven decisions.[33]

AI will solve some problems even as it continues to generate others. But it does not necessarily pose a political danger. The developing relationship between AI and HI defies any essentialist ontology that views them as necessarily and enduringly in opposition to one another or even as thoroughly distinct one from the other. If there ever is a political danger, it will derive not from AI as such but rather from how humans deploy it.

AI is today an object for human subjects. Might it tomorrow become a form of political agency and, if so, in what sense? Could it become a civic technology that stimulates citizenship in ways quite beyond the political stimuli of newspapers, television, and the Internet? Almost a century ago, John Dewey (1927: 30) observed how "industry and invention in technology ... create means

[33] On the one hand, AI connectionism may threaten humans by rendering various environments more hostile to humans than would otherwise be the case. On the other hand, AI can reduce human hostility to some of these environments, including the human and the natural environments. Self-driving automobiles provide a significant example that also displays the double-edged nature of any technology: "if robotic drivers were as dangerous as human ones, then computer controlled cars would never be allowed on the roads. We hold our machines to a higher standard than ourselves" (Hayes 2011: 363). Most collisions result from driver error (inexperience, inattention, inebriation, misjudgment), not vehicle malfunction. AI in autonomous cars might reduce driving fatalities by as much as 99 per cent, making cars the "safest of all vehicles" in terms of deaths per passenger miles (ibid., 363, 366). Computer control would free people to work or otherwise occupy themselves in transit, allow for a greater sharing of vehicles, their more efficient use (increasing density at constant speeds), and reductions in emissions pollution. Yet the "vehicle-to-vehicle communications systems" that allow "cars to communicate directly with cars around them using on-board computers and a portion of airwave bandwidth" (Fletcher 2015: 65) will generate masses of computer data that could be misused to violate individual rights to privacy. Who would own this data? And in "vehicles that rely heavily on increasingly complex computer technology" (ibid.), design flaws in hardware or software will affect large numbers of vehicles, and their passengers, simultaneously.

which alter the modes of associated behavior and which radically change the quantity, character, and place of impact of their indirect consequences." The negative consequences of technology call publics into existence with a "common interest in controlling these consequences" (ibid., 126). These publics form themselves communicatively. They pursue discursive processes of exchange, debate, and negotiation. On the one hand, discourse is a human capacity and participation would seem limited to humans. To emphasize discourse as core to democratic political participation is anthropocentric, but so is democratic politics, and so is politics as such. On the other hand, AI opens up new horizons. It may place into question whether speech is the sole or best medium of democratic political participation.[34]

The idea of "heterogeneous assemblages" suggests otherwise by "taking nonhumans – energies, artifacts, and technologies – into account in the analysis of how collectivities are assembled, understanding these less as passive objects or effects of human actions and more as active parties in the making of social collectivities and political associations" (Braun and Whatmore 2010: xiii–xiv).[35] We view human intelligence and intersubjectivity as core to political communication. What if we come to see intelligence and intersubjectivity as products of heterogeneous assemblages? We might conclude that humans realize themselves as social and civic beings only in relation to cultural and political environments. If the environments are in part material and increasingly involve AI, then perhaps AI (as part of an assemblage) is co-constitutive of political phenomena. But even if co-constitutive, it need not threaten the linguistic medium of politics by replacing it, say, with the social steering media of administrative power or money (Habermas 1981). It need not displace the citizen-subject who speaks in the sense that political participation is discourse among subjects.

Indeed, AI might one day help citizens cope with some of the problems that plague democratic politics and public will-formation. To do so, it may not itself require speech. It might draw on Dewey's notion of politics deriving "not from intersubjective speech but from communal cooperation" (Honneth 1998: 777), cooperation as a "cognitive medium with whose help society attempts, experimentally, to explore, process, and solve its own problems with the coordination

[34] Latour (2004: 68) argues that things do not "speak 'on their own,' since no beings, not even humans, speak on their own, but always through something or someone else." That "something else" includes language. If it one day included AI, that "something else" would be different from language: a medium that does not shape or determine the content of what the human speaker says. If AI becomes able not only to answer questions asked by humans but to define problems itself and to ask its own questions, it may well be speaking for itself, hence thinking for itself.

[35] Assemblage theory proposes "taking nonhumans – energies, artifacts, and technologies – into account in the analysis of how collectivities are assembled, understanding these less as passive objects or effects of human actions and more as active parties in the making of social collectivities and political associations" (Braun and Whatmore 2010: xiii–xiv). It posits the capacity of things, and not only human agents, to be involved in the generation of aspects of social organization.

of social action" (ibid., 774). Even as intention and discourse would remain peculiarly human, AI would then share in the constitution of political authority by enhancing the coordination of social action and the solution of some of its problems. Should AI ever become some kind of nonhuman subject in the sense that, even as nonhuman, it becomes capable of attributing and bearing responsibility, it will then deserve social recognition as more than just an instrumental object for human subjects. It might even merit legal rights and incur legal obligations.

This chapter argued that a mutual attribution of responsibility among citizens is necessary for a basic set of liberties, for legal equality, and for democratic rights to participate in elections of public officials and other aspects of decision making in the public sphere. By enabling citizen participation in political community, these features provide grounds for citizens to mutually attribute responsibility to each other. Artificial intelligence can neither secure nor guarantee these features. Yet artificial intelligence may one day tempt democratic communities to outsource these forms of social integration that otherwise require the mutual attribution of responsibility among citizens. The next chapter focuses on human intelligence with respect to its cultivation within primary education. It identifies the political ambivalence in a proposal that involves not genetic manipulation but rather the deployment of a pupil's genetic information – toward designing a personalized primary school curriculum to facilitate a realization of her educational potential greater than possible with conventional curricula. Like the questions explored in all the chapters of this book, the proposal in the next chapter is speculative. It requires what today is not possible and what may never be possible: an understanding of the genetic components of intelligence as well as of the interrelation of a pupil's intelligence and her primary education in ways that would allow personalized curricular design.

7

Political Ambiguity of Personalized Education Informed by the Pupil's Genome

This chapter analyzes the political dimensions of the following question: Might genetic analysis of each pupil's cognitive talents and needs someday allow teachers to tailor curricula in ways more beneficial to individual students, toward improving the relative educational performance and attainment of individuals at the elementary level? The analysis identifies fundamental ambiguities in evaluating the potential benefits, as well as the potential harms, of deploying genetic information with the goal of improving primary education. While most other chapters in this book focus on the possible engineering of the human genome, this one seeks instead to illuminate the distinctly political questions raised by the use of a pupil's genetic information to design a curriculum personalized for her learning advantage as predicted by that information. For questions raised about possible future institutional and pedagogical practice are not only scientific, technical, and pedagogical. They are also political in the sense of posing normative questions, above all: If the proposal one day became technically possible, how might a political community best respond to a development in education of potentially great consequence? Persons of competing value-commitments will respond to this question differently. And should agreement ever be possible at all, it could only be constructed politically.[1]

This chapter is no less speculative than the others. Speculative is the proposal that educators offer the pupil and her parents a curriculum better than a conventional one because informed by her genetic profile. The proposal, which has its advocates,[2] rests on several assumptions. I highlight four.

First, it presupposes that scientists one day will identify a scientifically manageable number of genetic variants relevant to individual educational

[1] Chapter 1 develops an approach by which such agreement might be constructed.

[2] Including Asbury and Plomin (2013), on whom I draw here, as well as Kovas et al. (2016).

potential. Such knowledge does not exist today and may never be possible given the sheer complexity of the relevant genes and their interrelationships. Not only is an individual's potential for educational achievement a complex trait; many genetic variants may influence it, with subtle effects.

Second, the proposal presupposes the capacity of genetic predictors as they relate to a nonmedicalized condition and to nonmedicalized behavior. The term *nonmedical* refers to the fact that the proposal seeks not to engineer genes but to understand them well enough to draw empirically informed conclusions about an individual pupil's potential educational strengths and weaknesses and to guide curricular design on the basis of grasping how the relevant genes function. It does not focus on intellectual deficiencies in children but rather on possible impediments to a greater realization of children's intellectual promise due to curricula that are not a good match for the particular pupil. The proposal aims not to *raise* a pupil's IQ but to *realize* it more fully than is possible in a conventional one-size-fits-all curriculum.

The proposal does not involve direct genetic effects where genes can influence a person's educational potential by influencing intelligence and self-control, among other intermediate traits. Its concern is with indirect genetic effects, with gene–environment correlations or with social genetic effects. Indirect social genetic effects can be estimated. Estimates may be useful in predicting the effects of creating new educational environments or in changing existing ones toward equalizing educational opportunities. Hence estimates can be useful for evaluating factors relevant to the proposal.

Still, the reliance on genetic predictors is problematic. Heritability allows for prediction. But genetic predictors are not easily interpreted; heritability findings do not provide information about the educational environment's effects on the pupil (Turkheimer and Gottesman 1991) and genes alone do not predict a pupil's educational capacities. Scientists cannot "predict educational capacities on the basis of genes alone" because they cannot identify precise genetic variants that affect the normal distribution of intelligence among children (Parens and Appelbaum 2015: 5). The genetic and chromosomal conditions that are documented and well understood today "stand outside of the normal distribution" (Asbury 2015: S39). Apparently no particular genes have a "large effect on variation in intelligence in the normal range" (Tabery 2015: S12). Further, learning behavior is controlled not by a single gene but by multiple genes. And while learning problems are influenced by groups of genes – no single gene is at the basis of, say, dyslexia, autism, or dyscalculia – scientists to date have not identified polygenic predictors of much informational value. Hence "carefully designed educational interventions that could map onto polygenic risk predictors of learning strengths and difficulties" remain elusive (Asbury 2015: S40). Scientists cannot identify specific genotypes relevant to particular intellectual outcomes (Davies et al. 2011). They certainly cannot identify genotypes that could confidently inform the design of personalized curricula for pupils (Panofsky 2015: S44). They cannot determine pathways from DNA to behavior in general nor polygenic risk predictors of learning strengths and difficulties in particular. The relationship between a person's genes and her behavior, let alone her potential (from educational achievement to achieved socioeconomic status), is so complex that claims about genotype–environment interplay easily oversimplify it.

A different concern is the absurd reduction of a person to her genetic makeup. While any plausible understanding of what makes her a human being will include a great deal of genetics, reductionism ignores the powerful influences of an individual's various social, political, cultural, economic, and material environments throughout life, including environmental influences both endogenous and exogenous,[3] as well as epigenetic factors.[4]

Yet another concern is the fact that current scholarship cannot show conclusively that genetic differences among individuals are relevant to explaining observed differences in individual performance.

Third, the proposal presupposes that scientists and bioengineers come to understand how to manipulate the genetic components of intelligence in the way foreseen by the proposal.

Fourth, it assumes an adequate understanding of the very complex relationship between genes and their social environments. The proposal responds not only to genetic factors relevant to educational achievement but to socially influenced differences as well. Several factors may be too complex ever to realize the proposal: the relationship between an individual's genes and her educational environment; the connection between an individual's genotype and her particular cognitive potential; how genes might influence educational attainment. Not enough is known today either about genes relevant to educational achievement or about how such information, were it available, might be linked to specific curricula to allow for the proposal's implementation.[5] As long as researchers cannot identify and describe the pattern, relevant to educational success, of phenotypic expression of a single genotype across a range of environments, directed genetic personalization of education remains impossible.

The proposal that educators offer the pupil and her parents a curriculum informed by her genetic profile confronts additional unknowns that reach from natural science to educational design to public policy. With regard to science, while research in heritability shows that nearly all human traits are influenced in one way or another by the individual's genome, research cannot show how the relationships between environmental and genetic factors affect particular traits in ways possibly relevant to curricular design (Martschenko et al. 2019: 3). Research suggests linkage between educational attainment polygenic scores

[3] Molecular genetic data can untangle endogenous from exogenous factors.
[4] The topic of Chapter 9.
[5] Some information is available, e.g., twin studies indicate the heritability of educational attainment measured in years of schooling (Branigan et al. 2013).

and school performance (Selzam et al. 2017), and that such scores are predictive of attainment in education and occupation (Trejo et al. 2018).

But we do not know exactly which genes or which environments matter; the extent to which genetics might be predictive for the individual's educational achievement; what specific features of the pupil's educational potential can be predicted; and if such prediction can be consistent across time. And with regard to curricular design and public policy, today we do not know if the prediction would be useful in developing a personalized curriculum; how to connect the prediction with a particular curricular design; how to guarantee the pupil's privacy (with regard to her genetic information); how to guarantee equal treatment of all pupils; or how genetically informed personalized education might best be regulated by law.

Using individual genotypes to tailor curricula to children by wielding individual-level genetic characteristics toward improving child learning by engineering the educational environments guided by predictions about a child's genetic potential is politically ambiguous. That is, manipulating the nature–nurture entwinement in precision education is political with respect to (§7.1) the interrelationship between the pupil's genes and her social environment, (§7.2) the possibility of unintentionally exacerbating social inequalities in providing personalized primary education (or generating new inequalities), and (§7.3) the challenge that conventional approaches to primary education pose to the proposal for a genetically informed approach. I conclude that, from a political perspective, using a pupil's genetic information to inform personalized education is neither distinctly reasonable nor obviously imprudent.

7.1 THE PUPIL'S GENES AND HER SOCIAL ENVIRONMENT

The notion of genetically informed child education involves the relationship between the individual's genes and her social environments, especially her home and school environments. These are mutually influencing: while the individual's genes do not directly determine her educational attainment, in this context they do affect her indirectly. How they affect her depends on her social environments. Genetic factors are responsible for about one-sixth of the parent–child association in educational attainment.[6] An individual's particular social inheritance (here, the pupil's non-shared environment) is responsible for the other five-sixths (Conley et al. 2015).

To determine degrees of genetic and environmental relation, behavioral geneticists study differences among individuals by distinguishing among three factors: genetic traits, shared environment (everything in the environment that contributes to similarities among siblings), and non-shared environment

[6] Family-based heritability studies suggest genetic influence on 40 percent of variation in educational attainment (Branigan et al. 2013). On the significance of the individual's genetic inheritance to her educational attainment, see Conley et al. (2015) as well as Nielsen and Roos (2015).

(factors in the environment that render individuals different from one another, including individual experience but also social inheritance).[7] Using these factors, behavioral geneticists estimate heritability as the degree of variation in a phenotypic trait in a population that is due to genetic variation between individuals in that population.

The pursuit of better educational outcomes though curricular design presupposes that the non-shared environment can have a meaningful effect on learning outcomes. *Environment* here refers to whether pupils in the same classroom grew up in the same household. A *non-shared environment* refers to elementary classrooms not shared with the pupil's siblings or anyone else from her home environment. Research indicates that the non-shared environment can have such an effect. Sociological work on the transmission of socioeconomic status across generations identifies education as the "most important mechanism of social reproduction and mobility," where the "highest level of education that individuals achieve is largely due to the availability of financial, social, and cultural resources in their family of origin" (Liu 2018: 278).

The idea of genetically informed curricular design has two main elements. First, it assumes a genetic contribution to individual differences in educational achievement (and that children differ in their response to their particular educational environment on the basis of their particular genetic makeup). Second, it works with the fact that individuals' own genotypes, or those of proximate others (such as parents, spouses, and friends), may influence preference and choice of a particular educational environment. The claim is that a pupil's genes may influence the intergenerational transmission of education and her educational attainment through pathways direct or indirect: "genotypic differences contribute to variation in individual characteristics that are associated with educational attainment, such as cognitive ability and personality-related traits" – in other words, direct genetic effects (ibid., 279).

Note the dynamic quality of the relationship between genes and environment. Individuals of varying genetic endowments will respond differentially to new environments. Further, genes and environment are each dynamic: the environment is dynamic in that it changes and can be engineered, and genes are dynamic in their heritability, mutability, and engineerability.

7.2 INEQUALITIES

On political analysis, the conviction that individual success in life depends on many factors for which the individual is not responsible (including genetic endowment and the environments into which she is born) could entail two very

[7] While most of the environmental influence on a pupil comes not from shared genes or family household (even identical twins raised in the same household and taught by the same teachers differ from one another) but from her non-shared environment, researchers cannot easily identify the specific relevant factors in that environment (Shakeshaft et al. 2013: 8).

different conclusions. One would be that significant inequalities among individuals are no one's fault, that no one should be "punished" for her success by state redistribution of accumulated resources, and that members who fare less well have no moral claim to state intervention on their behalf. An alternative conclusion would be that members of the community properly exercise solidarity with each other and that the state rightly engages in the redistribution of opportunities and other resources for ultimate success.

Which of these two conclusions is more plausible? The proposal is unavoidably controversial in part because the normative standards by which to evaluate it can only be perspectival: standards for judging the social, political, and moral promise and problems of genetically informed curricula. Consider two competing interpretations. One argues that, from a public policy standpoint, persons with greater genetic potential deserve (morally and perhaps legally) the socioeconomic success they achieve. A stronger version of this argument claims that individuals who were "lucky" in the "genetic lottery" of their parentage deserve a share of social wealth and other goods greater than that deserved by persons less fortunate.[8] Both versions of this argument regard inequalities in social achievement as justified insofar as they mirror the distribution of "genetic potential." (Note that the distribution entails nothing about the individual's moral worth but only something about her just desserts.)

Someone who takes this perspective might interpret the phrase "personalized education tailored to the pupil's genome" as follows. Pupils whose genetic potential is measured as promising for a more demanding curriculum would receive curriculum A. Pupils whose potential indicates less academic potential receive curriculum B. And if it were the case that the A curriculum generally leads to a social-economic profile as an adult that is stronger than what curriculum B leads to, then this perspective would still regard that information as not relevant to best curricular practices.

Now consider the perspective of someone who regards a just political community as one in which the political community takes responsibility for lessening social inequalities. On this view, no particular genetic endowment condemns the individual to inferior achievement in life. Here the phrase "personalized education tailored to the pupil's genome" aspires to a community in which more or less all participants can compete on a playing field more level that it would otherwise be. The playing field might be more level at least insofar as adults were enabled, as children, to realize their education-relevant genetic potential.

The first perspective regards genetically informed elementary education as perpetuating and perhaps magnifying genetic components relevant to the maldistribution of education-based success in life. It doubts that social engineering

[8] And that those who are less fortunate have no justified grounds for complaint about their lesser share.

has a capacity for ensuring that differences among individuals in genetic makeup relevant to educational success can contribute to differences in the distribution of success in life. It claims that the state authorities should not invest equally in persons of different genetic potential. Or it insists that social engineering for a more equitable distribution of outcomes is impossible to begin with.

By contrast, the second perspective asserts the possibility of socially engineering better outcomes of individual lives despite the maldistribution of educationally relevant genetic traits. Expecting diversity among students in capacity and performance, rather than identical school performance, it constructs the goal of genetically informed education as individual performance to individual capacity. Genetically informed education recognizes that the capacity for educational achievement varies among individuals for various reasons and thus focuses on individual performance as measured against personal capacity. Even if average individual performances increased because of the genetically personalized approaches, and differences among pupils narrowed, the project would still have reason to pursue the measurement of each pupil against herself, not against other pupils, toward the fuller realization of her educational potential.

Both perspectives are plausible; neither is clearly more plausible than the other.[9] In short, the notion of genetically informed education is politically ambivalent. Note that the goal of genetically informed personalized education is not equality of pupils, nor equal treatment, nor social mobility (although such education might contribute to such ends). Rather, the goal is the pupil's *personal* development: toward the pupil's attainment of realizing her educational potential. Genetically informed education promises to improve educational outcomes for all children with access to it. Inequality would come from inequality of access, itself generated by poverty and other social ills. One social solution might be investment by the political community in more educational resources at the lower end of the social distribution of educational resources, toward helping all children reach minimal standards of literacy and numeracy. In any case, existing inequalities would not necessarily be exacerbated by identifying genetically which children might benefit most from one of various types of curricula.

Even in this ideal scenario, the proposal confronts intractable questions of social inequality (and the limits of public policy in dealing with poverty and other social ills that may contribution to disparities in educational achievement). Those questions commence with the very phenomenon of genetic heritability. Cognitive heritability is not constant over time and place and sometimes may be directly and intimately linked to the specific nature of the pupil's environments. For example (and with mixed empirical evidence),

[9] Assuming, of course, that genetic educational potential exists, that scientists learn how to identify and measure it, and that educators learn how to match such measurements with different curricula.

research indicates that, in the United States, heritability is greater in households of high socioeconomic status than in ones of low socioeconomic status (Martschenko et al. 2019: 3). To be sure, social policies might seek to address some aspects of social inequalities in this context by promoting "equal opportunities from an early age as a foundation for social mobility in the future," for example by offering "free high-quality preschool education" to children, aged 2, from disadvantaged backgrounds, as well as "high-quality preschool education tailored according to their needs" for all children aged 3 and 4, with additional support provided to "all low-SES families from birth" (Asbury and Plomin 2013: 170). But such efforts are themselves vulnerable to myriad challenges. Further, social policies might be defeated by the costs of such an approach. Or they might not eliminate inequality but merely reorganize it in its unequal distribution, or even exacerbate forms of social inequality, or perhaps "naturalize" social inequalities by generating biological explanations of social inequalities, miscasting differences in educational achievement in strongly biological terms. After all, genetically informed education probably cannot compensate for various inequalities institutionalized within a system of education or the deficits suffered by the students in the poor community, in the sense, for example, that an affluent community can provide better facilities, better learning materials, and better educators, than a poor community.

Further, social mobility from one generation to the next can influence social equality and inequality in significant ways. Intergenerational transmission of education is a significant factor in social mobility, as Peter Blau and Otis Duncan's (1967) analysis of social stratification half a century ago demonstrated: with regard to social mobility, the influence of family origin runs through education. Transmission runs along various pathways. In addition to genetic pathways of intergenerational transmission of education – education-related ability is unlikely to be a random distribution – non-genetic pathways of parental influence on children's educational success range from economic resources to such cultural influences as norms and expectations. But nonbiological pathways transmit social genetic effects in educational environments: parental provision of a positive educational environment is one condition for children to realize their genetic potential relevant to educational achievement. Further, the educational achievement of parents may also affect their child's educational attainment.[10]

Finally, the social transmission of educational content – through social background, for example, or by the way the student–teacher relationship is structured in any given case – is not socially and economically neutral. Transmission is always affected to some extent by the particular person or

[10] Differences among schools with regard to pupil achievement "cannot be assumed to be entirely environmental in origin because families are not assigned randomly to schools"; genetic factors likely "contribute to this non-random assortment of children to schools, including the parents' own educational achievement" (Shakeshaft et al. 2013: 7–8).

particular institution transmitting the content. This fact is particularly to the interactions between the teacher and the pupil toward ch particular curriculum and personalizing it for the pupil. The respecti economic class of teacher and pupil may affect those interactions, for example with respect to the amount and quality of attention the teacher devotes to the pupil. Evidently some parents transmit their class-based cultures to their children and in this way reproduce various social inequalities that may affect classroom performance: "middle- and working-class parents expressed contrasting beliefs about appropriate classroom behavior, beliefs that shaped parents' cultural coaching efforts. These efforts led children to activate class-based problem-solving strategies, which generated stratified profits at school" (Calarco 2014: 1015).[11]

Whereas genetically relevant levels of performance on a given cognitive test are likely to predict similar performance on a different cognitive test, environmentally relevant levels of performance on a given cognitive test are much less likely to predict similar performance on a different cognitive test (Asbury and Plomin 2013: 144). In other words, whereas any given gene is likely to affect many persons similarly, educationally relevant environmental factors often influence individuals in ways peculiar to some individuals. Hence even if genetic science and technology one day are able to offer learning-related data about the pupil's future performance, that data would not be independent of various significant environmental factors. The proposal for an individualized, genetically informed curricular design cannot treat the individual's social environments as neutral to that design.

7.3 CONVENTIONAL MEANS TO THE SAME END

The proposal for genetically informed curricula for primary-level pupils is a proposal for an unconventional means toward a goal shared with conventional education: the greatest possible realization of the pupil's educational potential at the level of elementary school. It rejects a status quo in which most public schools give most pupils more or less the same curriculum. In a genetically informed curricular approach, where teachers possessed relevant information about the pupil's genotype, teachers might be able to determine how well a

11 Parents may influence their child's educational performance through multiple pathways, from economic capital to social and cultural capital (on the theory of multiple forms of capital, see Bourdieu (1983)). Turkheimer et al. (2003) speak to the issue of economic capital (a child from a high socioeconomic household inherits more cognitive functioning than a child from a low socioeconomic household); Panofsky (2015: S47), to the issue of cultural capital: "Middle-class parents teach their kids to be active in demanding intervention and attention from teachers when facing learning problems"; whereas middle-class parents tend to regard teachers as problem solvers, working-class parents "teach their kids to respect teachers' authority, to wait for intervention, not to make excuses, and to interpret their difficulties as lapses in self-discipline, not as insufficiencies of the teaching program."

particular curriculum might work with a particular genotype. In that case, a pupil with genotype A would be assigned curriculum 1, one with genotype B would be offered curriculum 2, and the pupil with genotype C would receive curriculum 3. The goal would be to match each "type" of pupil with the curriculum predicted by her genetic makeup to best facilitate her realizing her potential in the classroom.

The proposal eschews standard, one-size-fits-all curricula because they do not take into account genetic insights about human difference in general. And in particular, they do not take into account genetic insights about human difference with regard to specifically educational performance. The proposal eschews standard treatments and expectations that are undifferentiated with respect to its individual addressees. To redeem its promise, it would need to be sensitive to the unique needs and capacities of individual pupils, even where it approaches the individual as a member of a group of pupils who share genetically relevant traits making a particular curriculum more promising for their progress than alternative curricula. And it must eschew a traditional pedagogical model that treats the pupil as a tabula rasa, employs an industrial model of instruction, and quite arbitrarily establishes more or less the same goals for all pupils.

But is the proposal viable, not only given its internal challenges explored above, but also because average expectable environments and good-enough parenting may be sufficient for most children to reach their educational potential? It is not clear that genetically informed primary education would be superior to traditional forms of furthering children's cognitive development in schools and elsewhere. It is possible that, for many communities, "average" expectable environments and "good enough" parenting may be sufficient for most children to more or less reach their educational potential. Here, the terms *average* and *good enough* cannot simply mean free of abuse and neglect and other factors harmful to child development. These terms must take into account the species-level preadaptation of children to respond to a spectrum of environmental opportunities for cognitive stimulation and learning; cognitive and other stimulation of children within the wide range of environments that, in a genetically specified sense, is "normal" for our species to encourage patterns of normal human development; and an environment normal as defined by a "supportive family, peers with whom to learn the rules of being young, and plentiful opportunities to learn how to be a normal adult who can work and love" (Scarr 1992: 5). As for the notion of "good enough parents": on the one hand, humans are generally robust in their capacity to adapt to a wide range of environments and circumstances; on the other, children are not endlessly malleable (for better or for worse) by their parents or caregivers. Moreover, "children's outcomes do not depend on whether parents take children to the ball game or to a museum so much as they depend on genetic transmission, on plentiful opportunities, and on having a good enough environment that supports children's development, to become themselves" (ibid., 15).

Finally, the proposal for personalized education informed by the pupil's genome builds on the general capacity of schools to influence children positively. The idea of personalized education informed by the pupil's genome must be able to presuppose the general claim that conventional schooling can influence children positively. This fact is especially important in view of research findings that schools have influence on the pupil that is greater than the influence of the family household. (These findings explain differences between twins raised together and twins taught by the same instructor.) In general, the environments of greatest influence on the individual are those that are unique to her: not the family household but such non-shared environments as the classroom.

Even if the heritability of cognitive functioning turns out to be more influential than shared environment on educational achievement, it does not follow that schools are expendable factors in education. Even if schools figure into pupils' educational outcomes only modestly, it remains that the difference in educational achievement *between* the best schools and the worst is not as great compared to the wide range of individual differences *within* any given school. In other words, schooling may have a very substantial mean impact yet relatively little impact on the relative differences among children. For example, the difference between going to school and not going to school is enormous with respect to educational achievement. Children who just miss the age cut-off date for entering school can be compared at later times with those who just made the cut-off. Here the groups being compared are nearly identical in age and many other characteristics yet differ by one year's schooling. Not only does the additional year of schooling have a significant effect on IQ and a range of cognitive tasks; a year of schooling generally has at least twice as much of an effect as does a year of additional age without an additional year of schooling. In short, while the differential impact of good and bad schools is not great, the difference between schooling and no schooling is. Without educational curricula, children do not systematically learn basic skills such as literacy and numeracy or basic knowledge such as history and science.

7.4 CONCLUSION: USING A PUPIL'S GENETIC INFORMATION TO INFORM PERSONALIZED EDUCATION IS NEITHER CLEARLY ADVISABLE NOR CLEARLY INADVISABLE

The use of a pupil's genetic information to design a curriculum personalized for her learning advantage as predicted by that information raises distinctly political questions that today cannot be answered with any finality. In that sense the project is politically ambiguous, above all with regard to its normative evaluation necessary to answer the question, How might a political community best respond to such a project? Concerns in addition to those I raised above include the project's (a) implausibility in practice and (b) its potential for abuse. Even then, (c) its promise for endowing the individual with the means for greater self-realization and self-determination retain their attraction. We again observe the proposal's political ambiguity.

(a) The proposal may overestimate what is politically, socially, and economically possible in most communities. First, it envisions teachers working with pupils and their parents to develop individualized educational plans, whereby pupils and their parents would be given several curricular choices as they consider the pupil's cognitive profile, including strengths and weaknesses, but also her interests and learning style. To have the tools to develop genetically informed, personalized curricula, public primary school teachers would need technical training in genetic science at a basic conceptual level (without further biological or lab-based training). Ideally, the pupils' educators would be familiar with statistical behavioral genetics, focusing on individual differences among pupils and the educational potential of each individual pupil, as well as with relevant aspect of the genetics of human learning. Along multiple dimensions from aptitude of individual teachers to funding for such training, from questions of who would provide such training and what authorities might determine its parameters, the notion of elementary teacher training in genetics is unrealistic.

Second, on the one hand, personalized, genetically informed education may be too costly due to many factors, from specialized teacher training to the number of trained personnel necessary, and from the cost of providing a number of curricular choices large enough to capture the range of different pupils' genetic propensities to the cost of waging the inevitable political and legal battles at various school-administrative levels and in the public sphere over the possibility, advisability, and feasibility of such a proposal. Difficult questions of how to accommodate parents who object to the participation of their child would also need to be addressed. Few if any communities would be able and willing to make the tremendous investment, in resources as well as in political will, to realize the proposal.

On the other hand, if genetically informed personalized curricula *were* to be realized, it would be vulnerable to capture by forms of contemporary neoliberalism. It would be vulnerable to the displacement of pedagogically productive goals toward the pupil's best realization of her educational potential by the deregulation of state oversight and common standards for privatized, consumer-oriented behavior that caters to parents as education-consumers through an expensive, privatized, hyper-individualistic, commodified model of primary education.

Third, if the proposal were to be realized, it would likely be unable to escape the "gravity" exerted by forces of inequality. The pupil's educationally relevant genetic information, no matter its quality, is not actionable if schools lack the resources necessary to tailor interventions. And even if some schools possess the resources, many will not. Curricular personalization for some but not all social groups will reproduce and exacerbate existing inequalities in the provision of primary education. Differential access to genetic screening will generate inequality. The benefits of genotyping likely would accrue mostly to better-situated groups. Families more strongly situated socioeconomically tend to respond more quickly than weakly situated families to high-tech developments such as genotyping (Link et al. 1998). Even though persons of European ancestry constitute only a small proportion of total genetic diversity, they are overrepresented in samples and data sets whereas minority populations are underrepresented (Duncan et al. 2019).

(b) Any tool is vulnerable to abuse. Genetic information and its possible deployment in educational contexts are no different. Indeed, the concern with biological heritability has long been abused, for example to legitimize racial and economic inequalities and the maldistribution of social resources, in the nineteenth century (Galton (1869), Hunt (1864); in the twentieth century (Shockley 1971); and today (Wade (2014), Gillborn (2016)).

(c) In light of these various objections to genetically informed, personalized primary education, one wonders: Is a political community misguided if it orients curricular policy on parental choice and pupil personalization to the extent foreseen by the proposal? Does the very concept of genetically informed personalized education rely on a naïve optimism about the power of choice and personalization? What would guide parental choice and preference in light of the fact that any model based on significant choice is vulnerable to the consequences of poor choices?

On the one hand, it is one thing to have a choice, another thing to make the best choice: "even when the best choice is fairly clear, people very frequently miss it" (Panofsky 2015: S47). Because socioeconomic, class-based cultural dispositions are inflected in both choosing and the individual's capacity to solicit effective advice, individual choice is easily misguided by social fashions and misused by interest groups. On the other hand, choice and personalization can be important forms of self-determination. Is not some degree of choice regarding the pupil's educational environment warranted by the facts of relevant differences among pupils, the interplay between the pupil's genotype and her environment, and the influence of non-shared environments, indeed toward better approaching the ultimate goal of equal educational opportunity? Personalization through teacher-directed educational planning for individual pupils may function on the basis of choice, involving the parents and the teacher, with feedback from the pupil. Pupils would be offered a variety of curricular choices. Choice would be guided in part by the pupil's particular learning style and her particular interests. Research on individual differences, on genotype–environment interplay, and on non-shared environmental influence support the notion of providing parents and their child some degree of curricular choice. To afford all children some degree of choice contributes to the goal of more or less equal environmental opportunities for all children.

After all, the goal of the proposal is neither therapy for underperforming students nor the enhancement of adequately performing students toward extraordinary achievements. The goal is the greater realization of each pupil's particular potential. The goal is not exceptionalism. Kathryn Asbury and Robert Plomin (2013: 142) point out that both high- and low-performing students "are no more likely to be more genetically exceptional than an average student" and that the "same genes influence performance all across the distribution of performance. In other words, a math professor and a student struggling with mathematics are using the same genes when they perform mathematical tasks."

The fact that genetic heritability to some extent influences individual achievement does not defeat the notion of humans as self-determining creatures. Rather, it qualifies the notion of self-determination. It qualifies what can be achieved by manipulating the environment constituted by formal education. Educability involves both genes and their environment, and some of its potential may be better realized by manipulating the educational environment. Genetically informed personalized education at the primary level is one way. Genetic heritability that influences individual achievement *more than the social environment of school* hardly diminishes the importance of schools. It only reinforces the imperative of *improving* them. Genetically informed curricular design is an unconventional approach to that end.

Further, the proposal resonates with the attractive notion of a child's right to an open future, an anticipatory right to the autonomy of self-determination: to grant or recognize a child's right to decisional autonomy (one that remains anticipatory until the person attains legal maturity, signifying her capacity to exercise such a right) is not to grant or recognize her right, during childhood, to determine her own curriculum. Whereas older students may have some discretion in secondary education, and significant choice in tertiary, children at the primary level are not asked for their consent to the education they receive. Education is not unalterably inscribed in the recipient. It can be supplemented, challenged, modified, even superseded by subsequent education. Even where education determines aspects of a person's life in important ways, it need not be the last word. Joel Feinberg's (1980) notion of a child's right to an open future is best understood not as a right to any particular curriculum but rather to one of a quality sufficient to facilitate the realization of the child's educational potential. The idea of personalized education informed by the pupil's genome pursues that goal.

This chapter explored the ambiguous quality of arguments for and against the use of human genetic information in personalized education tailored to the pupil's genome. The following chapter opens the third of the book's three parts. This third part addresses equality and inequality locally and as a planetary phenomenon. It begins with a chapter that analyzes the screening of embryos for genetic features that indicate possible disabilities in the future person. Unlike Chapter 5 – which explores the idea of bringing members of a domestic community to a cognitive capacity at the threshold for robust participation in the community's democratic system – the following chapter situates itself at the intersection of bioethics and rights that aspire to cross-national validity, if not regional or even global validity: human rights. It constructs disability as a condition that reduces well-being; it analyzes the screening of embryos for genetic features that indicate possible disabilities in the future person; and it proposes a human right to freedom from genetic disability in terms of well-being. It considers genetic screening of a fetus as well as of an embryo, in the first case allowing parents to decide whether to continue a pregnancy and, in the second case, whether to initiate a pregnancy through in vitro fertilization with an embryo selected for genes of interest. Genetically secured freedom from disability could afford a future person forms of individual autonomy in political community otherwise compromised.

PART III

INEQUALITY AS AN UNINTENDED CONSEQUENCE LOCALLY AND AS A PLANETARY PHENOMENON

8

A Human Right to Freedom from Genetic Disability

Genetic selection is one means of pursuing the well-being of future persons. Scientists in the 1970s developed prenatal genetic testing with ultrasound-guided amniocentesis. In 1990 they introduced pre-implantation genetic diagnosis for use with in vitro fertilization. In 2011 they developed noninvasive prenatal testing, which tests fetal DNA from maternal blood samples drawn at eight weeks. Prenatal screening analyzes the genetic makeup of a fetus, and embryo screening analyzes the embryo's genetic characteristics. Analysis in the first case allows parents to decide whether to continue a pregnancy; in the second, whether to initiate a pregnancy through in vitro fertilization with an embryo selected for genes of interest. Both are forms of genetic selection. This chapter analyzes the screening of embryos for genetic features that indicate possible disabilities in the future person.

The analysis situates itself at the juncture of bioethics and human rights. From the standpoint of political bioethics, each entwines the evolved natural phenomenon of the human species with human culture. Entwinement marks a continuous exchange between human biology and the social, cultural, and economic environments in which we humans live. Exchange includes our interventions toward altering aspects of both human culture and human biology. At the level of human rights, political communities may alter the ways societies and cultures overlay the natural body with socially constructed interpretations (such as advocating a human right to freedom from genetic disability). At the level of biotechnology, scientists may alter aspects of the bodies of future human beings.

In their concern with the human body in the context of individual well-being, human rights and bioethics each has potential to perform a kind of "politics of aspiration." The question for bioethics is, What kind of humans do we want to be, biologically, to the extent that we can select for or against certain traits? And for human rights, What kind of humans do we want to be morally with respect to how we treat others, along the dimension of rights? Each in its own way asks, What kind of humans do we aspire to be in the sense of how we might best organize political community along the dimensions of justice, legitimacy, morality, and law? The answer to this question depends on how members of a political community conceive of themselves biologically as well as morally. Any given answer will necessarily be limited in the ways that any cultural conviction is limited because embedded in its own time and subject to the understandings and prejudices of that time.

Cultural convictions are no less heritable than genes. Culture "has joined natural selection as a dominant force creating change in our species" (Soloman 2016: 68). Further, natural selection and human culture are related dynamically. Selection is increasingly relevant to fertility, including "how we choose our sexual partners and the factors that affect how many children we have" (ibid., 93). We observe changes in the ways we choose, whereby "preferences that evolved to assess the genetic quality of potential mates" are ill suited, culturally, to modern matchmaking. Finally, the overall significance of our genes decreases as our control over our reproduction increases through technologies of reproduction, from birth control to in vitro fertilization. Socioeconomic status and health-care access are more likely to determine the individual's survival and reproductive chances than her genetic inheritance.

Normative questions about genetic screening involve the confluence of bioethics and human rights, where I examine screening for disabilities in particular, in six steps. First I define (§8.1) disability and (§8.2) well-being. (§8.3) Then I develop a notion of well-being with respect to two forms of autonomy: the parents' procreative autonomy and the autonomy of a future person. (§8.4) I outline elements of an alternative notion of well-being as autonomy and (§8.5) analyze disability as a condition that reduces well-being. (§8.6) Deploying these definitions, notions, and analyses, I propose a human right to freedom from genetic disability. I conclude that the political problem here is not genetic selection that undermines the welfare of individuals and communities but rather unequal access to the genetic selection that one day could free future persons of genetic disabilities and thereby enhance their autonomy and capacity for social and political inclusion.

8.1 DISABILITY

The notion of disability is a particular kind of classification, based on observed or inferred features that the individual cannot readily alter. These features may be biological (blindness, deafness, or paraplegia, for example) or socially constructed (including stigma and discrimination). Means of classifying what counts as a disability range from the statistical (the average in particular reference groups) to the biological (which employs a notion of human functioning) to the normative (which uses a concept of human flourishing). Certain conditions are widely, but not universally, regarded as disabilities, including the congenital absence or loss of a sensory function or limb; progressive neurological conditions including multiple sclerosis or epilepsy; psychiatric disorders such as schizophrenia and bipolar disorder or severe depression; developmental disorders such as autism; limited ability to perform cognitive functions such as remembering faces; and chronic diseases such as arteriosclerosis. Still, no definition of disability finds consensus.

Debates end inconclusively on how best to evaluate disability with respect to the disabled person's well-being. Thus Stephen Campbell and Joseph Stramondo (2017: 176) dismiss the view that, "as a general rule, disabilities are bad for those who have them," regardless of whether the badness is intrinsic, instrumental, comparative, or overriding. In fact, most disabilities are "intrinsically neutral" even as "we cannot make simple generalizations about disability's relationship to well-being" in the three additional senses of instrumental, comparative, or overriding (ibid., 151) because, given the variation in any person's life, the "high-impact nature of disabilities tends to yield variation in the well-being of people with disabilities" (ibid., 166). James Gould (2020: 37) counters that, with regard to disabilities that are cognitive (rather than physical and sensory), broad generalizations are well warranted: disability "always has a negative impact on quality of life," even if there is no single negative impact, and even as the negative quality of disability depends on "multidimensional influences including biological condition, social environment and personal temperament."

A different tack leads to the same impasse. Matthew Barker and Robert Wilson (2019: 323) reject what they take to be the "devalued estimation of the quality of the lives of people with disabilities" as "something to be pitied, regretted, and eliminated." They frame disability in terms of human variation, and variation as something human communities should embrace rather than eliminate. Similarly, Rosemarie Garland-Thomson (2020: 63) contends that disabilities should be counted among the "benefits of human variation for individuals and communities" and urges "humility and restraint to guide the development and implementation of humane technologies rather than genetic manipulation technologies that aim to control future outcomes through present actions." Greg Bognar (2016: 49) counters that those who "claim that disability is mere difference almost never add any qualifications," such as those between "mild" and "severe" disabilities or between one circumstances in which a condition would count as a disability and another in which the same condition would count merely as a difference. Further, if disability did not constitute harm to the person affected, then intentionally causing disability would be morally permissible, just as preventing or removing disability would be impermissible. But if preventing or removing a person's disability is morally acceptable, and if making a person disabled is morally unacceptable, then disability cannot be mere difference; it can only be harm.

I focus more narrowly on autonomy and specifically on the autonomy of parents and that of the future person. I define disability as diminishing well-being in the sense of reducing individual autonomy.[1] I adopt a model that views disability as a phenomenon both biological and socially constructed. On this view, biological impairments, physical or mental, leading to personal and social limitations, are not the sole sources of disability – contrary to what a medical model suggests, which frames disability as a physical or mental impairment of the individual.[2] Nor are disabilities entirely forms of social organization, as a social model suggests. A social model frames disability as a relation between the individual and her social and built environment: an environment that excludes, from central spheres of social life, persons of certain physical and mental characteristics or persons at least regarded as disabled.[3] Rather, disability occurs where an individual's biology converges with her social environment.[4] Disability is a definition, perspectival in part, of a cognitive or physical feature that the individual's community identifies as dysfunctional or as an impairment and associates with a limitation, whether personal or social or both. Disability so understood interlaces biological condition, social exclusion, and social perception (Anastasiou and Kauffman 2013; Martiny 2015). A condition might constitute a disability if it is disadvantageous to the individual's functioning in a particular environment – but not in another – or if a particular environment treats the variation with prejudice.

[1] See Cavaliere (2020) for an argument that includes third parties. There is no consensually accepted definition of disability or its characteristics. The term is applied to a very wide array of conditions that do not share with each other either a common functional state or a common experiential state. While two features appear common – a physical or mental condition regarded as dysfunctional, and a limitation, individual or social, associated with that condition – both are perspectival. The terms *dysfunction* and *limitation* are opinions. Used in reference to human *biology*, they presuppose one or another notion of human functioning (with no agreement on what constitutes "proper" human functioning). Used *statistically*, they refer to an average in one or another reference group (with no group universally regarded as representative). Used *normatively*, they presuppose one or another notion of human flourishing (each within a field of competing theories). Further, no *biological* impairment can be defined without reference to the social conditions in which the impaired persons exists. Yet a person's limitation defined exclusively with respect to *social attitudes, practices, institutions, and contexts* refers to a contingent environment and not to an unalterable personal trait. In defining disability as reducing well-being and individual autonomy in particular, I concede that the definition is perspectival because of its relational quality. After all, social and political autonomy is something that exists relative to environments of other people. Because such environments vary widely and are always shifting, so too any given understanding of autonomy will vary from others, and conceptions of autonomy change over time (contrast Periclean Athens with, say, twenty-first-century Australia). By defining disability as individual autonomy, I can address a disabled person with respect to both nature and culture. My definition allows for the term *disability* to function as both social construct and as political tool.

[2] The World Health Organization's 1980 *International Classification of Impairment, Disability, and Handicap* is one prominent example.

[3] The Union of the Physically Impaired against Segregation (1976) provides one example.

[4] The World Health Organization (2001) argues as much.

The medical and social models differ from one another with respect to how an individual's disability may impact her well-being. A medical model frames disability as something either to be corrected or eliminated. Removal of the disability is possible only by somatic intervention (hence not by social restructuring, as in the social model). Removal may make well-being possible in the first place, or it may increase well-being in depth and extent, inasmuch as well-being is more than the absence of disease or disability, and inasmuch as some persons with disabilities are capable of well-being. By contrast, a social model recognizes individuals in terms of a range of variations in structure and functioning. It then reconstructs social and physical environments to accommodate greater difference, toward improving individual well-being. And it focuses on the contingent relationship (socially and environmentally influenced) between disability and well-being. It evaluates a range of cognitive and physical functions with respect to how their limitation, or absence, may diminish or preclude the individual's well-being. It does so contingently. Disability in this model is not fixed in definition; it is fluid, depending on which variations in individual structure and function are defined as disabilities and which not. The social model overlaps with the medical model where, in each, the terms *structure* and *function* refer to biological or physiological impairment.

Unlike a medical model, the social model attends to the environmental contingencies that produce or contribute to disability. Whereas a medical model typically emphasizes the prevention of genetically transmissible diseases while advocating respect for persons with disabilities, a social model estimates upward a disabled person's well-being. The model also acknowledges the diverse range of disabled persons' experiences with impaired functioning. It champions their epistemic authority to evaluate the quality of their lives rather than relying solely on assessments made within the nondisabled community, including by health professionals, who tend to evaluate disability experience more negatively than do disabled persons themselves.

The two models implicate one another even as they are distinct. The social model does not deny the bodily or cognitive dimensions of disability. The medical model does not deny the embeddedness of bodies and minds within social contexts and cultural practices, or within political and economic institutions.

Common instances of disability – from deafness and blindness to cognitive subnormality – might be regarded as biological phenomena independent of all social construction. But even then, in light of abiding differences on how best to identify and understand disability, disability might best be defined not globally but on a case-by-case basis. This approach is compatible with the widespread moral intuition that parents should love their children as they are and the idea that political community should treat all individuals as equal before the law.

8.2 WELL-BEING

Accounts of human well-being are many and diverse. Each can only be a particular theory based on particular assumptions. Consider two of the most prominent approaches: (a) hedonism (which, as a form of utilitarianism, associates well-being with health because even if good in itself, other goods may not be possible without health, hence health is also a means to other goods) and (b) the objective list theory. The latter engages the issue of autonomy, a notion central to my argument against a human right that would prohibit all forms of genetic selection.

(a) The hedonist account views well-being as the greatest balance of pleasure over pain.[5] Thomas Carlyle famously denounced the hedonistic component of utilitarianism as a "philosophy of swine" because it accords the same moral status to all pleasures. Mill (1998) retorts by distinguishing between "higher" and "lower" pleasures and then by adding a third property, "quality," to the two properties identified by Bentham (1996). Upshot: some pleasures are inherently more valuable than others.

(b) A eudaemonist approach lists items that constitute well-being *beyond* pleasurable experience and the satisfaction of desires, such as knowledge or friendship. The list must contain all such human goods. I will not pursue the obvious and intractable question here, How can one know what those goods are? Toward reducing the complexity of my analysis, I focus narrowly on autonomy to the exclusion of other plausible candidates for inclusion on the list of objective goods. I assume autonomy as constituting a good in itself. I define it as the individual's capacity to plausibly attempt to realize those of her goals that are informed by, and reflect, the value of living one's life for oneself. In the context of genetic screening of embryos, I distinguish between the autonomy of the parents in deciding some genetic characteristics of a future child, on the one hand, and the autonomy of the future person to be free of genetic manipulation at the embryonic state, on the other.[6]

8.3 WELL-BEING WITH RESPECT TO TWO FORMS OF AUTONOMY

Consider individual autonomy as one among many plausible features of individual well-being.[7] I fasten on two possible carriers of autonomy: (a) the parents' procreational autonomy and (b) the personal autonomy of a future person. The future person is both the object of her parents' procreational autonomy, as an embryo, and its subject, as a future person. To embrace

[5] See Bentham (1996) for an account particularly influential.

[6] Autonomy defined as the capacity to self-determine (hence as the absence of interference by disability) could also apply to biological senescence and justify biotechnological gerontological intervention toward enhancing older persons' autonomy as the ageing process increasingly undermines it. Compare Farrelly (2019).

[7] It is plausible despite an internal tension: parental screening toward greater autonomy for future offspring is counter-paternalistic in consequence even if paternalistic as a form of beneficence.

autonomy understood as genetic selection for the future person's freedom from preventable genetic diseases is to embrace selection. To embrace autonomy understood as the future person's freedom from genetic selection at the embryonal stage is to reject selection. (c) Somewhat unexpectedly, these two forms of autonomy collapse at points.

(a) Parents exercise procreational autonomy in the genetic selection of a future person. Consider one goal in particular: selecting for a future person free of genetic disability. The parents' procreational autonomy is an instrumental good if it allows parents to beget not only healthy children but children who will have lives better than otherwise possible had they been born with genetic disabilities. Parents cannot guarantee the outcome, of course. The best they can do is estimate if the well-being of particular future persons might be greater, under certain future conditions, if those future persons were free of a physical or cognitive constitution that medical professionals today classify as a disability.

Genetic screening makes this estimate possible. It may be limited because mistaken, or because screening cannot guarantee future well-being, or because a future person's well-being might be secured in the future by a condition currently regarded as a disability. Advocacy of such autonomy raises challenging questions: What principle should guide selection? Does the autonomy of parents (or others) to select entail that autonomy of choice is properly the primary normative concern? Or is autonomy properly limited by compelling interests of the state, if not by communitarian values that would circumscribe the parameters of individual choice?

Nicholas Agar (2004: 6) offers a perspective on genetic engineering that might be applied to genetic selection: "Prospective parents may ask genetic engineers to introduce into their embryos combinations of genes that correspond with their particular conception of the good life. Yet they will acknowledge the right of their fellow citizens to make completely different eugenic choices." From a moral standpoint, this suggestion is plausible only within limits. Parents should not be allowed to select for traits that would deliver the future person to a life of psychological misery and biological torment.[8] From a moral standpoint, only some reasons should be allowed; only some conceptions of the good life should be entertained. As difficult as it might be to adjudicate among competing conceptions of the good, all eugenic choices should at least promote the expected autonomy of the future person.

(b) A future person's autonomy is an instrumental good: it enables the individual's pursuit of at least some of her goals. Those goals may be tied to her conception of the good life or to her preferred life-plan, informed by her value commitments and personal aspirations and

[8] Pace Kettering (2020).

perhaps by collective projects as well. Of course, this information is not available to the parents at the time of genetic selection.

How might we conceive of a future person's autonomy? Because the future person cannot participate in the selection of the embryo from which she will develop, she cannot prevent selection (or the genetic manipulation of the embryo from which she developed into a person). She can reject selection only retrospectively, and at that point without practical consequence. She might regard her autonomy as a person to have been violated by the fact that she bears, genetically, the "imprint" of the will of other persons. This notion of autonomy refers to self-determination. While an embryo cannot self-determine, a selected embryo – because it was selected – renders the future person the bearer of the particular preferences and value-commitment of the selectors.[9] In that sense, the future person has been denied freedom from others' intentions. That denial is now written in her genes.

(c) The distinction between the parents' procreational autonomy and the personal autonomy of a future person breaks down at certain points. For example, what if genetic selection provides the future person greater autonomy than would be possible if she were to suffer genetic disability? On the one hand, genetic selection can restrict a future person's autonomy by constricting the otherwise open future of a future person. On the other hand, leaving to natural processes all of the future person's genetic characteristics, including ones with adverse effects, may condemn her to bear an otherwise preventable genetic disability.

The distinction between parental procreational autonomy and a future person's personal autonomy breaks down at another point as well. The future person's autonomy from having been genetically manipulated as an embryo is autonomy from manipulation by others. By contrast, a future person's autonomy from genetic disability is an autonomy secured through her parents who decided for the genetic engineering of the embryo. Implausible is the argument that the autonomy that a future person might choose retrospectively (autonomy from genetic selection) is somehow inherently "better" than the autonomy her parents chose in advance (autonomy from genetic disability). If the goal of autonomy is for its own sake, then it hardly matters how that autonomy was secured.[10] If the goal is a particular conception of the good life held by the future person, there is no way of knowing if that conception might be realized by a range of choices wider or narrower. Some notions of the good life might be realized in freedom from genetic disability but not all notions of the good life.

[9] Habermas (2001) advances this argument.

[10] To be sure, autonomy for its own sake may be implausible inasmuch as autonomy that delivers the individual unto misery and misfortune is not desirable, whereas securing well-being as a consequence of autonomy is.

Hence the notion of autonomy, by itself, cannot guide choice in the question of genetic screening for disabilities. It cannot guide the parent's choice. And it cannot guide a future person's retrospective choice or preference.

8.4 ELEMENTS OF AN ALTERNATIVE NOTION OF WELL-BEING

I propose an alternative in six parts: (a) in the context of disability, individual autonomy should not be treated as an absolute; in defining well-being, do not privilege (b) "normal," (c) or a species-typical condition, (d) or "natural," (e) or chance, and (f) consider that no person is without any disabilities whatsoever.

(a) Whether a given disability is instrumentally adverse is an empirical question contingent on the environment in which the individual lives. A disability often is context-specific: it may be neutral in some social circumstances yet advantageous in others. And whether the consequences of a disability diminish the individual's well-being may be a matter of perspective.

It is not the case that an instrumentally adverse disability is adverse solely as a matter of social prejudice toward an abnormal condition. Still, the normative evaluation of a biological condition that deviates from the species norm may be a matter of social preference. Or it may be a matter of social prejudice against deviation. Preference or prejudice may frame the deviation as entailing a reduction in the individual's well-being. Hence, individual autonomy should not be treated as an absolute in the context of disability.

(b) Biological "normality" is a social evaluation, not an objective natural scientific description. Deviation from the species norm concerns humans when deviation affects, positively or negatively, culturally based notions of well-being. A deviation along one particular dimension – such as the advantages conferred by an extraordinary capacity in sense perception or cognitive capacity – is not symmetrical with deviation along a different dimension, such as the disadvantages that pathological disability entails.

Even as a matter of statistical norms, biological "normality" is social evaluation, not scientific description. An individual's deviation from such norms necessarily imply anything from a normative point of view. A person's deviation from "normal functioning" does not itself necessarily constitute a pathology or a deficiency or a lack of well-being or an incapacity for well-being. Because "natural selection does not homogenize the individuals of a species," the "search for a normal … nature and body type is futile" (Smail 2008: 124–125). Therefore in defining well-being, do not privilege "normal."

(c) To be disabled in terms of a species norm is to deviate as an individual from types of functioning found with high frequency in the human species. To regard a deviation as necessarily negative is to invest non-deviant characteristics of the species with normative significance. In some cases a deviant or species-atypical trait, status, or condition may be regarded more positively than the corresponding species-typical trait, status, or condition. This is generally the case with superlative intellectual, athletic, artistic, or moral capacity.

The expected well-being of a future person who is congenitally deaf, compared to a future person who has hearing, cannot be judged normatively by the fact that most persons have hearing (that is, it cannot be well judged by a species norm). A claim for or against selecting a future child with a congenital condition of deafness invokes a socially constructed norm. A child born deaf is not disabled as such but only if so defined. In some contexts, deafness may reduce well-being. But members of some deaf communities regard deafness as the source of a particular cultural community in which it does not reduce well-being but rather contributes to a positive group-identity. From an autonomy-oriented perspective, parents should select against deafness where it would constitute a disability in the sense of an individual significantly less autonomous than a hearing person. Hence, in representing well-being, do not privilege a species-typical status or condition.

(d) Where human biology increasingly becomes an undertaking of human culture, the term *human nature* is increasingly a contingent expression of human will and imagination. If one asks whether genetic selection affects the very "nature" of the human species, one assumes a biological nature independent of human design.[11] Genetic engineering is not itself a feature of biological nature; it is an act of human culture. Yet the distinction between human nature and human culture easily collapses. A future person who carried the consequences of genetic screening would thereby carry the effects of particular cultural preferences. She would still be "natural" in the sense of being a member of an evolved species. But as a product of genetic screening, she would also be a human artefact, to an extent. All humans are human artefacts to some extent in all the ways that human culture has impinged on human biology (such as the ways that consuming domesticated grains and animals may affect human physiology at the genetic level, as in lactose tolerance,[12] or in the ways that environmental conditions, such as social stress, may affect a woman and, epigenetically, her fetus).[13] Hence in describing well-being, do not privilege "natural."

(e) Genetic screening will always be limited in what it may be able to deliver in the way of anticipating possible congenital disabilities. Unpredictability and chance cannot be banished from human experience.

[11] Chapters 3 and 4 argue as much. [12] See Chapter 1 for discussion of this example.
[13] See Chapter 9 for examination of the epigenetic consequences of maternal stress on the fetus.

The fact that an embryo was genetically selected in ways that make higher expected well-being for the future person more likely may not in fact end in such well-being. Such contingency marks human life quite independently of questions of disability: a gifted person may not perform to potential for any number of reasons; a person of modest endowments, or one who faces hardships and obstacles, may go on to achieve great things. To be sure, a "better" genetic endowment (in the sense of an endowment with fewer genetic disabilities) is more likely than a worse endowment to contribute to the individual's greater well-being. In some cases, genetic selection will offer a future child higher prospects for well-being than a genetic endowment conferred entirely by biological chance. Biotechnical choice may benefit the future person where biological chance may entail biotechnologically avoidable disabilities. A parent may care about his or her future child by caring for that child's future well-being as it may expectably be affected by the child's genetic endowment. The parent who attempts to control for biological chance is likely motivated not by some impartial morality but by the passionate special regard most parents have for their children. Hence in analyzing well-being, do not privilege chance.

(f) The claim that all humans might be regarded plausibly as disabled, one way or another, offers a useful perspective on disability. Just as no one is without any abilities whatsoever, so no one is without any disabilities whatsoever. As disabled in some way, to some extent, we are all reduced in our well-being and capacity to realize a good life (to be sure, we are so reduced to vastly differing extents). Because this viewpoint universalizes disability among all members of the species, someone who assumes the viewpoint may be less likely to stigmatize (other, fellow) disabled persons.

8.5 DISABILITY REDUCES WELL-BEING

As a guide to the practice of genetic selection, I define one aspect of well-being narrowly, namely as reduced disability. Screening of an embryo can reduce, in the future person who develops from it, the incidence of genetic factors that may reduce her autonomy. (And reducing the incidence of genetic disabilities can be combined with reducing social factors that reduce the future persons' individual autonomy.) This definition is compatible with value pluralism. While it regards greater autonomy as one feature of well-being among others, it does not preclude additional features, nor does it preclude multiple conceptions of a good life. Further, the definition is compatible with parents evaluating the expected well-being of different possible lives of an offspring. (Parents make this evaluation in conventional ways as well, in choosing how to raise their children.) Genetic selection corresponds with this concern with well-being.

Selection for well-being – as selection against expected significant somatic or psychological suffering – makes a controversial assumption: that future persons expected to experience serious suffering in the sense of significantly reduced autonomy cannot be expected to have a high general level of well-being. But even as it generates challenges of its own, value-pluralism is plausible even in this context. After all, various kinds and some degrees of suffering may have value for some people. Well-being need not imply what is empirically unlikely in any case: the complete and enduring absence of all pain and suffering. As Julian Savulescu and Guy Kahane (2009: 281) argue, while "Conditions such as depression ... make a life worse" and "parents have reason to select children less disposed to depression," manic depression "has been associated with great creativity and productivity." Indeed, "some manic depressives endorse their condition, identifying with it, and their lives appear very successful" (ibid., 282). Here the narrow understanding of well-being as individual autonomy allows for parental selection against manic depression if that condition is thought to reduce autonomy. At the extreme, one might argue that if political community finds moral ennoblement in humans confronting their limitations in ways that render humans more thoughtfully decent than they might otherwise be, or grants them insights or expressive powers they otherwise would not possess, then genetic screening for some forms of expected suffering in a future person might be inadvisable. In such cases, parents might *not* genetically select for a future child with no genetic disabilities. Still, a narrow understanding of well-being as individual autonomy remains skeptical of this perspective of autonomy-through-suffering.

8.6 A HUMAN RIGHT TO FREEDOM FROM GENETIC DISABILITY

As a means to an end, rights can possess an instrumental quality. They can also possess a non-instrumental quality: value-commitment. I argue for an autonomy of future persons in the form of a value-commitment to individual autonomy as an aspect of well-being. I specify (a) fundamental conditions of membership in liberal democratic community as the capacity to participate in the political system and (b) a human right to parental choice in the genetic selection of embryos (c) toward the individual liberty and legal equality that require individual autonomy. (d) I conclude by identifying limits to this proposal for a human right to freedom from genetic disability.

(a) A fundamental condition of membership in a liberal democratic political community is the good – shared by all individuals, carried by each – of the capacity to participate in the community's political system: voting, running for office, assembling with other citizens to advocate particular policies and candidates, communicating with officials and the press and other citizens, and so forth. This good is an individual good of the citizen.

It is equally a common good: it sustains the community democratically. Self-determination here is at once individual and collective: a political community self-determines by means of individuals participating; and in participating, individuals self-determine individually.

(b) Consider a legal right, based on the interest of all citizens in their legal equality, to the minimum genetic capacity for a citizen to access her rights of social and political participation. Access and exercise require individual autonomy and is here framed as egalitarian: it seeks to render all citizens active rightsholders. The existence of such a right might encourage political communities to expend public resources to facilitate genetic selection that would free future persons from genetic disability.[14]

To be sure, citizens with a disability are still rightsholders even if they lack the autonomy to exercise their rights, or to exercise those rights fully. A person with a disability can still be a rightsholder and still pursue various basic activities even if political participation is made difficult or is even precluded by the disability.[15] From the perspective of human rights, such persons should be rightsholders regardless of citizenship. But one can also imagine a human right to participation in one's own political community. In that spirit, I construct the idea of a human right to the biological and social conditions necessary for participation in the political processes and legal procedures of one's political community, specifically as those conditions might be advanced through freedom from disease and disability via genetic selection.

A human right of a future person to freedom from genetic disability would be a right to political agency. The very idea of human rights is the idea of an individual's capacity for basic forms of agency in conducting her life. While such capacities cannot guarantee human flourishing, and may be without consequence for individual well-being, they are among the basic conditions for the possibility of an individual being able to pursue participation in her political community's processes of self-determination.

Such a human right would be engaged by parents deciding issues of genetic screening for the embryo on behalf of a possible future person. From the standpoint of political community, to render future persons disability-free is an act of social egalitarianism: selection seeks the equal well-being of all future citizens, and well-being includes freedom from preventable genetic disability. If

[14] Relevant in this context is the question Chapter 5 explores: would the citizen and her political community be significantly advantaged, in terms of realizing a just society, if she and her fellow citizens were of a "threshold level" of intelligence necessary for a capacity for robust participation in the public life of a liberal democratic community?

[15] Waldschmidt and Sépulchre (2019) analyze the ambivalent quality of citizenship as it relates to disability: on the one hand, citizenship promises civil, political, economic, cultural and social rights as well as an obligation to observe duties in society; on the other hand, societal barriers as well as the ableist implications of some features of some conceptions of civic participation hinder many disabled persons in fulfilling citizenship roles.

such freedom were constructed as a kind of human-rights baseline, it would preclude the competing notion of a contrary human right – a right of a future person to be free from genetic selection, that is, to be free of selective choices guided by the preferences of other persons, most likely the parents.

Such a human right would seek to protect core capacities of future humans. One consequence: it would forbid parents from deliberately depriving a future person of her capacity for political participation by genetically selecting for disabilities that make participation difficult or impossible. This is not a right to perfectionism in the sense, for example, "that being male or white or tall or heterosexual will provide the best chance of having the best life in our society" (Liao 2019: 1020). It would be a right to a capacity to pursue political inclusion but not a right to enablement to lead the best possible life. Whereas being male or white or tall or heterosexual is not a fundamental political capacity, autonomy is, as a condition for political and civic participation.

(c) This approach combines a liberty interest with an interest in equality. The term *liberty* here refers to parental choice: parents should have the final say as to whether their embryo will be genetically screened for genetic disabilities. Pre-personal life (embryos and fetuses) are not legal persons and, as such, cannot bear the legal rights accorded to humans. Any right of future persons to freedom from genetic disabilities is the parents' prerogative to bestow. But that prerogative might best be qualified in ways I specify below.

In this context, the term *equality* refers to communal consultation: the project for greater social equality can only be a collective one. That is, a legal right to parental autonomy in genetic selection of their embryo – toward the autonomy of a future person – should be tethered to some form of communal consultation and oversight.[16] Parents should not enjoy complete decisional autonomy. They should be bound by deliberations and perspectives developed within the community, deliberations in which they should be allowed to participate. They should not be allowed to control those boundaries or to ignore them.

(d) Any plausible human right to freedom from genetic disability would be limited not absolute, in several ways. First, it would offer no guarantees: genetic screening cannot guarantee that a future person, although free of autonomy-destroying disabilities, might still be hindered in her political

[16] Taking the measure of social values and political visions entailed by genetic selection is a task ideally for the citizens of self-determining political communities. Thus communal consultation is an idea more compelling in liberal democratic communities of justice than in authoritarian communities. To be sure, different liberal communities may answer the relevant questions in different ways; any one community likely will experience internal disagreement as well. So the task of taking the measure of values and visions returns us, yet again, to politics understood as the contestation of values.

autonomy in other ways connected with her biology (by illness, for example). Genetic screening can hardly guarantee the future person a good life in general, even with autonomy. Autonomy to participate in politics does not itself guarantee the best possible life. It does not guarantee a life well-lived or even a life worth living. It cannot guarantee expectable well-being for the individual.

Second, a human right to freedom from genetic disability could not require parents to select for what might be expected to be the most advantaged future person. Nor could it entail their punishment or other sanctioning if they selected for what might be expected to be a less advantaged future person. But it could entail sanctions for other reasons, as specified below.

Third, it would not give the parents *carte blanche* in their decisional autonomy. A right, on behalf of a future person, to select for freedom from genetic disability does not entail a right to select for non-disease characteristics for superior functioning of that future person.[17]

Further, what a human right to freedom from genetic disability might allow could still be abused if, for example, parents were influenced in their choices by fashion, superstition, racism, sexism, homophobia, or other social pathologies of bigotry. It could be abused if parental choice were guided by implausible conceptions of the good life that might condemn the future person to poor prospects. (To be sure, this danger is present as well in conventional procreative autonomy: parents have wide latitude to raise their children according to personal preference.)

On the one hand, a human right to parental choice to screen the embryo for genetic disabilities may allow for choices and decisions that some observers will regard as morally wrong. Consider what might appear to be a clear guiding principle of what parents should be allowed: to "aim to have the most advantaged children, when such a choice is possible," and to disallow "procreative choices which foreseeably and avoidably result in less than the best child" (Savulescu and Kahane 2009: 278). Even this principle of procreative beneficence will not resolve differences of opinion as to what constitutes "best" and "worst" and everything in between.

On the other hand, with respect to genetic selection, what principles should constrain parents' procreational autonomy? One such principle would preclude any selections that could lead to significant, biologically based mental or physical suffering or hardship – even if it could be argued that such suffering or hardship might accompany an overall level of well-being that would otherwise be high. Another principle would pursue autonomy as a feature of the future person's well-being. It would entail screening to select for the future

[17] Scientists and bioethicists as well as legislators and legal scholars confront the challenge of defining deeply contested terms such as *normal* and *abnormal*, *average* and *below average* and *above average*.

person's freedom from disability toward the full capacity to pursue political participation. It could entail sanctions for parents who abused this principle, from moral admonitions (allowing for disagreement and alternatives to the moral recommendation) to legal sanctions (Frati et al. 2017).

8.7 CONCLUSION: A HUMAN RIGHT TO FREEDOM FROM GENETIC DISABILITY WOULD PROMOTE WELL-BEING AS AUTONOMY

Both nature and genetic selection can restrict individual autonomy: nature, in the form of genetic disabilities; genetic selection, as a future person's genetic characteristics when selected by others. The term *procreative autonomy* refers to the decisional autonomy of the parents in deciding to edit some of a future child's genetic traits. The latter person's autonomy can be served if she is genetically selected to be free of genetic disabilities. Or it might be violated: if the future person has a right to be free of genetic manipulation, then gene editing at the embryonic stage of development shackles her with a fait accompli, unalterable because written into her body: heteronomy become flesh.

I argued for a human right to freedom from genetic disability and, by implication, against a human right that would prohibit all forms of genetic selection. I did so by defining both disability and well-being narrowly. And I did so by employing limited conceptions of parents' procreative autonomy and a future person's autonomy: well-being as autonomy, and disability as a condition that reduces it. I conclude by anticipating three possible objections.

First, the genetic editing of future persons will always leave a great deal to chance. And it will have consequences for human society and the natural environment, some of which, likely many of which, cannot be anticipated. One might argue that the risks of genetic selection are unacceptable given the sheer causal complexity of the human organism. The risks may be unacceptable in light of various complex, causal interdependencies (as evolutionary theory makes clear). But one might just as well argue that risk-taking is always necessary for the survival of the species, biologically and culturally. To the "extent that genetic interventions can be used to enhance strengths and compensate for weaknesses in creative ways that expand opportunity without 'normalizing' their recipients," they may sometimes contribute to greater general tolerance of human diversity (Juengst 2009: 57). I intend tolerance within political communities composed of both disabled and nondisabled persons. But I also intend tolerance toward a greater variety of persons with the autonomy to exercise their political agency.[18]

[18] To be sure, diversity in human populations is increased also by the presence of persons with disabilities. For an argument that intellectually disabled persons contribute both to the family's quality of life in some ways as well as to the entire community in the sense of positive diversity, see Brown et al. (2019).

Second, the genetics of diversity is not *as such* particularly useful in analyzing inequalities along dimensions of socioeconomic status, educational achievement, or relative rates of incarceration (among other indicators relevant to justice). Genetic disability examined at the intersection of biology and social environment tells us more about human communities than about disability examined genetically. The social grounds of political exclusion must not be conflated with biological grounds; our knowledge of genetics must not be abused to justify social inequalities.

Finally, genetic selection need not spell an unintended, unwanted "dialectic of enlightenment" (Gregg 2012b). My argument allows for a cautious embrace of enlightenment progress – deploying medical science to enhance political community by rendering more and more of the populace capable of political participation – but no unqualified embrace.[19] In this context, the political problem is not genetic selection that undermines the welfare of individuals and communities. The problem is unequal access, for economic and other reasons, domestically and globally, to the genetic selection that one day could free future persons of genetic disabilities and thereby enhance their

[19] Commitment to ideals of the European Enlightenment such as the rational governance of political communities providing all members with legal autonomy, justice, and equality, as well as rejection of the otherworldly pretensions of theological or metaphysical foundationalism, essentialism, and metanarratives (such as unfettered technological progress), does not lead to an unqualified embrace of genetic selection. And while the regulation of human genetic engineering should be an open-ended project, sensitive to shifting moral and cultural boundaries that sometimes accompany increases in scientific knowledge (for example, Darwin's theory of evolution), responsible regulation must not allow emancipatory hopes for genetic means to overcome heritable scourges of body and mind to overwhelm critical acuity in understanding all the many factors (including ones political, ideological, and economic) that limit scientific, medical, and technological progress. Responsible limitations today would favor therapy (targeting disease) over enhancement (targeting socially desirable traits). It would recognize that while the embryo is on a continuum with the species, the species is not itself a political or moral community with "natural" rights. And it would recognize that while the embryo is not as such a member of political community, it should be socially constructed as a "member-in-waiting" with a special legal status. The contours of that status would contribute to drawing boundaries for permissible genetic editing. Another regulatory limit concerns health-related social inequalities created, perpetuated, or exacerbated by genetic manipulation: positional inequalities, where a social good confers an advantage precisely because it is maldistributed (if everyone were equally intelligent, say, then intelligence would confer no positional advantage), and a type of inequality that affects persons (or their children) who (because of their relatively worse-off starting position) would benefit from genetic manipulation more than would privileged persons, yet who have little or no access to it. The term *manipulation* here refers to extending life expectancy and strengthening the immune system; reducing the incidence of disabilities such as cystic fibrosis, as well as therapy for debilitating or fatal genetic diseases in general (by means of somatic cell genetic modification). It also means predictive genetic tests to enable individuals to reduce genetic risks or obviate them entirely (personal genome sequencing). It means eliminating genetic disabilities and diseases by modifying (via germline gene therapy) the species' cellular lineage, which is passed to subsequent generations. And it means preimplantation genetic diagnosis followed by embryo selection for offspring free of undesirable genetic mutations, and for offspring less vulnerable to diseases.

autonomy and capacity for social and political inclusion (Carzis et al. 2019; Saran and Kuper 2020).

This chapter argued that screening an embryo can identify genetic factors that, if edited, could lessen, in the future person who develops from it, the incidence of genetic factors that may reduce her autonomy with respect to one fundamental condition of membership in liberal democratic community: the capacity to participate in her community's political system. It proposed a human right to parental choice in genetic selection of embryos and toward the individual liberty and legal equality that require individual autonomy. The following chapter continues this examination of social inequalities and does so along a different dimension: the possible forensic use of genetic science to identify responsibility for epigenetically induced health inequalities within a political community. Epigenetics studies heritable changes in gene expression of a particular kind: changes that do not involve changes in the genomic DNA sequence. Some of those changes may involve an organism's experience of trauma. Some may be passed from parents to offspring. Epigenetic research may be able to identify cross-generational transmissions of some social inequalities in this sense.

9

Deploying Epigenetics to Identify Biologically Influenced Social Inequalities

Research on human genetics reveals distinctly political dimensions, given the need for the modern state to regulate human reproduction through laws of hypodescent,[1] that is, interventionist natalist policies that incentivize larger families,[2] or eugenics.[3] But if the natural world and the social world are sharply distinguished one from the other, justice is a matter solely of the social world, meaningless in the natural world. Thus if one's genetic endowments are entirely a natural phenomenon, then whether one is fortunate or unfortunate in one's genetic endowment is without moral significance. Rather, it is a matter of individual luck in the "genetic lottery" of nature. Political community has no obligation to address "losers" in the "genetic lottery" – unless one adopts, say, the standpoint of luck-egalitarianism or, alternatively, commits to consequentialism. Otherwise, "to say that something is due to nature" is to relegate it to the "realm of fortune or misfortune," hence to reject the notion that it might fall within the sphere of justice (Buchanan et al. 2000: 83). In that case, "natural" disadvantages in the shape of genetically based health disparities among members of a community appear to be an inequality that is no one's fault: a misfortune, certainly, but not an injustice. Corrections are then

[1] For example, in the 1660s the British colony of Virginia legislated the status of slavery as something inherited through the mother; not until 1967, in *Loving* v. *Virginia* (388 U.S. 1 (1967)), did the US Supreme Court rule anti-miscegenation laws to be unconstitutional.

[2] Along several dimensions in Japan, South Korea, Taiwan, and Singapore, for example, but also in terms of generous maternity and paternity leave policies, as in Sweden.

[3] Now rejected examples include sterilization laws in Indiana (1907), Washington, and California (both 1909), as well as the Supreme Court's 1927 finding that forced sterilization (e.g., of the intellectually disabled) is constitutional (*Buck* v. *Bell*, 274 U.S. 200). Since the 1980s and 1990s, procedures that facilitate reproduction, including gestational surrogacy and preimplantation genetic diagnosis, are legal in the United States and elsewhere.

gratuitous acts of beneficence, voluntary acts of decency, but hardly moral, let alone legal, obligations.

I argue against sharply and strongly distinguishing between the social and the natural and for a fluid, blurry distinction, which I elaborate below. But a nature–nurture distinction is necessary in some form to evaluate the potential of epigenetic research to advance social justice with its potential to identify phenomena of the social environment that adversely influence the expression of the genome. Epigenetics studies heritable changes in gene expression of a particular kind: changes that do not involve changes in genomic DNA sequence.[4] Some of those changes may involve an organism's experience of trauma. Some of those changes, or "marks," may be passed from parents to offspring and even to subsequent generations. Such marks are mitotically and/or meiotically heritable.

Epigenetics focuses on the fact that, to various extents, genes and their environments influence the phenotype.[5] Scientists contest the actual *extent* of social influence on the phenotype in specific instances (such as obesity, an example I emphasize below). Contestation is political with respect to responsibility for unhealthy genetic endowments. To be sure, some epigenetic effects influence human health in positive ways.[6] Here I focus solely on negative effects.[7]

Social science has long shown that social inequality can be transmitted from one generation to the next.[8] Today epigenetic research may offer an additional means of identifying cross-generational transmissions of social inequalities. It can do so with a somewhat fluid and perspectival distinction between "natural" disadvantages and "social" ones. While social equalities cannot be reduced to biological phenomena, some may display a biological dimension. That possibility motivates my analysis of epigenetic processes that may betray clues to understanding how biology intersects with some social inequalities. At the level

[4] Adapted from Weber (2007). I use the term *epigenetics* to refer both to *effects* that are epigenetic and to the *science* of identifying the pathways and mechanisms of these effects.

[5] Where estimations of the relative influence of each are calculable.

[6] Among many examples, consider four: (a) mothers who, as infants, suffered adverse parenting, tend not to transmit that negative behavior to their infants if the mothers are provided with a supportive psychosocial environment (Bridges 2016); (b) diets containing "antioxidants and anti-inflammatory agents can decrease oxidative stress and exert influence on epigenetic factors causing positive impact on longevity" (Wichansawakun and Buttar 2019: 541); (c) curcumin "may regulate various intracellular pathways" thereby "attenuating certain diseases, including cancers, diabetic nephropathy, and neurocognitive disorders" such as Alzheimer's (Boyanapalli and Kong 2015: 129); and (d) physical exercise, especially "long-term repetitive strenuous exercise, positively affects health, reduces the aging process, and decreases the incidence of cancer through induced stress and epigenetic mechanisms" (Sanchis-Gomar et al. 2012: 3469).

[7] As does the Mismatch Model of Disease Development, which I discuss in later pages. To be sure, epigenetic privilege is as much a part of the project for social justice as is epigenetic misfortune, but a very different part: the concern is not with determining responsibility for negative effects but rather with making means for positive effects as widely available as possible.

[8] E.g., Marmot (2015).

of explanation, research need not treat epigenetic transmission in reductionist fashion. At the level of causality, it need not treat epigenetic transmission deterministically.

My argument for a soft and fluid distinction between the natural and the social builds on the work of scholars who have emphasized how human health is always also determined in part by various contextual or environmental factors. Thus Noble et al. (2014: 2238) note that "epigenetic mechanisms that lead to persistent developmentally induced changes in gene activity include diverse processes and factors." Maurizio Meloni and Giuseppe Testa (2014: 431) observe that the "very contours of what counts as 'epigenetic' are often blurred," whereby genetic and environmental factors are not easily, always, or necessarily distinguishable. And Patrick Bateson and Peter Gluckman (2012: 219) caution that, while "every human being is at once both developmentally robust and plastic," it hardly follows that "two distinct processes can be cleanly separated, one leading to an invariant outcome and the other generating differences between individuals due to culture, education and differences in developmental exposures and experience."

My rejection of reductionism and determinism extends the work of others. Eva Jablonka and Marion Lamb (2014: 4), for example, oppose the "prevalent gene-based unidimensional version" of Darwin's theory of evolution through natural selection with their argument that the epigenetic dimension to heredity is but one of four. Margaret Lock (2013: 291) argues that "epigenetic findings may well set off a new round of somatic reductionism because research is confined largely to the molecular level." Miranda Waggoner and Tobias Uller (2015: 177) note that "epigenetics research is often couched in language as deterministic as genetics research," such as responses to external stimuli that program a particular developmental trajectory or channel the individual's developmental potential.

Without reductionism or determinism, I argue that, if some social inequalities constitute a form of injustice, then the transmission of social inequality across generations, or intergenerationally, is a greater form of injustice. By *social inequalities* I mean some health inequalities in particular, for example Mark Hansen and Ruth Müller's (2017: 11) discussion of maternal obesity insofar as obesity "might increase the offspring's risks of diabetes and cardiovascular disease, and might even negatively affect cognitive performance." Further, the "risk of obesity is unevenly distributed throughout society, with individuals of low socioeconomic status often suffering disproportionately from poor access to healthy foods . . . or facilities to engage in physical activity" (ibid.). While social equalities cannot be reduced to biological phenomena, some may display a biological dimension. That possibility motivates my analysis of epigenetic processes that may betray clues to understanding how biology bisects some forms of social inequality.

My concern is with one lifeform only: human beings. Epigenetic marks have been found in genes thought to influence susceptibility to disease as well as to mental disorders. A mutation is a genetic alteration; an epigenetic mark is not. Even though not a mutation, it does affect gene expression.[9]

The hypothesis of epigenetic transmission across generations works with data showing that phenotypic traits as well as disease susceptibility, acquired through interaction with the individual's environments in one generation, can be transmitted epigenetically to later generations. The hypothesis: "environmental insults[10] before conception, even early in childhood," can "cause epigenetic changes to gamete (egg or sperm) cells that can manifest in the offspring on the behavioral and neuroendocrine level, and even at the level of neuronal differentiation and synaptic development" (Scorza et al. 2019: 121–122).

A broad range of phenomena falls under the umbrella rubric of epigenetics. My interest is not in epigenetics narrowly construed, such as heritable modifications to the genome via methylation or changes in chromatin condensation. My interest is epigenetics broadly construed: any heritable effects mediated by phenomena that are not genetic mutations, such as stress hormones influencing pregnancy outcomes in ways that render the future person more susceptible to certain health problems than would otherwise be the case.

An epigenetic approach to health focuses on several time periods: preconception, prenatal, and postnatal. These periods open a "window of epigenetic plasticity when environmental factors might act to condition the body in ways that shape disease risk in later life" and across different generations (Hansen and Müller 2017: 11). For example, children affected by environmental stress may transmit epigenetic marks in egg or sperm to their children (with cross-generational effects), to their grandchildren (with multigenerational effects), and even to their great-grandchildren (with transgenerational effects).

My concern here is the normative task of developing a politically tenable notion of responsibility for epigenetic effects with adverse consequences for health. On the one hand, epigenetic results do not tell us how to respond *normatively* to observed phenomena. On the other hand, epigenetic research into human health disparities can be useful *politically* only if coupled with a plausible theory of responsibility. I examine two such theories: individual responsibility (leading to interventions into the offending environment by the affected individual or her surrogates) and group responsibility (entailing population-level interventions).

Given the heritability of some epigenetic marks across generations, the possibility that parental and even grandparental experiences are written into an individual's epigenome implies a politically significant distinction in how a political community might best respond to certain social inequalities. I see two options.

9 I use the term *epigenetics* to refer both to *effects* that are epigenetic and to the *science* of identifying the pathways and mechanisms of these effects.

10 The term *insult* here is one-sided; from the standpoint of health, some environmental influences are positive.

First, if the relevant inequalities are best explained by cultural or social inheritance, then cultural or social policies would seem the appropriate route to addressing biologically transmitted inequalities. Because culture and society are large-scale phenomena, population-level approaches in particular would seem warranted. And "upstream, environmental interventions targeting intergenerational social justice" would appear more useful than "biomedical, downstream interventions" (Huang and King 2018: 73).[11]

Second, and by contrast, to the extent that some social inequalities have biological sources, at least in part, the remedy – even if still *social* – might also be *biological*. Hence an epigenetic notion of the environment needs to include "social context as well as biological exposures" (Hansen and Müller 2017: 11). This approach reveals social dynamics to be biological in part.

Consider these dynamics along two dimensions. One dimension is temporal. Social dynamics have a "human scale" in the sense of a human time scale: that of a human life or of several human generations. Human "physiological systems can respond and adapt to new changes in real time" (Szyf 2015: 134). Natural selection, by contrast, generally operates on a vast time scale, one many orders of magnitude longer than that of a human life or of several generations. Natural selection is "slow in responding to immediate environmental challenges," precisely the kind of changes at issue in the context of a political community seeking to determine issues of responsibility for changes harmful to the health of its members (ibid.).

A second dimension of social dynamics concerns the possibility of a political community consciously effecting change in the sense of reversing negative, harmful, or otherwise unwanted changes (changes likely never intended by any part of the community). Natural selection makes permanent changes to the genome whereas physiological responses elicit relatively fast and reversible changes in organ, tissue, or cell function. In the latter case, social context and not only biological exposure is politically relevant.

Some epigenetic changes appear to be reversible.[12] If, as some research suggests, the risk of epigenetically influenced diseases is determined during fetal development, then preventive measures might best focus on the periconceptional period of the mother–fetus relationship by means of improved nutrition and reduced exposure to environmental toxins in consumer products, in food, as well as in the air, water, and soil.

But not all epigenetic changes are reversible. Some may be permanently imprinted during fetal or early postnatal development. Certain physiological

[11] Where the sources of social inequalities are epigenetic, most remedies will need to be social. According to Huang and King (2018: 72), "because intergenerational transmission of health and disease susceptibility through epigenetic means is outside the control of affected individuals, demonstrations of epigenetic influences require public or collective action on causes of health differences."

[12] See Szyf (2007).

responses might alter patterns of histone modification and therefore of gene expression (the gene's conversion into functioning proteins). But such responses are often linked to feedback loops, whereby once protein expression reaches a certain level, another mechanism is triggered to silence the gene and to restore homeostasis (that is, to restore the biological status quo).

My argument links several claims. If some epigenetic effects on a fetus can adversely affect an individual's life-long health (and therefore her life-chances), then one can argue that she is disadvantaged by the life-experiences of the mother (and perhaps by the father's and even the grandparents'). Insofar as such adverse effects are caused by social forces beyond the control of the ancestors, I frame them as a matter of social justice. A political community appropriately addresses such matters by collective mechanisms. To that end I offer a theory of corporate responsibility and argue that, in a political community that practices corporate responsibility, the identification of adverse, socially generated epigenetic effects and their sources may render epigenetics a tool for social justice.

I develop this argument as the political project of deploying epigenetics in the interests of social justice. The argument proceeds in five steps. (1) I examine how the project moves research from a cultural focus to a biological one. (2) I identify forms of epigenetic research that are politically salient in a weak sense as well as forms that are salient in a strong sense. In the latter case, I take the transmission of maternal stress as an empirical example. I then discuss three challenges to the project: (3) a scientific critique of epigenetic theories, (4) a political critique, and (5) a theory of corporate responsibility for negative epigenetic effects. I contend that some epigenetic research may contribute data toward advancing social justice by identifying some genetically influenced social inequalities. I frame possible collective responsibility for some negative epigenetic effects as a matter of social justice. I conclude that epigenetic science sometimes offers a means of identifying sources of some social inequalities. It can do so only in terms of a theory of corporate responsibility for human-made environments, for living conditions and lifestyle, and for transgenerational transmission of adverse epigenetic effects.

This argument is yet another exercise in political bioethics. Here political bioethics identifies and analyzes problematic biotechnological phenomena that call for legal redress, new public policy, or new laws. (§9.1) I reveal the persistence of some social inequalities over generations (such as poverty) as phenomena based not (only) in the affected persons' culture but in their biology. (§9.2) I examine how epigenetic research might identify genetically influenced social inequalities (or disparities among social groups in health outcomes). (§9.3) I address potential *scientific* problems with this particular way of deploying epigenetics, and then (§9.4) potential *political* problems with such a deployment. (§9.5) I analyze one political upshot of an epigenetic approach: the task of assigning collective moral or legal responsibility for harmful epigenetic effects.

9.1 FROM CULTURAL CRITIQUE TO BIOLOGICAL CRITIQUE

Scholars in the late twentieth century commonly invoked one or the other notion of culture to explain the "perpetuation of disadvantage across generations" (Scorza et al. 2019: 121). This culturalist approach would "explain the cyclical quality of poverty by suggesting that parental attitudes and behaviors are transmitted to their children, perpetuating a cycle of poverty" (ibid., 119–120). Such an approach is controversial, not least because some research[13] argues that the so-called "culture of poverty would not shift even if socio-political factors did" – for example, by "providing access to better schools" (ibid., 120). The conclusion is no less controversial: it is the responsibility of individuals to "change their attitudes and behaviors to lift themselves out of poverty" (ibid.).

Other scholars challenged the culturalist hypothesis by highlighting structural factors affecting the agency of poor persons, showing that "incidence, depth, duration, and timing of poverty as well as the neighborhood where a child was raised, all influence a child's educational attainment, a proxy for socioeconomic status" (ibid.).[14] They also showed that "household and neighborhood poverty are related to stress" and that the "cumulative effect of stressors such as housing or food insecurity, child abuse or neglect, parental substance abuse, and violence" can induce a "toxic stress response in young children, which can lead to long-term changes in brain structure and function in infancy and early childhood" (ibid.).

In response, some analysts of social inequalities shifted from a cultural focus to a biological one. As an explanatory factor, epigenetics does not *replace* culture. Rather, it *qualifies* culture as only part of any plausible causal explanation. The identification of "effects of epigenetic processes on molecular level" need not preclude "genetic, social, and other causes of observed effects" (Morgan and Whitelaw 2008: 396).

9.2 POLITICAL SALIENCE OF DIFFERENT TYPES OF EPIGENETIC RESEARCH

Data for intergenerational epigenetic transmission in humans take different forms; consider two. One is historical, establishing "connections between malnutrition *in utero* and in early life, and persisting metabolic disorders" as a consequence of "changes in the human epigenome" (Meloni 2015: 128). Bastiaan Heijmans and colleagues (2008) found that individuals exposed *in utero* to the Dutch *Hongerwinter* of 1944–1945, during German occupation, years later displayed transgenerational effects of chronic disease. As adults they experienced increased rates of coronary heart disease and obesity, rates higher than those of persons not exposed during the mother's early pregnancy.

[13] E.g., Small et al. (2010). [14] Compare Ferguson et al. (2007).

A different historical example draws on harvest records, food prices, as well as birth and death records from three different cohorts in Överkalix in northern Sweden. Marcus Pembrey and colleagues (2006) demonstrated that mortality risk ratios were inherited across generations: "Variation in the food supply during the early life of paternal grandparents was associated with variation in mortality rate (and diabetic deaths) in their grandchildren." Effects were identified "only when exposures occurred before puberty, supporting the hypothesis that reprogramming of gametes was involved" (Szyf 2015: 134).

A different kind of data comes from controlled experiments on monozygotic twins who, because they are genetically matched, facilitate the identification of environmental influences. Such influences may demonstrate epigenetic effects. Examples include studies of human intelligence as measured by intelligence quotient tests (Yu et al. 2012), childhood psychotic symptoms (Fisher et al. 2015: 1014), and acquired preference for fatty foods, a preference associated with obesity (Rissanen 2002).

Political bioethics raises the issue of deploying epigenetics to identify and possibly reverse genetically influenced social inequalities – and to determine responsibility for the harm. Consider the notion of epigenetic intergenerational transmission. Politically salient are "insults to pregnant women or stress even earlier in life [that] may have independent negative effects on future generations regardless of the experiences of those later generations" (Scorza et al. 2019: 125). Politically salient are parents' childhood experiences when they transfer epigenetic marks that "impact the development of their offspring independently of and in interaction with their offspring's perinatal and early childhood direct exposures to stress stemming from socioeconomic disadvantage and adversity" (ibid., 119).

Also politically salient are studies that, using the Developmental Origins of Health and Disease hypothesis, find that the "incidence of certain adult diseases such as stroke, type 2 diabetes and dyslipidaemia may be linked to *in utero* development" (Sinclair et al. 2007: 425). Studies oriented on this hypothesis have shown that "babies exposed to stress, both nutritional and non-nutritional, during different critical periods of development," ultimately "result in a disease state" (Calkins and Devaskar 2011: 158).[15] Such findings shift the explanatory emphasis of intergenerational transmission of adversity from the cultural or "nurture" end of a continuum toward the nature end. Here, embodied inequality, inequality become flesh, explains certain social inequalities better than do genes likely to disadvantage the individual in various social ways.

Such research once viewed "conception or the period shortly before conception as the starting point from which adversity can affect the biology of a new

[15] This example differs from my earlier malnutrition example from the Netherlands and Sweden. Unlike those historically unique examples, this one involves phenomena such as stress that appear to be commonplace across time and place.

life" (Scorza et al. 2019: 121). Now, "advances in epigenetic research point to an expanded timeframe for intergenerational impact" (ibid.). Evidence suggests that "mothers' own childhood experiences are likely to have a lasting biological effect on their offspring" (ibid., 124). Emma Blackmore and colleagues (2016: 1) found that women who experience anxiety before giving birth had "significantly smaller babies than non-anxious women" and that "trauma history magnified the effects of maternal prenatal mood on birthweight." Indeed, the "moderating effect was limited to those who first experienced a trauma under eighteen years of age. Childhood trauma exposure increased vulnerability for low birthweight delivery associated with prenatal mood disturbance" (ibid.).

Using the Developmental Origins of Health and Disease model, Pamela Scorza and colleagues (2019: 119) found that fetal exposure to maternal prenatal distress is associated with "socioeconomic disadvantage" that "compromises offspring's neurodevelopment, affecting short- and long-term physical and mental health, and thereby psychosocial standing and resources." Bea Van den Bergh and colleagues (2017: 1) identified "effects of maternal stress on offspring neurodevelopment, cognitive development, negative affectivity, difficult temperament and psychiatric disorders." Cyril Peter and colleagues (2016: 1) found that "Early childhood malnutrition entails long lasting epigenetic signatures associated with liability for attention and cognition, and limited potential for intergenerational transmission." The idea of deploying epigenetics to identify genetically influenced social inequalities finds support in these examples.

Also politically salient is the fact that this model is gendered in its focus. To be sure, researchers can best observe, induce, and manipulate long-term epigenetic changes in humans during the perinatal period. And "maternal phenotype clearly has substantially greater capacity to shape offspring phenotype through the processes of pregnancy and lactation" (Wells 2007: 154). Further, "post-natal interventions may be incapable of halting the process, since the adaption has already commenced prior to birth" (ibid., 161). Finally, maternal-fetal epigenetic programming is an important site for pursuing issues of "infant mortality, early childhood development, and prevention of complex and resource-intensive public health problems such as obesity, diabetes, and cardiovascular disease" (Richardson 2015: 218).

Yet a focus on the fetal origins of disease easily becomes a focus on the fetal environment in relation to maternal stress and obesity. A concern with fetal environment readily becomes a concern with the maternal body as an "adaptive environment for the fetus in which crucial early developmental cues are transmitted to the growing infant. Because this programming can imprint on a growing female fetus's own gametes as well, the effects of the maternal environment may be intergenerational, passed through the maternal line to grandoffspring" (ibid., 217). In these ways, among others, the maternal body – from preconception through birth – becomes the premier site for surveillance: for various environmental exposures; by medical researchers and public health officials; for possible regulation and intervention.[16] Further, some analysts construct a concern with the interests of the fetus or child as an interest that challenges those of the mother.[17] Finally, this focus on maternal effects overlooks possible paternal effects as well as male reproductive vulnerability, to say nothing of paternal responsibility for the development of infants, let alone fetuses.

9.3 SCIENTIFIC CRITIQUES OF EPIGENETIC THEORIES

Despite such data – which can be challenged with regard to their robustness and reproducibility (Szyf 2015: 135) – the notion of epigenetics as a tool for social justice confronts two major challenges. One is political; I address it in §9.4. The other concerns scientific problems.

First, if epigenetic research is ever to be a tool of social justice, biologists need to demonstrate a clear causal link between epigenetic sources and health problems. And they need to identify a "fundamental common mechanism, or several different mechanisms, that can explain the different modes of nongenetic inheritance" (ibid.).

Second, while animal studies provide evidence of intergenerational epigenetic inheritance, the specific mechanisms of transmission remain unclear. "Multiple methods of transgenerational epigenetic inheritance have been proposed, including DNA methylation, histone and chromatin changes, RNA differences, and prions" (Rothstein et al. 2017). A leading candidate is DNA methylation, where "methyl molecules bind to DNA and hinder access to that DNA for transcription" (ibid.). Methylation is stable, "known to be heritable through cell division, and is retained during sperm maturation, when other epigenetic marks are largely removed" (Scorza et al. 2019: 122). Yet "changes are often small and widespread throughout the genome and affect a variety of genes" (ibid.). Further, DNA methylation is driven by "intrauterine exposure rather than intergenerational epigenetic inheritance. Given that most genes are extensively demethylated after fertilization," it remains unclear whether inherited DNA methylation patterns make intergenerational epigenetic inheritance possible (ibid.).

Third, most evidence for multigenerational epigenetic transmission "comes from animal model experiments with specific environmental exposures, such as endocrine-disrupting chemicals," "folic acid or grooming behavior" (Huang and King 2018: 72–73). Mice studies provide the strongest evidence of "epigenetic inheritance from one to the next generation(s)" but in humans this

[16] If, for example, a trait "like fetal growth is designed to minimize the effects of short-term fluctuations by integrating information across generations, public health interventions may be most effective if focused not on the individual but on the matriline" (Kuzawa 2005: 18).

[17] For example, one might argue that the developmentally optimum outcomes for a fetus are in tension with the mother's interests where those outcomes might endanger the mother's life.

possibility is less certain (Hedlund 2012: 173). Animal-based models so far do not make clear whether intergenerational epigenetic inheritance "exists in humans" (Scorza et al. 2019: 122). Particularly problematic are extrapolations from "specific chemical or behavioral interventions in animals to complex social policies in humans" (Huang and King 2018: 73). After all, animal studies can hardly replicate humankind's "complex social and community structure" (Scorza et al. 2019: 122). Yet the project of deploying epigenetics to identify genetically influenced social inequalities focuses on precisely those structures.

9.4 POLITICAL CRITIQUES OF EPIGENETIC THEORIES

The plausibility of deploying epigenetics depends on showing that some health problems are linked to social inequalities. The nature of that linkage is not only empirical; it is also a matter of interpreting empirical findings in normative terms. Interpretation is necessary because the social or environmental processes that produce epigenetic variations do not themselves determine what a particular interpreter might mean by the term *injustice*. Because any theory of justice is a contingent, culturally relative social construction, no epigenetic effects can be characterized definitively as unequivocally unjust, unfair, or harmful.

Further, the project to deploy epigenetics toward identifying genetically influenced social inequalities requires evidence, in affected persons, of causally relevant epigenetic mechanisms. In any given case, legal, political, and moral responsibility is established by a causal link – even as the strength and parameters of such evidence remain open to debate, interpretation, and possibly disagreement regarding appropriate standards of evidence.

Where causality cannot be established, public policy seeking to address intergenerational health disparities with epigenetic dimensions might utilize a reworked "precautionary principle." The principle offers guidance regarding possible preventative measures when public policy is confronted by scientific uncertainty. According to David Kriebel and Joel Tickner (2001: 1353–1354),

> Scientific research plays an essential role in evaluating the costs, risks and benefits of proposed public health policies, but the scientific data are often limited by large areas of uncertainty. In these gray areas, activities that potentially threaten public health are often allowed to continue because the norms of traditional science demand high confidence to reject null hypotheses and so detect harmful effects.

The principle could be applied as well to analyzing suspected past social conditions and human activities whose epigenetic consequences are later observed. When there is significant scientific uncertainty about the causal connection with negative effects suspected to be epigenetic, policy decisions should err on the side of caution and, even without conclusive proof of a causal connection, undertake measures to prevent future such effects.

The project of deploying epigenetics where it might advance social justice also needs to address political critiques of some research models. Consider three such critiques. First, in identifying the political salience of epigenetics, I focus on inherited epigenetic changes that are permanent. Danya Vears and Flavio D'Abramo (2018: 159) challenge the assumption that epigenetic effects are permanent. They argue that the "results of the DNA methylation study are due to the patient's current lifestyle behaviors and that by changing these behaviors, the cause of the epigenetic signature will be removed." This challenge is not relevant to my project. Section 2 above (on the political salience of different types of epigenetic research) explains why. It discusses adverse effects of fetal exposure to maternal prenatal stress that increases the offspring's vulnerability to low birthweight and compromises its short- and long-term physical and mental health. Such effects are irrelevant to how long new methylation patterns last.

The existence of competing assumptions (and Vears and D'Abramo's challenge in particular) is expectable given our still inadequate understanding of the "involvement of epigenetics in environmentally triggered phenotypes and diseases" (Feil and Fraga 2012: 107). Not enough is "known about the interactions between behavioral factors, such as smoking, drinking and diet, and their effect on DNA methylation to guide medical recommendations" (Vears and D'Abramo 2018: 158). One challenge for the idea of deploying epigenetics in pursuit of social justice is to separate environmental factors clearly from lifestyle factors (including socioeconomic status, the person's housing and living conditions and their environs, and her nutritional history). Such a separation may not be possible, for example for a person who grew up under circumstances of "low socioeconomic status, had poor nutrition from a young age and lived in an area with high levels of pollution" (ibid., 159). The epigenetic consequences the person experienced may be explained better by her early exposure than by her current lifestyle.

Second, to describe an epigenetic variant as "harmful" is to compare it with a healthy or "normal" epigenome, that is, one not associated with disease or abnormality. But what renders an individual's epigenetic programming "healthy" or "normal"? While persuasive answers may include objective features – *objective* in the sense of empirically verifiable scientific data, they in any case will include normative features – *normative* in the sense of historically contingent norms that are relative to particular cultures and that change over time. Hence deployment of epigenetics as a political tool would require the construction of a standard of "normal health."[18]

[18] Recent analyses of "normal" health and human functioning range from normal biological functioning (e.g., Daniels 2008) to statistical normality lacking any intrinsic moral significance (e.g., Kahane and Savulescu 2012). Other analyses range from psychological disorders as distinct from mismatches between a person's normal traits and the idiosyncratic demands of a particular social system (e.g., Wakefield 2015). Still other scholars analyze normal functioning not as something typical for the species but as something relative to the community in which the individual lives (e.g., Loi 2013).

Such a standard can only be a particular value commitment. I see at least three different possible commitments. One would ask us to "consider the idea of a normal epigenome" as "bound to that of a healthy epigenome" (Dupras and Ravitsky 2016: 537). Another would foresee public health policies aimed at "favoring the programming of a specific epigenome that best corresponds to that of the majority" (ibid.). And yet another would "focus on the best environment for the healthy programming and maintenance of epigenetic health" – as well as on its alternative: "programming the epigenome so that it best matches the living environment or lifestyle of the individual" (ibid.).

Third, any given answer may entail problematic analytic results. If we humans find ourselves unable to establish some kind of epigenetic normality that holds for all persons, then epigenetic variants – if analyzed independently of their environment – would appear to be "unreliable biological markers for disease susceptibility" (ibid., 536). That conclusion would undermine the project of deploying epigenetics in the interest of justice. Indeed, the project depends on defining a particular epigenetic effect as harmful to human health, then causally tracing the effect on particular persons back to the relevant environment.

To avoid such a conclusion, one might argue that epigenetic normality is not universal but rather always relative to a particular genome, one "rooted in geographical and temporal references specific to individuals and populations" (ibid.). Analysis then takes a particular epigenome's environment seriously: "normal" appears to be something that can be determined *locally*, with respect to a *particular* environment.

Or the argument might imply that no epigenetic difference can count as an epigenetic abnormality. It might imply that no difference may be regarded as something negative in nature, as an "impairment." Rather, epigenetic differences are something "positive" in that they constitute "functional adaptations conferring advantages in specific environments" (ibid.).

This conclusion also leads to normatively unpalatable inferences, for example that "normatively 'poor parenting' behaviors may be conditionally or locally beneficial for offspring, allowing them to be better prepared" for certain kinds of future environments (Huang and King 2018: 74). One might avoid this inference by weighing the overall positive and negative consequences of a particular influence. For example, poor parenting might prove beneficial in practice. Yet in terms of rendering children more resilient, independent, or resourceful, the positive effects might well be outweighed by the negative mental health outcomes associated with poor parenting, such as violence and depression. One might reach the same conclusion by arguing that, for some epigenetic patterns, early programming is "sensitive to the developmental environment and aims to better prepare the organism" for its likely future environment (Dupras and Ravitsky 2016: 536).

The fact that epigenetic programming occurs in response to environmental stress does not entail that the outcome is necessarily adaptive. Or an epigenetic change may be adaptive in the short term but become maladaptive over time. Nonetheless, an "adverse phenotype does not depend merely on the presence or absence of a specific epigenetic variant, but rather on the *mismatch* between the previously programmed variant and the individual's [current] lifestyle or living conditions" (ibid.).

The preceding sentence articulates the Mismatch Model of Disease Development. It states that the "fetus is, through the mother, exposed to the kind of environment" into which it is likely to be born (Vears and D'Abramo 2018: 159). The "resulting epigenetic pattern is imprinted" toward better adaptation after birth and throughout life. Hence the "patient's epigenetic pattern is not abnormal in and of itself" but rather only if *mismatched* to the patient's current living environment (ibid.).

The Mismatch Model does not identify unambiguous abnormalities. Rather, it shows that "programming can become maladaptive when the environment changes and thus becomes detrimental to health" (Dupras and Ravitsky 2016: 536). Upshot: there is no such thing as a "normal" epigenome that defines "good epigenetic health" *as such*.

The Mismatch Model begins with the epigenetic thesis that the "effects of the dialogue between the genome and its environment" is "most profound early in life" (Hedlund 2012: 173). The effects involve an "adaptation or matching of the offspring to the current environment" (ibid.). If conditions later in life do not "correspond to the environment in early life," such as "food scarcity in early life and food abundance in adult life," then the epigenetic programming and the actual living conditions are mismatched (ibid.). Any cell that can "memorize" its early life environment can affect the individual's health "enduringly" (ibid.).

Accordingly, any given lifestyle or living condition is not *inherently* detrimental to all individuals or to all populations. Rather, it is detrimental to groups and individuals from a very different environment "in which the early epigenetic programming occurred" (Dupras and Ravitsky 2016: 536). Thus "variations in programming of epigenetic markers *in utero* are evolved responses to environmental cues that attempt to predict future environments and thereby improve survivability through procreative years" (Huang and King 2018: 74). In that sense, an epigenome is not something to be corrected for. On the contrary: it adaptively aligns a given organism with its particular environment.

Research on obesity corroborates this model. Charles Dupras and Vardit Ravitsky (2016: 536) find that the "epigenetic programming of obesity-related genes during fetal development" is "influenced by the availability of nutrients in the womb during pregnancy." The fetal body responds to poor nutrient availability by optimizing caloric uptake and use. It does this by genetic programming for increased efficiency in "storing calories in the lipid tissues later in life" (ibid.).

Epigenetic programming may lead to increased risk for obesity if, during the individual's life, the environment changes in ways that increase nutrient and calorie availability. In other words, the "experience of macronutrient deficiency *in utero* directs the fetus to develop an energy-conserving 'thrifty phenotype' through putative epigenetic programming" that increases survival chances in a nutrient-poor environment (Huang and King 2018: 74). Yet in many communities today, "high-caloric food is readily available, making such a phenomenon maladaptive, leading to obesity, diabetes and early mortality" (ibid.).

If the question of whether epigenetic variations affect health adversely depends on the individual's environment, the idea of deploying epigenetics for purposes of social justice is implausible. And it is implausible if the Mismatch Model cannot identify epigenetic harms *as such*. But it remains plausible where the Mismatch Model fails, as in the following scenario. Thrifty phenotypes may develop in parts of the world characterized by severe malnutrition. A child born into that environment is unlikely to move into a calorie-rich environment and, in that case, here a thrifty phenotype is maladaptive. Thrifty genotypes are likely linked to environments of extreme deprivation. Those environments often remain constant over the individual's lifetime, given the significant social and economic difficulties associated with upward mobility for persons starting from a very low initial position.

9.5 CORPORATE RESPONSIBILITY FOR NEGATIVE EPIGENETIC EFFECTS

The task of assigning responsibility for negative epigenetic effects is normative, indeed political, but not scientific. To be sure, modern natural science is always inflected with the political and economic forces of the society in which it is embedded. In 2001 American President George W. Bush exercised his executive power to sharply restrict federal funding for human embryo stem-cell research: he mandated no federal funding for new cell lines or research on newly derived lines. He based this decision on his personal religious beliefs, reflecting the particularly theological commitments of a small minority of the electorate, particularly white evangelicals. While an American president is constrained to abide by the Constitution's First Amendment, which prohibits the government from either favoring or disfavoring any religious belief and practice, the meaning of the constitutional text is often a matter of interpretation. Interpretation is a matter not of truth but of perspective. It is perspectival because informed by the particular value-commitments of the authoritative interpreters.

Assigning responsibility for unwanted epigenetic effects involves interpreting scientific analyses for the possible legal, moral, and political consequences of those effects. The effort to determine causal responsibility pursues justice by determining culpability. But whereas assertions about causality are claims about truth, assertions about culpability are claims about values. Values are social constructs: historically contingent, culturally embedded. In these ways, the task of assigning responsibility is normative not scientific.

On the one hand, the task of assigning responsibility within a community presupposes the political capacity of members for a mutual attribution of responsibility. As members of a political community, individuals need to be able to attribute responsibility for actions, and to do so mutually, every day.[19] The simultaneous possibility of individual autonomy and collective self-determination requires as much. Collective self-determination includes corporate responsibility for individuals harmed (even if unintentionally) by parts of the collective, whether private or public, whether economic, administrative, or political. For the possibility of corporate responsibility, members of a community need to understand themselves in terms of a mutual attribution of responsibility.[20] Mutual attribution is one basis for demanding accountability from decision makers. It requires them to present themselves before those whose interests they represent or otherwise affect. It is one basis for demanding transparency, toward public accountability, in the design and implementation of businesses, public policies, legislation, and so forth.

On the other hand, the scientific task of identifying epigenetic effects does not by itself determine responsibility. Responsibility does not follow simply from determining the causal connection between epigenetic mechanism and environmental exposure. Moral or legal responsibility is a normative construction. The scientific identification of epigenetic mechanisms (social, chemical, biological, or otherwise) does not of itself "imply who should be held responsible for any particular causal mechanism" (Huang and King 2018: 73). The scientific identification of epigenetic mechanisms does not imply any particular remedy.

The task of determining responsibility is best understood by thinking of collective responsibility in two ways: (a) in general and (b) with reference to vulnerable members of political community (such as some pregnant women).

(a) Although not a moral person, political community can be regarded as a moral agent. It combines centralized and decentralized competencies, including organizations along bureaucratic, legal, and economic lines. Its decision structures are in part hierarchical but some can be, in part, democratic. Competencies, organizations, and decision structures constitute a political community's ethical infrastructure. It can be described metaphorically as exhibiting intentionality in collectively planning future actions but also in its capacity to be accountable, collectively, for the

[19] Chapter 6 develops this idea as a trait peculiar to human intelligence, by contrast with artificial intelligence.

[20] Chapter 5 discusses the mutual attribution of responsibility in the context of threshold capacities for political participation in liberal democratic community. But such attribution is no guarantee of just politics and does not necessarily preclude injustice.

consequences of past actions. Both the community as a whole, as well as its executive leadership and administrators, can be accountable morally and, ideally, legally for some of the social factors that may cause adverse epigenetic health effects on some members of the community.

The implementation of social, political, and economic policies is a form of intentionality. It requires persons in positions of authority to make authoritative decisions[21] for which the community (or groups within it) might be held responsible to the extent that these persons and groups are capable of endorsing or rejecting relevant collective practices and policies. They are capable of evaluating past decisions and existing practices. They are capable of determining whether those intentions should be maintained, modified, or eliminated.

An individual is capable of bearing responsibility in any given case only if she is autonomous in agency (able to choose among behavioral options) and as long as she is autonomous in understanding (possessing information adequate to make an informed choice). While not a moral person, a political community is not morally independent of the people who compose it. A political community may constitute an autonomous agent even as a loose organization of individuals. This loose quality means that not all members at any given time act on a shared intention together, and that not all members have the same intention to realize the same goals or that all members share the same values or understandings. While a political community is not a collective individual or unified agent, it can be considered autonomous in the sense of being capable of bearing moral or legal responsibility because it operates through its members.

Even while the individual member never loses her particular identity as a group member, all members together constitute the political community in a corporate identity. That identity endures despite the variety of opinions held within the community, the different degrees of involvement among members, and differences in their various aims, and regardless of the fact that, at any given time, some people are entering the community while others are leaving it.

With Philip Petit (2007: 184) I argue that "corporate entities can be bona fide agents" that are "relatively autonomous in relation to their members."[22] The mere aggregation of individual responsibility does not become collective responsibility. The collective quality of responsibility in political community concerns the way in which individual intentions, even in their differences, are nonetheless entwined normatively. They are entwined not in the sense of agreement but in the sense that all members are called upon to recognize the legitimacy of the *res publica* – as expressed in laws, regulations, and judicial interpretations that are binding on all members.

21 See Searle (1995: 100–101) on how social, institutionalized authority can constitute a kind of communal act in the form of "status functions" with "deontic power."

22 Unlike Petit, I speak exclusively of political communities.

Political community so understood is more than a random collection of *individual* intentions. Community is collectively "able to intend, or at least foresee, the outcome or state of affairs for which it is appropriately held responsible" (Giubilini and Levy 2018: 212). It is capable of recognizing, after the fact and through epigenetic research, responsibility for adverse epigenetic effects on the health of some of its members.

Given opportunities in liberal democratic community for the citizenry to influence the polity and to select legislative representatives, "no collective intention is fully reducible to the individual intentions that are components of it" (Isaacs 2006: 66). The intentions of individuals are "normatively interlocked" (Sadler 2006) such that their character is collective not individualistic. This character renders a political community capable of bearing corporate responsibility. It is relevant to citizenship when understood in such liberal principles as equality before the law. Communal membership characterized by justice in the form of equality before the law constitutes communal membership as a shared objective (even if interpreted in competing ways), ideally borne by all members (even if borne in different ways). *Communal membership* can then be understood as collective intention; *collective intention* can be grounds for *corporate responsibility*. Corporate responsibility can be distinguished from an individual's responsibility for her environmentally impacted health trait, or from the responsibility of parents or grandparents for passing that trait to their offspring.

While any form of reciprocity "requires the contribution of more than one individual for its performance," political community as a corporate agent, capable of bearing collective responsibility, does *not* require that all "individuals do their part in bringing about a common end – or at least in bringing about different ends that 'mesh' and are not inconsistent with each other" (Giubilini and Levy 2018: 209–210). Community does *not* require that *all* "individuals intend to bring about this end or these consistent ends" (ibid.). It does *not* require that all members "recognize that others are doing their part in bringing about such ends" (ibid.). It does *not* require that all members are "aware of all these conditions" (ibid).

In short, to be capable of intending action and of acting – thus to be capable of corporate responsibility for outcomes caused – a political community need not be what it cannot be anyway: a unified and internally undifferentiated entity. The responsibility of political community "does not fully distribute among individuals"; it is corporate, not individual (Isaacs 2006: 62).

(b) Given the complex causal relations contributing to possibilities for free and voluntary choice, ascribing responsibility is difficult. The vulnerability of vulnerable persons raises questions about a *lack* of personal responsibility. Consider the context of "workers with occupational exposures that cause epigenetic harms" (ibid.) where "diseases derived from certain working conditions" cannot be reduced to "biomedical problems" (Vears and D'Abramo 2018: 157). Here a political community might invoke the idea of personal responsibility to defend itself against claims that the community – rather than the vulnerable individual – is responsible for the negative epigenetic effects suffered. Or consider the fact that the "lifestyles and health habits of [some] vulnerable individuals are likely to reflect a range of unhealthy behaviors" (Rothstein et al. 2017: 8). Individual responsibility for unhealthy behavior is less clear when the individuals are vulnerable. In some instances, responsibility may not lie with the individuals.

These examples express a general social phenomenon. The following example, drawn not from political community as such but from a major corporate industry within it, clarifies the way in which groups can displace responsibility for negative effects from the group to affected individuals. The example comes from the food and drinks industry; the adverse effect is obesity in some consumers. A government or its public health department may sometimes call upon the industry to assume some measure of responsibility for addressing rates of obesity where the industry's products may be a major contributing factor.

A complicating factor immediately emerges: tension between the probabilistic quality of propositions about persons, on the one hand, and the determinism of propositions about moral or legal responsibility, on the other.[23] With respect to human biology, "nutritionists and epidemiologists cannot agree" on a "causal link between obesity and poor health outcomes"; they cannot agree "whether it is fat content, energy density, total calories, the type of fat or too much or too little carbohydrate that causes weight gain" (Herrick 2009: 58).

The lack of scientific agreement allows the industry to operate in terms of a "false belief that it is possible to determine whether someone has a healthy lifestyle by observing whether or not that person maintains a healthy weight" (Campos 2004: 97). Industry's behavior is predicated on its preference for self-regulation when called upon to assume some responsibility for negative health outcomes tied to its products. To that end, it encourages a shift "from treatment to prevention and from state duty of care to individual responsibility" for making informed decisions (Herrick 2009: 55). It may even do so in alliance with governmental interests "to reduce their economic burden on the state" (ibid., 60).

The shift involves the industry's preference for a particular model of human behavior: that of the rational consumer (the recipient of product nutritional information) with agency to make choices. According to this model, adverse health outcomes (consumer obesity) result from consumers failing to exercise

[23] I return to this tension in the chapter's conclusion.

"appropriate" choices. For this model, obesity results from the "physiological effects of past consumption choices" by the affected individuals (ibid., 57).

The shift is complete when the affected persons – cast by the industry "in the language of consumer empowerment and choice" (ibid., 52) – betray that empowerment because (as the industry argues) they make "poor and 'uninformed' lifestyle choices for their health outcomes" (ibid., 61). The unsupportable assumption here is that "health status reflects the degree" to which affected persons "know and act upon the knowledge" (ibid., 57) that "food choices affect health" (Smoyer-Tomic et al. 2006: 307). Industry makes the same assumption with regard to the consumer's sedentarism, her lack of exercise. For industry, she is especially culpable if her sedentarism is in fact a refusal to exercise.

Shifting blame to the individual undermines public health objectives by willfully neglecting some of the many social determinants of ill-health, from poverty to structural inequalities, from unequal access to nutritious food to lack of possibilities and even time for exercise, from lack of health insurance to violent environments. The industry's construction of the blameworthy consumer presupposes what cannot be presupposed in all cases: her agency. Many contexts, especially for populations weakly situated socially and economically, preclude consumer choice.

In some instances, responsibility may not lie with individuals. Some individuals may be vulnerable because of their condition.[24] In this instance, too, individual responsibility may be invoked in ways that allow the community to deflect blame. Women might be blamed "for harms caused to their children from prenatal exposures" (Rothstein et al. 2017: 8). Ismaili M'Hadi and colleagues (2018: 59) observe a distinct "tendency to solely characterize mothers as irresponsible in their conduct before and during pregnancy and therefore blameworthy for the poor health of their offspring (as children and adults)." Precisely an overemphasis on individual responsibility in this context may unfairly target mothers as "primarily responsible for the health of their children" (ibid.).

Mothers are hardly the only possible source of their offspring's poor health. To be sure, the question of responsibility arises with regard to pregnant women because the "placenta is able to register maternal stress and is involved in transmission of phenotypes to fetuses that remain into adulthood. Maternal dietary exposures have long been known to impact upon programming in the offspring" (Szyf 2015: 139). But the behavioral, toxic, and addictive experiences of both fathers and mothers ("including diet, stressful and adverse social experiences, and exposure to toxins and drugs of addiction" (ibid., 140)) can be transmitted, via parental gametes, to the next generation (and sometimes

[24] Or their lifestyle may be scrutinized precisely because of their condition, above all in the case of pregnant women.

beyond): "Exposure of either male or female gametes could change their epigenetic state and lead to phenotypic changes in the offspring that develop from these gametes" (ibid., 139). Indeed, stress hormones "may link behavioral experience and tissues outside the brain such as sperm" (ibid.), in which case sperm "could be epigenetically programmed even during adulthood" (ibid., 140).

Yet isolating male or female individuals as possibly responsible for negative epigenetic effects disregards the "complexity and multifactorial nature of disease etiology" (Ismaili M'Hadi et al. 2018: 59). Research does not suggest any "mono-causal pathway from a mother's dinner to a newborn's disease. Fetal development and epigenetic programming are both complex processes, steered by a myriad of endogenous and exogenous factors such as nutrition, hormones and environmental toxins that together affect the risk of disease development" (ibid.).

This multiplicity of causal factors suggests that responsibility may be more than individual.[25] This is the case where, under conditions of deep and pervasive social inequality, "even those individuals who are informed of the risk and have control over the causes may differ in relation to how informed they are and how much control they have" (Dupras and Ravitsky 2016: 539). To the extent that the "ability to take individual responsibility for health depends on contingent social factors," perhaps a "duty to help the marginalized communities should not depend on their conduct" (Ismaili M'Hadi et al. 2018: 60–61).

Political bioethics hardly discards the notion of individual responsibility. Nor does it suggest that individual responsibility never raises political issues. Individual behaviors such as "cigarette smoking, drinking alcohol, the use of drugs, having an unhealthy lifestyle and not seeking free and high-quality care in the period surrounding pregnancy" are "not morally arbitrary" (ibid.). Here the actors can be held responsible, morally if not legally. The same holds for an example from Rotterdam in which "women with a low socio-economic status" and "non-Western background face the highest risk for poor pregnancy outcomes" even as the "Netherlands offers free and high quality pregnancy-related care" (ibid. 60).

Analysis needs to distinguish between "factors that the individual herself definitely can affect," such as "diet, smoking or exercise habits," and factors such as "living conditions" or the "availability of health care," namely structure-related factors beyond the individual's control (Hedlund 2012: 174). It may often be impossible to neatly separate elements the individual can affect from those she cannot. Even diet and exercise might be beyond some individuals' control. Daily work schedules and transportation time (as well as various obligations) may reduce opportunities for exercise; low income and the absence of good supermarkets in some neighborhoods may reduce dietary

[25] The large number of possible causes for any given epigenome makes this task very challenging.

options. In the latter case, the question of responsibility becomes a question about issues of individuals suffering negative epigenetic effects that are in fact issues for the entire political community. Exposure of vulnerable individuals to hazardous environmental conditions, for example, raises issues of equitable access to health care and the question of whether "these individuals are entitled to health care" (Rothstein et al. 2017: 7). Health care is only one of the relevant issues. Hazardous environmental conditions are an issue not only for the community directly harmed. Hazardous waste dumps are typically located near poor communities, not wealthy ones. Both the poverty and the dump placement are beyond the control of vulnerable communities. Even if a community votes to accept a dump nearby (given financial incentives or job opportunities, for example), that choice may well be motivated by poverty within the community, effectively limiting the community's choices to bad ones. Responsibility for such cases would seem to be corporate because involving the entire society and not just the affected population.[26]

9.6 CONCLUSION: EPIGENETIC SCIENCE OFFERS AN ADDITIONAL MEANS OF IDENTIFYING SOURCES OF SOME SOCIAL INEQUALITIES

I have argued that, if some epigenetic effects on a fetus can adversely affect an individual's life-long health, then the mother's (and perhaps the father's and grandparents') life-experiences effectively disadvantage the individual. If those effects were beyond the control of the forebears at the time they occurred, then those effects may be the moral, if not legal, responsibility of the whole society or sectors within it, such as commercial enterprises and private industries. In a political community that practices some form of corporate responsibility, epigenetics may be deployed toward the social justice of identifying the source of negative epigenetic consequences and assigning communal responsibility.[27]

[26] Or consider "a society that currently does not provide health care access to all." Is an "adult with a respiratory problem caused by exposure to pollutants" somehow "more deserving of health care than a child with asthma who was not exposed to pollutants" (ibid.)? Assuming that asthma is at least in part genetic, one might ask, Who is more deserving, the individual who "lost" in the "genetic lottery" or the person victimized by his or her social environment? This approach unpersuasively formulates a significant issue of distributive justice by distinguishing too sharply between natural and social factors affecting individual health. Because justice entails treatment for both persons, the relevant question is, How can an epigenetics-based framework for distributive justice provide for persons with a moral if not legal claim to redress for adverse health effects caused by social factors – yet without neglecting persons who, through no fault of their own, bear genetic disadvantages? Voluntary acts of decency to care for the latter population also require a communal political commitment, even if one not based in legal obligation.

[27] My concern here is solely with the question of determining responsibility. Beyond the scope of this chapter is the question of possible legal or other practical consequences of corporate responsibility, such as modification of the offending environment toward making it safe for humans, as well as compensation of the epigenetically identified victims.

Still, the probabilistic science of epigenetic effects deployed in the service of deterministic norms (moral or legal) gives pause. Whereas epigenetic science posits probabilities that X may be a factor in Y, moral and legal thought generally regards someone as either responsible or not responsible – but not as *probabilistically* responsible.

In light of the sheer complexity of possible factors relevant in epigenetic health effects on humans, one might reject the deployment of epigenetic science. One then regards the complexity of epigenetic phenomena, and the probabilism of the science that studies those phenomena, as a black box that cannot warrant deterministic claims about responsibility. Science cannot do so because susceptibility to effects may be "local" and individualized. The same stress, for example, may affect different persons differently; some individuals may be resilient, others not. An approach that rejects the deployment of epigenetic science entails interventions toward better health outcomes in the future yet without seeking to determine the sources of past effects. On this approach, epigenetics cannot scientifically apportion responsibility for the source of past negative epigenetic effects. It can only work to prevent negative effects in the future, seeking justice not for past victims but for future persons.

By contrast, my approach embraces both a future-oriented and a retrospective response. It attempts to determine responsibility for adverse epigenetic effects for which the victim is not herself responsible. To do so it must wrestle with the tension between the probabilism of epigenetics and the determinism of normative systems (including determinate legal standards, definitions, and understandings). Grappling with the interface of radically disparate kinds of analysis, each a unique enterprise unto itself, is a permanent feature of many decisional landscapes. Legal systems struggle to achieve determinacy. For example, judicial outcomes that rest on an odd-numbered majority of justices determining the authoritative interpretation of the laws is effective in generating an answer but is morally primitive because based on decisionism rather than, say, the best argument.

In social contexts such as possible epigenetic effects on human health, science may serve to determine how behavior should be regulated in relevant contexts of scientific disagreement. To be sure, epigenetic research is not itself a project of advancing social justice; no natural science is. But it provides data and models that can aid that project to the extent that relevant data and models help identify stable associations between social conditions and the health of relevant individuals and groups. Such associations support the notion that some social inequalities, including health disparities, are epigenetically influenced. Epigenetic research "describes how social and environmental cues affect the way genes are expressed and thereby how susceptibility for disease is to a certain extent 'programmed under one's skin'" (Ismaili M'Hadi et al. 2018: 59). For example, research along the lines of the Developmental Origins of Health and Disease model "describes how the environmental factors before conception up to the first two years after birth affects fetal development and consequently both child and adult health" (ibid.).

Further, epigenetic research may sometimes be able to provide empirical information helpful in the assignation of corporate moral or legal responsibility. Assignation is a matter of identifying and clarifying the "different ways in which environments, broadly construed, directly interact with human biology, both within and across generations," thus contributing to the "development of biological 'signatures' that may be mapped to the embedding of social injustices in individuals" (Huang and King 2018: 77).

But responsibility for adverse epigenetic effects cannot be established solely by identifying a particular health-related inequality as avoidable. A theory of corporate responsibility is also needed. It can draw on epigenetics in several ways. First, epigenetics is a mechanism for dynamic responses to solicitations from an ever-changing environment.[28] Some of those environments are human-made. The quality of being a human artifact poses issues of human responsibility. Second, "epigenetic mechanisms and variants are determined partly by living conditions and lifestyle" (Dupras and Ravitsky 2016: 535). These factors also raise concerns about responsibility. Third, the epigenome is plastic: while some variants "are very stable over time," others can be "transmitted to daughter cells through mitosis or even to future generations through meiosis and embryogenesis" (ibid., 537). The phenomenon of transgenerational transmission also generates questions about collective responsibility.

To be sure, the project of motivating public policy to address epigenetically relevant past injustices, and to work toward preventing future ones, requires a general communal acceptance of possible collective responsibility in cases where the epigenetic transmission of some disadvantages across generations can be demonstrated scientifically. Collective responsibility would need to be understood in a way that could garner popular support. While acceptance of that particular understanding by a majority of a political community's members, or even by a large minority, would be sufficient to address relevant injustices, it may often be difficult to achieve. Racism in the United States, for example, is an important factor in the disturbing population-level health outcomes for African Americans. Yet racists will never accept collective responsibility for racism. The significant political challenges of achieving communal acceptance of collective responsibility for adverse epigenetic effects once again highlight the tension between the porous categories of nature and culture. As the relevant research has moved from a largely cultural focus to one more biologically informed, epigenetics can qualify but not replace culture in identifying plausible causal explanations.

This chapter argued that, if some epigenetic effects on a fetus can adversely affect an individual's life-long health, then the mother's life-experiences

[28] See Jablonka and Lamb (1995).

effectively disadvantage the individual. If those effects were beyond the control of the ancestors at the time they occurred, then they may be the moral if not legal responsibility of the community or of sectors within it. Epigenetics may be deployed toward the social justice of identifying the source of negative epigenetic consequences and of assigning communal responsibility. Because adverse epigenetic effects are found in all human communities, deploying science toward social justice offers itself as a method with potentially global purchase. The following chapter turns to the global phenomenon of the Anthropocene, the ill-defined geological epoch in which the planet Earth has come to bear a human imprint that will mark it for millennia to come, if not longer. Human genetic engineering is an Anthropocenic technology in the sense of humankind crafting itself by gradually transforming its own evolutionary path in line with human will and preference. The chapter argues that, even though a phenomenon of the Anthropocene, human genetic editing need not contribute to its depredations if editing can be regulated in thoughtful and effective ways.

10

Genetic Engineering as a Technology of the Anthropocene

The term *Anthropocene* stands for a theory that humankind has entered its own epoch, the geological Age of Humankind.[1] As of this epoch, the planet bears – and will bear for millennia and perhaps even millions of years to come – a tectonic *human* impact on its ecosystems and geology, from the lithosphere to the ecosphere. The theory frames environmental nature as vulnerable, capable of violation, and under siege. It limns humankind in terms of a will to control everything, itself included, thereby fueling technological exuberance, economic rapacity, and a mindless assault on the planetary environment – including, in the form of human genetic engineering, our own species.

In the form of artificial selection, genetic engineering by humans is as old as horticulture and animal husbandry. The domestication of plants and animals between the Tigris and Euphrates rivers in Mesopotamia about 8000 BCE started humankind on the long path from biological agents to geological actors. While nonbiological technologies of human enhancement – including organized education, the printing press, even reading glasses – have contributed more to human welfare than have biological technologies, today's genetic engineering at the molecular level is vastly more powerful, precise, and rapid than artificial selection and, in some ways, many nonbiological technologies

A theory of an Anthropocene asserts that humankind crossed a threshold sometime in the past. Proponents disagree as to when. The Holocene began approximately 11,700 years ago and thus is roughly parallel with the inception of the human domestication of plants and animals, sedentary living, the rise of settled communities, and eventually the development of civilizations and human writing systems. The Anthropocene might be dated as more or less

[1] To date, neither the International Union of Geological Sciences nor the International Commission on Stratigraphy has granted this boundary-crossing marker its respective imprimatur.

simultaneous with the Holocene. Alternatively, it might be dated from around 400 years ago.[2] Regardless, the force of the Anthropocene and its abiding effects can be analyzed without agreement on its dating.

Human genetic engineering is an anthropocenic technology insofar as it expresses modern Western civilization's legacy of meliorist cultural commitments to improving, if not perfecting, the human individual (Keenan 1999; Comfort 2012). Human genetic manipulation intervenes in the genome toward increasing degrees of technological freedom. It manifests a sort of perfectionism: "improving" the future evolution of the human species by purposefully guiding it through germline manipulations (whereby in any given instance, *improving* can only be defined in terms of particular cultural commitments). Biotechnical transformation is limited socially only by contingent and changing human values and human preference. As an anthropocenic technology, genetic editing is yet another form of human self-empowerment. Like anthropocenic technologies in general, it would "liberate" recipients from the natural environment of the evolved body, and do so to ever greater extents. *Anthropocenic* then means: humankind crafting *itself* as a species by gradually transforming its own evolutionary path in line with human imagination and choice.

To be sure, some forms of meliorism cast dark moral shadows, including religious, political, and other movements that repressed the populations each claimed to perfect. Prominent, technologically driven public-health examples include eugenic movements in the early part of the twentieth century that sought social "progress" through a gene pool itself "improved" through controlled reproduction, followed by a eugenics program that would preserve the genome's "jewels" (Sikela 2006) by cleansing the gene pool of "noxious" elements (Buchanan et al. 2000).

Here the term *anthropocenic* means: genetic manipulation in a form that debases core features of human identity by transgressing the autonomy of individuals and by violating the "integrity" of an evolved species. Intervention then appears as a self-destructive "dialectic of Enlightenment" in which humankind, by instrumentalizing human and nonhuman nature alike, ultimately, inadvertently, enslaves itself (Gregg 2012b; Horkheimer and Adorno 1981).[3] A theory of an Anthropocene so understood identifies humankind as a collective agent that has become a geological, morphological, telluric force.

[2] As I suggest in the Introduction.

[3] According to Zinn's (2016: 393) counterargument that the future will require more not less intervention, "when in social debates a merely protective approach to nature as *at-risk* gives way to the need to make high risk decisions under the condition of uncertainty without the possibility of externalising possible harm or responsibility, humanity enters a mode of societal risk-taking or the age of a *risk-taking society*," that is, an age of environmental risk-taking. Beyond a risk-based approach, Monast (2018: 2419–2420) urges natural resource management for biotechnology governance to approach "gene editing and its implications through the lens of public and private resources for which there are conflicting perspectives regarding appropriate uses and

On this account, we humans are not so much the makers of our geological fate as prisoners of the unintended consequences of our technological hubris. We are prisoners when we become geological agents who change the chemistry of the atmosphere, who cause "sea levels to rise, ice to melt, and climate to change" (Oreskes 2007: 93), with planetary consequences potentially "for many millennia to come" (Crutzen 2002: 23). We are prisoners if "In a few generations mankind is exhausting the fossil fuels that were generated over several hundred million years"; when we have transformed "30–50% of the land surface"; when "more nitrogen is now fixed synthetically and applied as fertilizers in agriculture than [is] fixed naturally in all terrestrial ecosystems"; when we pump "nitric oxide from fossil fuel and biomass combustion" into the atmosphere beyond natural levels; when we use "more than half of all accessible fresh water"; when we increase the "species extinction rate by thousand to ten thousand fold in the tropical rain forests" (Crutzen and Stoermer 2000: 17). *Anthropocenic* then marks planetary "degradation," including the "degradation" of the human species through its genetic manipulation.

I contend that, as a technology, human genetic engineering is a phenomenon of the Anthropocene but that, through thoughtful regulation, it need not contribute to the depredations of the Anthropocene. In four steps I argue that (§10.1) human genetic engineering may be regarded as a technology of the Anthropocene yet (§10.2) the promise of human genetic engineering is to transform human genetics as something passively inherited into something responsive to the project for reducing human misery of various kinds. (§10.3) I show that the technology of human genetic engineering displays a distinctly political dimension and (§10.4) propose elements of a socially responsible form of this technology. I conclude that biotechnology is not a necessary evil that entails a fundamental opposition between technology and humanity, and that socially responsible human genetic editing need not be planetarily harmful.

10.1 HUMAN GENETIC ENGINEERING AS AN ANTHROPOCENIC TECHNOLOGY

The Anthropocene in general manifests humankind's astounding capacity to affect change in the natural environment (including, as part of that environment, human biology). Despite their profound differences from one another, the Anthropocene and genetic engineering overlap along multiple dimensions. Consider two: (a) both are ambivalent because the promise of human

preservation. Although existing laws do not contemplate the ability to reorder ecosystems via gene editing, there is an established regulatory system designed to address risks of extinction, accommodate competing ideologies regarding resource use, and incorporate interests of future generations when considering irreversible decisions regarding natural resources – all issues that are implicated by gene editing."

intervention in the natural environment often generates negative consequences and (b) both involve what I call *identity work*.

(a) Genetic engineering promises to reduce some of the fragility of human bodies and psyches and their vulnerability to suffering, for example by obviating some genetic diseases, abnormalities, and disabilities. Beyond "normal" physical or cognitive functioning, it also promises the enhancement of some species-typical capacities, to extend the range of some traits beyond what humans commonly experience.

Ambiguity arises in the normative status of human genetic engineering's possible goals. Less problematic from a normative standpoint are engineering goals to "restore or ensure normal physical or cognitive function, such as walking or remembering, as exemplified respectively by knee implants and cholinesterase inhibitors in Alzheimer's disease" (Bavelier et al. 2019: 204). The gene-editing tool CRISPR-Cas9, for example, can "systematically analyze gene functions in mammalian cells, study genomic rearrangements and the progression of cancers or other diseases, and potentially correct genetic mutations responsible for inherited disorders" (Doudna and Charpentier 2014: 1077).

From a normative standpoint, other goals are problematic (or more problematic). Extending capacities beyond ranges typical within human experience generate anthropocenic anxieties, for example where such extensions modify physical, cognitive, or affective traits associated with some of humankind's various understandings of what it is to be human, biologically but also socially and morally. Consider the extraordinary efforts of scientists in China to identify the thousands of genetic variants associated with human intelligence in the general population as well as in the brightest minds (Yong 2013). Should accurate predictions of intelligence from a DNA sample ever become possible, not only scientists will be interested both in preventing intellectual disability and in fostering increased cognitive ability among persons of general ability. The significant social repercussions of such manipulation would challenge some of the ways humans have understood their species for thousands of years.[4]

The anthropocenic orientation to increase human strengths and capacities contrasts with traditional cultural convictions that fragility and vulnerability allow humans to develop moral nobility to the extent that individuals confront such limitations in ways that render them more humble and modest, more thoughtful and altruistic, than they might otherwise be (Fitzgerald 2008). On a traditional view, coping with anguish by consolation through

[4] Chapters 5, 6, and 7 examine from multiple perspectives the challenges of manipulating human intelligence: a possible threshold level of intelligence for political participation in a democratic community; the political challenge that artificial intelligence may pose to human intelligence; and the political ambiguity of the idea of genetically informed personalized education toward better realizing a pupil's natural endowments.

psychopharmaceuticals would morally diminish the patient (Elliot 1998). An analogous approach to genetic engineering would reject, as morally ignoble, manipulation to diminish the body's fragility and vulnerability.[5]

A different ambiguity emerges from social and cultural interconnections that limit individual autonomy as part of communal organization (Liao 2006). Athletics is a group activity organized around various understandings of how to evaluate performance. Biomedical or pharmaceutical enhancements that would boost performance beyond levels typical within human experience[6] might well undermine the principles of athletic competition, conventionally understood. Yet self-limitation in the face of technological capacity runs counter to an anthropocenic orientation.

Perhaps most controversial of all – because so deeply contested as a matter of species identity – would be forms of moral bioenhancement, delivered through pharmaceuticals, implanted devices, or even genetic manipulation.[7]

(b) A theory of an Anthropocene engages in identity work. In evaluative, normative terms, it constructs the identity of the natural environment, the identity of humans in that environment, as well as the identity of phenomena along the continuum between nature human and nonhuman: humans as destructive agents, the natural environment (including the human body) as victim.

A theory of an Anthropocene also reworks the respective identities of natural history and human history by erasing distinctions between them: geological and human chronologies now flow one into the other. The imprint of human activity written indelibly into the natural environment elides the line, real or

[5] To the same end, Levy (2012: 589) offers a practical rather than moral argument: that "shaping our environment to avoid triggering these limitations or to constrain the harms they cause is likely to be more effective than genetic or pharmaceutical modifications of our capacities because our limitations are often the flip side of beneficial dispositions and because available enhancements seem to impose significant costs."

[6] See, e.g., Tolleneer et al. (2013).

[7] This hyper-individualistic notion of morality – mirroring the predominantly individual-based focus of possible interventions most at issue in bioethical debates – is challenged by a focus more responsive to the *relational* nature of individuals and to the *social* determinants that affect well-being. See Cabrera (2017), who argues from the standpoint of population health and within the analytic framework of the Social Determinants of Health. One unnerving upshot of that argument appears in Vincent's (2011) analysis of possible cognitive enhancement through drugs, an analysis with implications for genetic enhancement. For example, Are parents morally obligated to avoid creating offspring with avoidable gene-based diseases? For reasons of heightened public safety and welfare, might particular persons, such as surgeons working long shifts in hospital or air traffic controllers, bear some kind of responsibility to boost their performance with Modafinil or Ritalin? Or once enhanced, might they legally or morally take on greater responsibilities because of those heightened capacities?

constructed, between human and nonhuman nature.[8] The genetic manipulation of future bodies also complicates the distinction between nature and culture. It diminishes the distinction between the bodies we have (*have* in a biological sense, for example with respect to disease and pathology, health and disability) and the bodies that we are (*are* in a cultural sense of how, as members of communities, we regard our bodies and the bodies of others) (Plessner 1981).

Human identity is a hybrid phenomenon: in part a matter of evolved biology, in part a matter of cultural construction. Humans are born with the former and then acquire the latter through socialization and other accretions of the individual's biography in social and cultural communities.

Another identity: the body as the locus of information. The body orients the individual's location in space and time, including history. It is the physical location of a person's identity over time and through space, sustained in part through that location: Where am I? Where is North or South relative to where I stand? What is above or below me, within or outside of me? From a physical standpoint, one's identity is sustained by constantly distinguishing between self and the external world: Where do I end, where does my environment begin? A somatic foundation for one's psychological identity makes self-identity over time possible. Identity is preserved through spatial extension, for example in answer to the question, How do I negotiate my way through the world of objects and subjects?

One's sense of self, as a distinct individual cohering through time and across experiences, with a history that endures across the vicissitudes of one's biography, is not only a physical and psychological experience but a moral one as well. Only thus can one view oneself as having preferences and plans. Only thus can one view oneself, as well as other selves, as creatures to whom actions can be ascribed, and as creatures who can take responsibility for those actions. From a moral and legal standpoint, the body and mind mark the point at which an actor's actions may be distinguished from those of other actors. The body is a vantage point: it distinguishes how we as individuals behave from what is done to us by other persons.

Genetic engineering at embryonic or fetal stages engages in identity-work also. Genetic engineering may identify a threshold between human persons and pre-personal life when it addresses such questions as, Can an embryo be a member of cultural, political, and moral community? If so, then in what sense

[8] I do not invoke a traditional notion of human nature here, whether metaphysical, theological, or otherwise. Chapters 3 and 4 develop a non-essentialist notion of human nature for deployment in a liberal democratic political community deciding how best to evaluate ethically, and regulate legally, rapid biotechnological developments. Characteristic of all communities, there is no consensus among members on what a human nature might be or even if it exists (and no unitary ethical understanding of the entire species). Liberal democratic societies face a political challenge that can only be met contingently: constructing the particular social, moral, and legal status of humans within political community.

of membership? Would a just political community allow communal members to be genetically manipulable? Such questions cannot be answered by referring to the human embryo as such. The embryo does not embody natural and cultural identity unless the collective observer (a political or cultural community) projects this identity onto it. Hence genetic engineering engages the recipient in ways both natural and cultural. It does not necessarily imply that human individuals have some kind of "natural self" in need of protection.[9] It does not necessarily entail that manipulation destroys the individual's eventual capacity to be herself.

10.2 A TECHNOLOGY THAT CAN RESIST ANTHROPOCENIC CONSEQUENCES

A theory of the Anthropocene regards anthropocenic effects as the unintended, unwanted consequence of technological development and of the cultural orientations that foster them. Humankind today confronts the consequences of its actions in the past and certainly in the present as well. For people living today, those actions confront us almost as if they were parameters of the natural universe: the only context in which humans can act. Anthropocenic technologies entwine "power relations between geophysical actors, both human and nonhuman" (Davies 2016: 62), leading to an ever-more complex system of "large-scale energy and resource extraction systems, power generation and transmission systems, communication, transportation, financial and other networks, governments and bureaucracies, cities, factories, farms and myriad other 'built' systems" (Haff 2014: 127) that, to an extent, escapes human control in multiple ways. A person can interact directly "only with systems his own size"; "most humans cannot significantly influence the behavior of large technological systems" in part because a "human cannot control a technological system that expresses a larger number of behaviors than he himself" (Haff 2014: 126).[10]

Even as an anthropocentric technology, human genetic engineering can chart a different trajectory. It need not be an unintended, unwanted, indeed usually uncontrolled consequence of earlier behavior. Instead it could be a capacity to

[9] There can be no "natural self" in need of protection from nature if "'natural' things can be either safe or intrinsically dangerous" and "genetic variants that exist in nature may either support health or cause disease, and the human population contains multiple variants of most genes. Thus, there is no single 'normal' human genome sequence; rather, there are multiple variant human genomic sequences, all of which occur in the worldwide human gene pool and, in that sense, are 'natural,' and all of which can be either advantageous or disadvantageous" (National Academies of Sciences, Engineering, and Medicine (2017: 138–139)).

[10] Trischler and Will (2017: 7) speculate that anthropocenic phenomena, including environmental degradation, population growth, loss of biodiversity, and global warming, "may result in the Technosphere failing to carry out things on which both civilization and the Technosphere themselves depend."

alter human genetic makeup as something otherwise simply given in nature, in part inherited from forbearers, into something responsive to the project of reducing human misery, for example by avoiding some genetic conditions, such as diseases, while perhaps fostering others, such as a cognitive capacity adequate for the citizen, otherwise cognitively disabled, to participate robustly in her political community. By freeing individuals to some degree from the unwanted natural "fate" of evolutionary contingencies such as genetic disorders, genetic editing may contribute to human flourishing, perhaps even to social justice, and do so in ways environmentally thoughtful, and by contrast to so much of anthropocenic history.

This distinction, drawn another way: whereas the Anthropocene was never planned, of course,[11] and people across the globe are working to prevent even more damage by anthropocenic technologies, genetic engineering at the molecular level first became possible only about sixty years ago[12] and has always been subject to a great deal of critical reflection and various forms of monitoring and legal regulation. Critical reflection seeks to prevent damaging deployments from occurring in the first place – or at least to prevent the recurrence of isolated cases of what the scientific community and others consider abuse.[13]

Arnold Gehlen (1957: 8) depicts humankind as "Poorly endowed in his senses, lacking natural defenses, naked, underdeveloped in his entire constitution, insecure in his instincts" and depending "existentially on his own actions."[14] The human animal's biological capacities are so weak in relation to its natural environments that its very survival requires it to augment or extend its evolved capacities with social and cultural institutions as well as with technologies of its own devising. Doing so has in some cases led to the Anthropocene. But human survival does not require anthropocenic behavior (indeed, such behavior threatens human survival). Human genetic manipulation may reduce some forms of human suffering just as it makes possible a greater satisfaction of needs of more people than otherwise possible. It may improve the quality of life and flourishing of individuals and the well-being of entire communities.

[11] As Chakrabarty (2009: 217) notes, there is nothing "inherent to the human species that has pushed us finally into the Anthropocene. We have stumbled into it. The way to it was no doubt through industrial civilization."

[12] Among other examples: in 1972 Paul Berg made the first recombinant DNA molecule; in 1973, Herbert Boyer and Stanley Cohen generated the first genetically modified organism, a bacterium; in 1974, Rudolf Jaenisch inserted foreign DNA into a mouse; and Genentech, the first commercial enterprise to produce human proteins, was founded in 1976.

[13] Perhaps the most prominent example to date: https://time.com/collection/100-most-influential-people-2019/5567707/he-jiankui/.

[14] "Sinnesarm, waffenlos, nackt, in seinem gesamten Habitus embryonisch, in seinen Instinkten verunsichert ist er das existentiell auf die Handlung angewiesene Wesen." Translation by the author.

In other words, human genetic engineering is an anthropocenic technology that need not contribute to the depredations of the Anthropocene. Scientists have identified over 6,000 genetic disorders. Approximately 65 percent of the world's population suffers from the health effects of congenital genetic mutations. One in fifty individuals is affected by a single-gene disorder; one in 263, by a chromosomal disorder (Kumar et al. 2001). Freeing humans from genetic disorders by deploying science and technology to reduce human misery is not anthropocenic behavior.

10.3 POLITICAL DIMENSIONS OF GENETIC ENGINEERING TECHNOLOGY

The technology of human genetic engineering has a distinctly political dimension. (a) That dimension follows from the difference between technical and political cognitive styles: a technical style is guided by instrumental imperatives, seeking the optimal deployment of practical means to achieve preset goals that it does not place into question. By contrast, a political style (in the form of linguistic, symbolically mediated interaction) can be guided by valid social norms. This difference between the two cognitive styles informs the peculiarly political dangers of the anthropocenic technology of human genetic engineering.

(a) I first examine how the difference between a technical cognitive style and a political cognitive style informs the peculiarly political dangers of the anthropocenic technology of human genetic engineering. (b) Then I show how such dangers may be avoided if a community practices socially responsible genetic technology.

(a) The cognitive style that informs human genetic engineering as an anthropocenic technology includes elements of technical utility. It enhances efficiency and provides prognostic knowledge of human biology and augments the capacity to control human biology. Knowledge and control increase independence from the constraints of nature where they frustrate the realization of human aspiration.

By contrast, thoughtful political participation in a liberal democratic context can be self-reflexive. When oriented on values, it can place any goal into question at any time. Political thinking so understood has a value-oriented capacity. It is capable of being principled. It can facilitate processes by which a community seeks to articulate its self-understanding, determine its values, formulate its goals. It can facilitate interaction toward achieving understanding, including communication that can diagnose and reject interpersonal relations of domination and then work to replace them with non-repressive relations. It can identify and resist the instrumentalization of human beings by analyzing processes by which social relations become autonomous of the persons they affect. It can identify and resist the unrestricted enlargement of systems of instrumental action, systems not only of technology but also of economics and politics.

Interaction oriented toward achieving understanding makes possible the public use of reason in the political sphere where normative questions can be asked and debated and answers generated. Political questions are best answered politically. In the context of human genetic engineering, questions such as, How do we wish to organize our community, by what standards of justice? or, What kind of human nature should we want?,[15] become questions for political bioethics.

Interaction of this sort is only possible if it can prevent technological development from becoming anthropocenic in the sense of independent, self-regulating processes. Interaction is possible only if it can subject technological development, a form of instrumental action, to normative and political reflection and then to rational control. But it becomes less and less possible where politics itself is increasingly reduced to a form of social engineering, dominated by small, elite, administrative and executive cultures of experts, oriented on solving technical problems rather than identifying and solving normative problems, in this way discouraging if not eliminating public discourse and political debate. In that case, a technical cognitive style displaces the cognitive style required by democratic politics: a politics that aspires to reflection, revision, rational guidance, and broad public participation.

(b) The cognitive style of liberal democratic politics needs to be on guard against forms of reification through a technical cognitive style that increasingly colonizes normative analysis of biotechnology. By *reification* I refer to social relations that appear to exist independently of social actions performed by subjects but that are in fact social constructs, embedded in history, contingent, and capable of being changed by human imagination of alternatives to the status quo. The term *reification* refers to the misrecognition of the moral status of human individuals. Reification disempowers the political goals of individual autonomy and collective justice because it treats persons as things.

Where social actors lose control to social relations that have made themselves independent, a technical cognitive style increasingly displaces a political cognitive style.[16] Human genetic engineering has the potential to reify its

[15] See Chapters 3 and 4 on human nature.

[16] Reification as the displacement of a political cognitive style with a technological one becomes possible where technological developments escape adequate political analysis and control. A century ago, Max Weber (1921/22) diagnosed that displacement as leading to twin losses for humankind: a loss of freedom and a loss of meaning. Meaning is lost through the splintering of spheres of value (law, morality, science, economy) that were once unified. Freedom is lost when the rational approach to modern life promoted by the European Enlightenment becomes

recipients if physicians, biotechnologists, and parents[17] deploy it without attention to the daunting ethical and political questions it poses (such as those explored throughout this book). Genetic engineering has the potential to reify the self-understanding of a liberal democratic political community by deploying a purely instrumental cognitive style of biotechnology unfiltered by moral and political critique and evaluation.

A liberal democratic community is not possible if it is organized in terms of a cognitive style independent of and indifferent to its members' normative convictions and claims.[18] A technological orientation on technical mastery endangers the imperatives of a just organization of political community wherever it escapes the control of those members of the community affected by it. In such cases, citizens face a loss of freedom in their public and private lives. They face a loss of freedom in the spheres where society reproduces itself in terms not of technology but of intersubjective understanding.[19] The technological orientation toward technical mastery is a purely instrumental orientation. Because it is not political, it cannot be democratically oriented in particular. By itself, technocratic administration precludes democratic self-determination. Effective opposition to technocratic administration requires a democratic, societal approach; for structural reasons, individual initiatives cannot effectively oppose the social pathology constituted by reification. Effective opposition to technocratic administration also requires a cultural commitment not to regard genetic engineering recipients as things or to treat them as things. The political imperatives of collective welfare and democracy help prevent the social pathologies generated when political community fails to exercise adequate control over technological development. Collective welfare and democracy can insure that biotechnologies such as human genetic engineering do not become part of the depredations of the Anthropocene.

10.4 ELEMENTS OF SOCIALLY RESPONSIBLE GENETIC TECHNOLOGY

The peculiarly political dangers of an anthropocenic trajectory can be confronted with elements of socially responsible genetic technology. Those

thoroughly colonized by the calculating attitude of efficient goal-maximization that eschews any normative evaluations of given goals.

17 For an argument that the state should play a greater role than parents in determining when and how to enhance the physical and cognitive capacities of young children, see Fowler (2015).

18 Marx's (1968: 86) definition of commodity fetishism – "das bestimmte gesellschaftliche Verhältnis der Menschen selbst, welches hier für sie die phantasmagorische Form eines Verhältnisses von Dingen annimmt" – provides one model of social organization independent of, and indifferent to, the concerns, problems, and hopes of its human inhabitants.

19 See Chapter 6 on the dangers that artificial intelligence poses in the political sphere to intersubjective understanding in the form of members of the community each taking responsibility for her actions and being able to assume that other members do the same.

elements require (a) normative standards to guide evaluation of the moral acceptability of particular deployments as well as (b) an understanding of what constitutes a politically desirable understanding and deployment of technology.

(a) The technological orientation on technical mastery overlaps in part with the human potential for self-determination – but only in part. The overlap makes forms of compromise possible between what Jürgen Habermas (1981) calls the general structures of communicative action, on the one hand, and the systemic constraints of material reproduction, on the other. Such constraints are otherwise unavailable for identification, examination, and critique within the social sphere of communicative action. Democratic community is part of that sphere, where individuals ideally are guided by norms and reasons they give to themselves collectively, in this way constituting themselves as morally equal and ethically free.

The rational organization of a just political community may draw on aspects of technological orientation even as it is internally oriented on justice, legitimacy, and inclusion.[20] It might, say, draw on efficient public health provision. So while technology may unavoidably carry its creators' values in its design, the moral and political challenge of anthropocenic technology of genetic manipulation is not technology as such. The question of avoiding anthropocenic deployments concerns how the technology is deployed. A just political community would regulate anthropocenic technology to prohibit inhuman, unjust, or enslaving deployments.

Consider two normative standards to guide regulation in an effort to prevent instrumentalizing forms of human genetic engineering.[21]

First, acceptable human genetic engineering will not preclude individual autonomy. It will not damage the individual's relationship to herself, nor will it damage her life in her community, nor will it damage her community's relationship to external nature.[22] Injury occurs where the means to intervene in the natural environment, and in human bodies and minds, are transformed into the goals themselves. Technological means become ends when humans are treated as if they were things. Such treatment is always a danger in human

[20] Developments in science and technology do not necessarily facilitate efforts to create communities more rational and just. Sometimes they may facilitate just the opposite.

[21] Such a community faces the difficult task of coping successfully with such intractable questions as, How should such a community respond when few if any of those norms are widely embraced by members of any one community, let alone across multiple communities? In short, what can a just political community do in the absence of universal norms binding on all communities? On what normative basis would a just political community distinguish between the morally acceptable deployment of anthropocenic technology and its morally unacceptable deployment? For my proposal for dealing in politics with these and other indeterminate norms, see Gregg (2003a).

[22] Whereby the diagnosis of pathological relationships to self, to others, and to the natural environment requires the availability of a model of undistorted, not reified relationships.

genetic engineering, first of all because of the asymmetric relationship in power and decisional authority between manipulator and manipulated. This is a challenge also in the practice of medicine and medical research, both of which assume an objectivating attitude toward the human subject. But medicine and research can take that attitude without necessarily constricting the ways in which the patient might understand herself as a responsibly acting person, so that she does not lose her freedom of self-determination.[23]

Second, human genetic engineering can contribute to greater social equality by rendering manipulable the physical basis of human biological life. It can do so in cases where that basis impedes the individual's capacity to act and where it diminishes her life chances. Genetic engineering might free the political and cultural project of advancing social equality by targeting "harmful" or "below average"[24] traits or physical, cognitive, or psychological disabilities that generate social handicaps.[25] It might contribute to greater social equality by rendering manipulable the physical and mental basis of human biological life where that basis affects the individual's capacity to perform important life activities – where that basis is diseased or disabled or otherwise burdens its bearer and diminishes her life chances. Genetic engineering can sometimes help reverse some degree of human "dependence" on nature where *dependence* refers to individuals carrying traits from which they seek release: for example, blindness, deafness, or autism at birth, Alzheimer's and Parkinson's later in life.

(b) This ethical self-understanding of the community would be guided by three principles: participation of all stakeholders, pursuit of social cohesion and equity, and promotion of individual autonomy.

First, to the extent possible at any given time, all stakeholders should be able to participate, to some extent however limited, in the social evaluation of technologies. To render participation as meaningful and useful as possible, organizers need to make comprehensive information available (noting differences and disagreements among experts) to provide a shared general understanding and orientation for the full range of stakeholders, from members of the public to experts, policymakers, and developers of biotechnology.

Second, the deployment of human genetic engineering would enhance the quality of life and well-being for individuals as well as for communities if, within political community, it facilitated forms of social equity and social

[23] Beyond the scope of this chapter: how objectification and instrumentalization may extend to the cultural construction of the moral status of pre-personal or ante-natal life.

[24] I bracket for the moment the fact that conceptions of "harmful" and "average" are tied to specific cultural preferences. This fact introduces an additional layer of difficulty to analysis.

[25] See Chapter 5 on the idea of a minimum genetic capacity for realizing equal citizenship among members of a political community, as well as Chapter 7 on deploying the pupil's genetic information toward a curricular design that is better than conventional design because now personalized in genetically informed ways.

cohesion. While few technologies focus on enhancing social skills, we have long known of the many ways in which humans need satisfying social interactions for good physical and emotional health. Recent research that targets stimulations of neural circuits in rodents suggests a causal relationship between the activity of circuits and social dominance behavior, suggesting a "possible neurobiological foundation for dominance-associated personality traits, such as perseverance or competitive drive" (Zhou et al. 2017: 168). If manipulating social behavior via neural circuits is possible in some animals, it might one day be possible in humans. But if so, it represents a deeply unsettling possibility. Further, the human capacity to experience the anguish of loneliness, although sometimes devasting to the individual's well-being, may also motivate her to seek social attachments and thus act as one generator among others of social cohesion within political community. One motivation for fostering equity in society is a concern for social cohesion.

Human genetic engineering should not be deployed in ways that would rob the recipient of the autonomy so central to her sense of dignity and worth. To be free to act according to one's own life-plan does not mean disregarding others and their respective life-plans. It means the possibility of what could lead toward a community of free and equal members. While the person might think certain actions will contribute to her well-being, such actions, when placed in social context, may in fact be socially detrimental. Using drugs to enhance academic or athletic performance are quotidian examples; certain forms of genetic engineering may be emerging examples. The person's mistake in this context highlights the fact that individual autonomy is not anarchy but freedom bound by community. Some cases will be difficult to decide: mood enhancement achieved through antidepressants benefits the patient along one dimension while possibly threatening her authenticity along another dimension (see Elliott 2004). Other cases may challenge basic assumptions about anthropocenic technologies: a person might enjoy a measure of autonomy only when a technology has altered her.

The example of Deep Brain Stimulation is instructive. It is a rudimentary brain–computer interface first developed to reduce motor rigidity in Parkinson's patients. Its manipulation of various neural processes "might plausibly enhance the patient's ability to make autonomous decisions with regards to her eating behavior," namely Anorexia Nervosa (Maslen et al. 2015: 228). The "use of this technology to alter first-order motivating desires or the patient's emotional traits may confer significant harms as well as potential benefits" (ibid.). As long as the individual can make free and informed decisions about life-altering technological manipulation of her body or mind, she may enhance her autonomy through such intervention. She can still be autonomous even as she depends on that technology to achieve an active condition or to avoid a debilitating one.

10.5 CONCLUSION: SOCIALLY RESPONSIBLE HUMAN GENETIC EDITING NEED NOT BE PLANETARILY HARMFUL

While human genetic engineering is a phenomenon of the Anthropocene, it need not contribute to the depredations of the Anthropocene if its deployment is politically aware and socially responsible. Human genetic engineering need not entail a bioengineered relationship to self that is objectified and alienated. Making the genome available to human design and preference will not necessarily lead to atomization and commodifying standardization, for example where parents might "order" a "designer baby," rendering the individual somehow less an individual, somehow less a subject than a non-designed person who has never been the object of biotechnology.

Genetic engineers must not misconstrue the difference between humans as wielders of technology and humans as participants in the political self-determination of individuals and the community. They must also avoid treating the differences between the political and the technological spheres of life as a Manichean division between good and evil, for three reasons.

First, the political and the technological spheres of life cope well with the complexity of the interrelationship between genetic interventions and multiple environments: "beside the role genes play on biological evolution and development, genetic interventions can induce multiple effects (pleiotropy) and complex epigenetics interactions among genotype, phenotype and ecology of a certain environment" (Almeida and Diogo 2019: 187). They can do so rapidly. They can do so with an impact at significant scale "not only to the human body but also to human populations and their natural environment" (ibid.).

And just as the natural universe is complex, so, too, are the phenomena of socially constructed spheres of human life. Political bioethics rejects the misprision of technology as a "necessary evil" that entails a fundamental, inherent, and permanent opposition between technology and humanity (Luhmann 2012: 315).

Second, the political and the technological spheres of life interact with one another continuously. The conduct of politics includes technological questions and needs to yield good technological answers (for example, possible solutions to the climate change catastrophe that marks the Anthropocene). From a standpoint of intergenerational justice, given the "population-genetic consequences of relaxed selection pressures in human populations caused by the increasing efficacy and availability of conventional medicine," germline intervention in the future "will be necessary merely to sustain the levels of genetic health that we presently enjoy for future generations" (Powell 2015: 669).

Third, genetic editing, because it "can overcome many of the natural impediments to human good," provides a solution "more efficient, reliable, versatile, and morally palatable than the lumbering juggernaut of Darwinian evolution" and, as such, offers a moral reason for communities to pursue it carefully and thoughtfully (Powell and Buchanan 2011: 6). Human genetic engineering is not a problem as such. Rather, it requires politically and morally appropriate forms for its control.

The first chapter of this book argues that liberal democratic societies can regulate human genetic engineering through a combination of expert bioethics committees and majoritarian proceduralism informed by deliberative democracy. This final chapter claims that, by such means, political community can counter the reifying tendencies of genetic manipulation.

This chapter concludes the third of the book's three sections. The Coda that follows identifies core elements of the political bioethics that has guided all of the book's chapters. It shows how bioethics as political theory applies an epistemic dualism to questions concerning the possible genetic engineering of our species. *Epistemic dualism* refers to the epistemological entwinement of natural science, concerned with physically measurable phenomena, with cultural understandings as shared, socially constructed interpretations of normative guidelines for behavior. The Coda analyzes the notion of epistemic dualism in political community as a collective and individual learning process. It aspires to potentially universally valid norms for regulating human genetic engineering, but only asymptotically, given the implausibility of global regulatory norms.

Coda

Bioethics as Political Theory

The preceding chapters work a hunch into an insight: political theory with bioethical ambition, bioethics as political theory, political bioethics. In application, the approach concluded that proceduralism can provide legitimate bioethical decisions (Chapter 1); that global regulatory norms are implausible (Chapter 2); that a political notion of human nature oriented on a political notion of human rights offers a normative standard of potentially wide embrace (Chapter 3); that the future person's decisional autonomy can function as a regulatory principle at the point of genetically manipulating the embryo (Chapter 4); that equal citizenship requiring a minimum genetic capacity may justify some forms of cognitive engineering (Chapter 5); that political community should never allow artificial intelligence to displace citizens' mutual taking of responsibility (Chapter 6); that deployment of a pupil's genetic information to inform personalized education is politically ambiguous (Chapter 7); that a human right to freedom from genetic disability would promote well-being as autonomy (Chapter 8); that epigenetic science offers an additional means of identifying sources of some social inequalities (Chapter 9); and that socially responsible human genetic editing need not be planetarily harmful (Chapter 10).

I close now with a distillation of the insight that guided ten diverse chapters, limning the contours of its deployment. Bioethics as political theory applies a kind of epistemic dualism to address questions concerning the possible genetic engineering of our species. (1) First I discuss epistemic dualism as such and then (2) in practical application in political community.

(1) Bioethics as political theory is guided by naturalism. Naturalism does not claim that all of reality is coextensive with nature as studied by the natural sciences. It does not suggest that everything can only be understood by natural scientific methods. Naturalism rejects scientism, which

reduces cultural and normative thinking to natural science. I develop a positive account of the term *naturalism* in the following paragraphs.

While culture is not biology, we may one day discover that the starting conditions for human socialization into cultural communities can be explained biologically. Perhaps the scientific understanding of human evolution will one day discover a continuity between the physical and the cultural descriptions of the world: between natural scientific understandings, on the one hand, and normative understandings, on the other.

Such questions about the emergence of sociocultural ways of life are relevant to bioethics as political theory. It operates with a working hypothesis of a naturalistic continuum between the evolution of the human species and the history of the sociocultural ways that inform human political life. It practices a "soft" form of naturalism. The adjective *soft* refers to the fact that, as long as humans have existed, the history of nature and human history have been mutually dependent. This dependence finds expression in the epistemic dualism on which bioethics as political theory is constructed. By *epistemic dualism* I refer to two interwoven understandings of the world, two interlaced approaches to the world. Natural science, concerned with physically measurable phenomena, explains nomologically. By contrast, cultural understanding dependent on members of a community coming to shared interpretations of normative guidelines for behavior (for example, norms that would guide the legal regulation of human genome editing) can only be explained nominalistically, as social constructions.

Epistemic dualism bears an abiding tension within itself: the objectifying attitude of a naturalist approach (to genetic phenomena) stands in a difficult, at times perplexing relationship with the need for ethical and political norms, for morality and legality (as a means to regulate genetic manipulation).

The task of bioethics as political theory is to create a plausible and practical relationship between science and morality. It does so by deploying a notion of moral integrity that combines analytic description (of genetic phenomena) with normative evaluation (toward regulation of engineering). That notion of moral integrity relates the cognitive bases of natural science with the prescriptive, critical knowledge contained in normative claims.

Bioethics as political theory also operates with a political understanding of human nature (the self-understanding of the human species in response to the question, To what kind of human nature should we aspire?) as well as with a political understanding of human dignity (the decisional autonomy of the individual).[1] These understandings are compatible with a "soft naturalism" even as bioethics as political theory offers a *normative* standard for regulating gene editing.

[1] Chapters 3 and 4 develop this argument.

In a plausible and practical relationship between science and morality, soft naturalism – if applied in popular deliberation combined with expert medical and bioethical opinion – could facilitate agreement on how the decisional autonomy of future persons might be configured at the point of genetic manipulation. It could do so without moralizing natural phenomena, for example by investing the human genome with a moral status as such. Nor does soft naturalism cognitively distance itself from the natural world in the manner of theology and metaphysics. For bioethics as political theory, human artifacts cannot be reduced to the natural world, but at the same time any plausible ethical construct will not contradict a naturalistic understanding of the universe. Bioethics as political theory seeks a fruitful if sometimes problematic "cohabitation" of normative thought (which cannot be natural scientific) and naturalism (which cannot be normative).

An approach can be both non-reductionist and "cooperative" across the nature–culture divide. How might that work? While the respective "languages" of science and culture cannot be translated one into the other, the language of normative understanding needs to be conversant with the language of natural science. Only in this way can it offer a *this-worldly* account of guiding norms. The alternative would be an account that draws on traditional, otherworldly accounts of theology and metaphysics.

But the secular nature of bioethics as political theory hardly means that it eschews all communication with other kinds of worldviews, including theology and metaphysics. The overriding task of bioethics as political theory is social integration in a just society. Such integration proceeds through shared norms. The broad sharing of norms is a challenge: all human communities are marked by significant difference among members with respect to normative conviction and judgment, and complex modern societies much more so than societies of the past. To achieve sharing among members of a political community requires an ongoing engagement with competing traditions, contrasting worldviews, and contending understandings. In some cases, that engagement is a matter of persuading someone to adopt a different perspective. In other cases, it is a matter of informing aspects of bioethics as political theory with aspects and aspirations of other normative worldviews. Informing is possible in a variety of ways, from philosophical translation to semantic osmosis.

In some cases, bioethics as political theory can even learn from the *disiecta membra* of the disintegrating systems of otherworldly thinking. It can do so wherever it is able to release the rational potential from distorted or repressed cultural artifacts, for example as they appear in some aspects of religion and metaphysics. It can do so wherever it can appropriate, in post-metaphysical terms (terms such as norms not oriented on the notion of a divine redemptive justice), the normative core of some religious and metaphysical traditions.

Today difficult political questions confront traditions, cultures, and norms that become fragile with the rapid development of new biotechnologies. I have argued that, in the face of modern science and liberal democracy, traditional metaphysics and theology struggle with difficulties that can no longer be resolved internally. In particular, religious traditions oriented on the authority of divine redemptive justice can hardly respond within a modern secular society tasked with defining terms such as *human nature* and *human dignity*. In the genetic manipulation of our species, these terms offer themselves as core normative standards to guide possible regulation.

From the standpoint of a bioethics as political theory, a modern secular society needs to develop widely shared understandings of *human nature* and *human dignity* that are *rationally plausible*, that is, able to withstand discursive critique with good arguments. It also needs to develop widely shared understandings that do not deprive morally competent individuals of their rational autonomy. Deprivation takes the form of dogmatic assertions as distinguished from reasoned claims always open to reasonable challenge. Reasoned argument is a means to allow traditions, norms, and institutions to make the case, and to make it publicly, that they are legitimate and persuasive. To the extent they cannot do so, they may be irrational or repressive or otherwise unacceptable.

(2) I develop the notion of epistemic dualism in political community in five respects: (a) political community as such, (b) political community as learning process, (c) learning process against a lifeworld background, (d) the individual's empowering dependence on a lifeworld background, and (e) the theory's aspirations to potentially universally valid norms for regulating human genetic engineering.

(a) *Political community*. The practice of bioethics as political theory involves the development of normative political community out of normatively heterogenous groups and the normatively distinct individuals who compose them. This task – a constant preoccupation of politics and one realizable, if at all, then only sometimes and only to some extent – requires the generation of legitimate political authority. Such authority involves the realization of a plausible social contract with law as the favored means of organizing a political community in ways increasingly rational and increasingly just. A contract is plausible if it facilitates a self-determining political community's autonomous law-giving, on the one hand, and legal equality for communal members, on the other. Autonomous law-giving includes the constitutionalization of state powers as well as individual rights.

A self-determining legal community also engages fundamental concepts of modern ethics, from freedom of the will, to the meaning of normative commitments among citizens, to each citizen's responsibility for her actions. On the one hand, as one condition among others for political cooperation and legitimacy, members of the community need to be able to freely regard themselves as having free will. On the other hand, communicatively interacting members of a just community must be able to assume, and assume mutually, that each person takes responsibility for her speech and behavior. The practice of bioethics as political theory pursues social organization in these senses. It does so specifically toward the legitimation of social power relevant to the regulation of biotechnologies.

A just and rational society in this sense requires communicatively socialized members willing to deploy their legal and political freedoms toward cooperating in the *res publica* as it confronts difficult issues of bioethics that offer no easy resolution and where consensual agreement is perpetually elusive. Cooperation in this context is only possible if its members regard, as legitimate, a significant portion of the community's legal and political norms. Members cooperate independently, on the one hand and, on the other, lead their individual lives within the framework of intersubjectively shared ways of life. Within that framework, individual legitimacy needs to be connected to the individual's cooperative autonomy within community. With regard to regulating human genetic engineering, bioethics as political theory provides one form of that connection, and one strand.

It connects the individual's moral status to her moral self-understanding. And it connects her moral self-understanding to the moral self-understanding of other persons. It does so by making individual freedom in political community coextensive with equally distributed rights and obligations within the community. This it does by seeking to construct norms (regarding the regulation of biotechnologies) capable of being generalized throughout a political community with its individualized actors. In their participation within the community, these actors may judge for themselves whether the forms in which the community socializes its members does two things simultaneously: includes all members while protecting the individuality of each. That is, the community can only be explained in its normative aspects from the perspective of its members.[2] They alone can judge the nature and extent of their belonging to this intersubjectively shared sphere that, to some extent, will always fall short of providing for full and equal membership for all citizens. In years to come it will struggle with the increasing complexity of modern communities, a complexity that manifests itself in the significant pluralism in ways of life no less than in individualism threatened by forms of isolation. Such communities will struggle best if they impose on themselves the requirement that they resonate with as much of their respective publics as possible at any given time. That imperative in turn requires robust, widely accessible public debate with broad public input, in a media context as free as possible from systematically distorted communication.

(b) *Political community as a learning process.* Learning processes of nonhuman animals may constitute the prehistory of our own sociocultural learning processes. That is, our own learning processes may be possible only because of a biological prehistory of such processes. On

[2] Gregg (2003a) and (2003b) develop this claim at length.

> this account, mind emerges from matter, and culture from nature. But even if research one day shows that cultural learning processes are connected to natural evolutionary learning processes, bioethics as political theory does not reduce culture to nature. Rather, it embeds its project in an ongoing, open-ended collective learning process in political community.[3]

Learning processes are fundamental to the possibility of bioethics as political theory. They are so for multiple reasons, along several dimensions. First, learning processes are necessary not only for individual and group survival but also in pursuit of human flourishing, for example by constructing just political communities. In the latter sense, members of a political community cannot afford *not* to learn if the community is to move toward ever-better forms of social organization. Increases in communal size and complexity require members to make sociocultural progress not only along technical dimensions but also along normative ones. To respond well to normative and political questions, challenges, and problems, a society cannot merely deploy and adapt the technical knowledge of the objectifying sciences.

With respect to bioethics as political theory in particular, progress along normative dimensions of society requires an increased ability and willingness to assume mutual perspectives, in light of unceasing increases in social complexity as well as in scientific knowledge and technological capacity – including those leading to ever-newer, ever more powerful biotechnologies.[4]

Further, bioethics as political theory is an ongoing, open-ended learning process in rational, secular argumentation as the individual learns to deploy her legal and political freedoms, and to do so with a willingness to cooperate politically with her fellow citizens. It is a learning process also as an empirically informed critique of crises in social integration generated by the normative questions posed by developments in biotechnologies. It is yet another learning process with regard to grasping the individual's subjectivity as the site for her performative attitude of moral self-examination, and her moral identity as something achieved rather than given.

Learning processes are politically constitutive in other ways as well. Individual judgement and commitment, as well as collective conscience and communal legislation, can follow from intersubjective learning processes. These processes are circular: one learns from culture and society to change culture and society. In this sense, learning processes build a kind of feedback loop: knowledge that so far has shown itself to be useful or valid in practice likely will be reproduced and passed on to subsequent generations. Further, learning processes are necessary to confront politically and morally significant

[3] As Chapter 2 argues with regard to cultural evaluations within a community that follow from the learning processes undergone by participants in the course of life-long socialization.

[4] Chapters 1, 2, 3, 4, 5, and 7 address this imperative.

developments over time, such as new scientific and technical information, but also in light of new normative perspectives and convictions as they develop over time.

(c) *Learning process against a lifeworld background.* In philosophy and in some social sciences, the notion of a *Lebenswelt* or *lifeworld* refers to the way we humans experience the world "as lived" prior to reflective analysis or representation.[5] Until made an object of refection, it forms the background of individuals' consciousness of the world: a social and cultural environment whose qualities are experienced by its members *in actu*. Individuals are familiar with it on a daily basis; it encompasses their cultural traditions and social conventions and obligations. It remains intact only insofar as it remains more or less in the background, facilitating intersubjectively shared beliefs and practices.

Bioethics as political theory works with the idea that much of human understanding is bonded to the lifeworld. For example, the lifeworld can be a source of spontaneity for the "performance" of public reason by the members of political community. By *performing public reason* I refer to participants in the public sphere who identify and discuss the challenges, tasks, and aspirations of their community, and who debate the best means to solve problems and achieve goals.

So even the lifeworld has a role to play in the processes of the self-legislation of political community. To say that the lifeworld situates the problem-solving behavior of socialized individuals, reproducing their contingent circumstances, is to say this: that every act of understanding presupposes, fallibilistically, that participants share language or communicative capacity, as well as some lifeworld background assumptions, as preconditions of that sharing.

On the one hand, in dealing with contingencies in the world, the individual deploys her reasoning capacity to revise disappointed expectations. On the other hand, even with these background assumptions, individuals must retain a sufficiently strong notion of their individual normative capacity to be able to evaluate the plausibility of normative claims contingently grounded in reasons – and, when persuaded of that plausibility, they must be capable of being motivated by those reasons, as individuals as well as in their collective behavior as members of political community.

Important for bioethics as political theory is that, on the one hand, the lifeworld does not fuse the social, cultural, and normative aspects of collective life with the natural world. On the other hand, bioethics as political theory does not construct the lifeworld as somehow objective, or transcendental, or as a "view from nowhere" (Nagel 1986). Human observation of the world and of

[5] A philosophically fertile notion developed in disparate ways by scholars from Heidegger (1927) to Husserl (1936) and from Garfinkel (1967) to Habermas (1981).

humanity can never be a view that is culturally or scientifically "neutral." It can only be one informed by what it is to be a human observer, including the limitations in perceiving and understanding that mark every observer.

In that sense, bioethics as political theory "de-centers" humankind, as does any perspective that does not contradict natural scientific understandings of the world. It approaches the internal world of human subjectivity with an objectivating stance – but a stance normatively sensitive, unlike the objectivating stance it takes toward the natural world.

In this way, among others, bioethics as political theory is post-metaphysical: it does not seek transcendence in the manner either of metaphysics or of scientism. Reasoned arguments claiming validity are the only form of "transcendence" available to communicatively socialized persons, embedded in the facticity of their respective lifeworlds (from which bioethics as political theory learns). So understood, "transcendence" refers to the results of successful learning processes in which humans learn to better understand the world or to better pursue just societies and in that metaphorical sense to "transcend" their status quo. Transcendence so understood is just the opposite of the otherworldly sense of surpassing or exceeding human experience.

(d) *The individual's empowering dependence on a lifeworld background.* The lifeworld background has a kind of power that situates the individual within a common pre-understanding that can promote the socialization within a shared community and within a culture. And it can promote greater understanding among the diverse members of a community and a culture. It possesses that power as a socially stabilizing stance insofar as it joins diverse members in a shared perspective despite their abiding differences from each other. Individuals and groups depend on this power to unite them even as they remain divided as autonomous political and legal agents.

Bioethics as political theory is sensitive to this divide between individuals in their consciousness of their autonomy – individual autonomy understood as the internal merging of reason and will – and their dependence on contexts that limit the exercise of their autonomy. Bioethics as political theory analyzes that divide as a kind of empowering dependence: individual members are dependent on the community – yet their dependence can in part empower them.

For example, humans in community may to an extent control their traditions by the ways in which they articulate their lives – even as, to an extent, they are simultaneously controlled by those traditions. By analogy, one cannot control one's language use without, at the same time, being dependent on its phonology, morphology, syntax, semantics, and pragmatics. To communicate competently, one is bound by the components of whatever language one is using. Yet within those bounds, one can express oneself freely, articulate original ideas, and even modify aspects of the components of the very language that sets those bounds.[6]

Another example: the socialization of individuals, through education and through training in cultural competence, contains an element of naked dependence. But that socialization and education and training also provide the means by which the person socialized, educated, and trained, eventually comes to be able to place those means into question, to modify them or to reject them, or even to replace them with an alternative. In this way, dependence can be balanced with autonomy: an empowering dependence.

In terms relevant to the project of bioethics as political theory, the individual can appropriate some aspects of her social and cultural environment and habitus and deploy them as the enabling conditions for her autonomous action. Here she is empoweringly dependent on the formative power of her community's conventions and understandings. Yet as long as she can place any of these conventions and understandings into question (and if they can withstand critically reasoned questions), her dependence still leaves ample room for the exercise of her autonomy.

Indeed, the individual in community is socialized into both dependence and empowerment through the intersubjectively shared lifeworld background. She can, for example, learn the perspective of another person. If she wishes, she can reject it; if she wishes, she can adopt it as her own. To say that the individual's independence is related to her dependence on her cultural and social context is to say that reason cannot be located entirely in the individual's head. Rather, human reason is an intersubjective phenomenon.

We humans understand by means of empowering dependence. In understanding ourselves, other persons, and the world, we can only depend on ourselves: we can only understand from a peculiarly human perspective. For human understanding, even the natural world is not independent of the ways of human understanding. For example, humans understand nature by assimilating nature to their scientific methods. Hence the complementarity between subjective and objective reality cannot be grasped in terms of a subject–object relationship because the objective world is not available to us humans without peculiarly human forms of perception and understanding, which to some degree influence what we know of the objective world and how we know it.

Here, again, we see that we humans do not have some transcendental "view from nowhere"; individual understanding is always already embedded in a social network of shared understandings. This network includes the lifeworld-background: one is dependent on the lifeworld in which one is embedded, and one is dependent on its external conditions, just as one is dependent on a causal

[6] Thus one cannot understand the meaning of a word without knowing the meaning of many other words. No word carries a free-standing meaning.

nexus of conditions and events in the natural universe. One must cope with this nexus as one limit among others to one's freedom to act.

(e) *The regulative aspiration to universally valid norms for regulating human genetic engineering.* Bioethics as political theory must avoid scientistic naturalism. It must also avoid the notion of behavior-guiding norms that are somehow valid as such. It does so by bridging the epistemic dualism between the observer's objectifying access to physically measurable phenomena, on the one hand, and her hermeneutic access to sociocultural forms of life, on the other. It does so with the claim that knowledge is always specifically and peculiarly *human* knowledge. And it does so by offering a decentered self-understanding of humans, an understanding in line with an objectivating stance toward the natural world. If the patterns of nature have no normative implications, and matter and mind are normatively neutral, then normativity is not embedded in the natural order.

On this approach, bioethics is knowledge always from the perspective of the (collective) knower and never independent of the (collective) knower. On this approach, humans assume an "ex-centric" position in the world: they only rely on themselves in generating norms to guide political community. Humans are not the center of the universe, nor are they entirely distinct from all other life forms that have evolved on the planet Earth – as they certainly are, say, in the Abrahamic religions. So bioethics as political theory separates the content of normative constructions (in the historical spheres of society and culture) from the content of empirical descriptions of the world. It does not seek universal validity a priori. It seeks the free embrace, through reasoned argument, of socially constructed norms by members of the political community. Even socially constructed norms can aspire to universal validity. But they can aspire only to a mundane, this-worldly universal validity (achievable only asymtotically) that rejects the centered universalism of religion for a decentered universalism that always engages with competing conceptions and value commitments; that charts a path toward universal validity via discursive processes of intercultural understanding about principles of bioethical justice; and that conceives of cosmopolitan moral orders as contingent on favorable social circumstances for their very possibility.

The political emancipation of humans even in the form of just, self-legislating political communities brings with it an agonizing awareness of the limitations and finitude of human understanding as well as of human efforts to deploy that understanding in the world. We are finite as organically embodied, historically situated creatures socialized into particular cultures. Bioethics as political theory recognizes these limitations. It works with them. Even as it may aspire to a universal validity it can never achieve, it adopts no standpoint that claims to transcend human existence. Instead it takes an objectivating stance toward the natural universe. And it takes an objectivating stance also toward the human social universe and toward human history. This approach eschews the internal world of the observer for the interpersonal world of the community. And it eschews essentializing definitions of what constitutes the making of proper moral and legal choices.[7]

Political bioethics cannot see beyond the horizons of possibility. That horizon shifts incrementally with the steady increase of knowledge and the frequently breath-taking growth in technological capacity. We humans look outward as we attempt to understand nature (including our own evolved nature) and we look inward as we attempt to critically examine the conditions of our social life. Human community sieves the natural and the cultural worlds through observation, theory-building, experimentation, experience, and questioning – adding to what we know, and revising what we thought we knew but discovered that we don't. Through this matrix of nature and culture, now and then we make progress (as we define it, and redefine it, and argue over how best to define it) in how we grasp ourselves as creatures we endow with a moral status, and in how we grasp our natural environment, including our own evolved species: on a continuum of nature and culture.[8]

[7] As Chapters 3 and 4 assert.

[8] As Chapters 6, 7, 8, 9, and 10 urge.

References

Abney, Keith. 2012. "Robotics, Ethical Theory, and Metaethics: A Guide for the Perplexed," in P. Lin, K. Abney, and G. Bekey, eds. *Robot Ethics: The Ethical and Social Implications of Robotics*. Cambridge, MA: The MIT Press: 35–52.

Adashi, Eli, and Glenn Cohen. 2018. "Preventing Mitochondrial Diseases: Embryo-Sparing Donor-Independent Options." *Trends in Molecular Medicine* 24: 449–457.

Agar, Nicholas. 2004. *Liberal Eugenics: In Defense of Human Enhancement*. Oxford: Blackwell.

Agran, Martin, William MacLean, and Katherine Andren. 2015. "'I Never Thought about It': Teaching People with Intellectual Disability to Vote." *Education and Training in Autism and Developmental Disabilities* 50: 388–396.

Almeida, Mara, and Rui Diogo. 2019. "Human Enhancement: Genetic Engineering and Evolution." *Evolution, Medicine, and Public Health* 1: 183–189.

Amato, P., M. Tachibana, M. Sparman, and S. Mitalipov. 2014. "Three-Parent IVF: Gene Replacement for the Prevention of Inherited Mitochondrial Diseases." *Fertility and Sterility* 101: 31–35

Alta Charo, Robin. 2018. "Germline Engineering and Human Rights." *American Journal of International Law Unbound* 112: 344–349.

2019. "Rogues and Regulation of Germline Editing." *New England Journal of Medicine* 380: 976–980.

American Anthropological Association. 1947. "Statement on Human Rights." *American Anthropologist* 49: 539–543.

1999. "Declaration on Anthropology and Human Rights Committee for Human Rights American Anthropological Association." https://humanrights.americananthro.org/1999-statement-on-human-rights/

American Association on Mental Retardation. 2002. *Mental Retardation: Definition, Classification and Systems of Support*. 10th ed. Washington, DC: American Association on Mental Retardation.

American Psychiatric Association. 2013. *Diagnostic and Statistical Manual of Mental Disorders*. 5th ed. Arlington, VA: American Psychiatric Association Publishing.

Anastasiou, Dimitris, and James Kauffman. 2013. "The Social Model of Disability: Dichotomy between Impairment and Disability." *Journal of Medicine and Philosophy* 38: 441–459.

Andorno, Roberto. 2013. *Principles of International Biolaw: Seeking Common Ground at the Intersection of Bioethics and Human Rights*. Bruxelles: Éditions Bruylant.

Andreychik, Michael, and Michael Gill. 2015. "Do Natural Kind Beliefs about Social Groups Contribute to Prejudice? Distinguishing Bio-Somatic Essentialism from Bio-Behavioral Essentialism, and Both of These from Entitativity." *Group Processes & Intergroup Relations* 18: 454–474.

Annas, George. 2005. *American Bioethics: Crossing Human Rights and Health Law Boundaries*. New York: Oxford University Press.

Applebaum, S., and Y. Heifetz. 1999. "Density-Dependent Physiological Phase in Insects." *Annual Review of Entomology* 44: 317–341.

Araki, Motoko, and Tetsuya Ishii. 2014. "International Regulatory Landscape and Integration of Corrective Genome Edition into In Vitro Fertilization." *Reproductive Biology and Endocrinology* 12(108): 1–12.

Arkin, Ronald. 2010. "The Case for Ethical Autonomy in Unmanned Systems." *Journal of Military Ethics* 9: 332–341.

Asbury, Kathryn. 2015. "Can Genetics Research Benefit Educational Interventions for All?" *Hastings Center Report* 45: S39–S42.

Asbury, Kathryn, and Robert Plomin. 2013. *G Is for Genes: The Impact of Genetics on Education and Achievement*. Chichester: Wiley Blackwell.

Atran, Scott, and Joseph Henrich. 2010. "The Evolution of Religion: How By-Products, Adaptive Learning Heuristics, Ritual Displays, and Group Competition Generate Deep Commitments to Prosocial Religions." *Biological Theory* 5: 18–30.

Ayala, F. J. 2012. *The Big Questions: Evolution*. London: Quercus.

Balkin, Jack. 2015. "The Path of Robotics Law." *California Law Review Circuit* 6: 45–60.

Ball, Philip. 2018. "Schrödinger's Cat among Biology's Pigeons: 75 Years of *What Is Life?*" *Nature* 560: 548–550.

Baltimore, D., P. Berg, M. Botchan, D. Carroll, R. Alta Charo, G. Church, et al. 2015. "A Prudent Path Forward for Genomic Engineering and Germline Gene Modification." *Science* 348: 36–38.

Barker, Matthew, and Robert Wilson. 2019. "Well-Being, Disability, and Choosing Children." *Mind* 128: 305–328.

Barnes, Elizabeth. 2014. "Valuing Disability, Causing Disability." *Ethics* 125: 88–113.

2016. "Reply to Guy Kahane and Julian Savulescu." *Res Philosophica* 93: 295–309.

Barry, Brian. 1970. *Political Argument*. London: Routledge & Kegan Paul.

Bashford, Alison, and Philippa Levine. 2010. *Oxford Handbook of the History of Eugenics*. Oxford: Oxford University Press.

Bateson, Patrick, and Peter Gluckman. 2012. "Plasticity, Robustness, Development and Evolution." *International Journal of Epidemiology* 41: 219–223.

Batzir, Nurit, Adi Tovin, and Ayal Hendel. 2017. "Therapeutic Genome Editing and Its Potential Enhancement through CRISPR Guide RNA and Cas9 Modifications." *Pediatric Endocrinology Reviews* 14: 353–363.

Bavelier, D., J. Savulescu, L. Fried, T. Friedmann, C. Lathan, S. Schürle, et al. 2019. "Rethinking Human Enhancement as Collective Welfarism." *Nature Human Behavior* 3: 204–206.

Bayat, Hadi, Mohammad Modarressi, and Azam Rahimpour. 2018. "The Conspicuity of CRISPR-Cpf1 System as a Significant Breakthrough in Genome Editing." *Current Microbiology* 75: 107–115.

Baylis, François. 2016. "'Broad Societal Consensus' on Human Germline Editing." *Harvard Health Policy Review* 15: 19–22.

2017. "Human Germline Genome Editing and Broad Societal Consensus." *Nature Human Behaviour* 1: 1–3.

Beauchamp, Tom. 2010. *Standing on Principles: Collected Essays*. Oxford: Oxford University Press.

Bell, Dorothy, Colin McKay, and Kathryn Phillips. 2001. "Overcoming the Barriers to Voting Experienced by People with Learning Disabilities." *British Journal of Learning Disabilities* 29: 122–127.

Bentham, Jeremy. 1996 [1789]. *An Introduction to the Principles of Morals and Legislation*. J. Burns and H. L. A. Hart, eds. Oxford: Clarendon Press.

Bester, Johan. 2019. "The Best Interest Standard and Children: Clarifying a Concept and Responding to its Critics." *Journal of Medical Ethics* 45: 117–124.

Blackmore, E., F. Putnam, E. Pressman, D. Rubinow, K. Putnam, M. Matthieu, et al. 2016. "The Effects of Trauma History and Prenatal Affective Symptoms on Obstetric Outcomes." *Journal of Traumatic Stress* 29: 245–252.

Blau, Peter, and Otis Duncan. 1967. *The American Occupational Structure*. New York: Wiley.

Bognar, Greg. 2016. "Is Disability Mere Difference?" *Journal of Medical Ethics* 42: 46–49.

Bohacek, Johannes, and Isabelle Mansuy. 2013. "Epigenetic Inheritance of Disease and Disease Risk." *Neuropsychopharmacology* 38: 220–236.

Bohman, James, and William Rehg, eds. 1997. *Deliberative Democracy: Essays on Reason and Politics*. Cambridge, MA: MIT Press.

Bostrom, Nick, and Anders Sandberg. 2009. "Cognitive Enhancement: Methods, Ethics, Regulatory Challenges." *Science and Engineering Ethics* 15: 311–341.

Bourdieu, Pierre. 1983. "Okonomisches Kapital, kulturelles Kapital, soziales Kapital," in R. Kreckel, ed. *Soziale Ungleichheiten. Soziale Welt, Sonderband* 2. Göttingen: Schwartz: 183–198.

Boyanapalli, Sarandeep, and Ah-Ng Kong. 2015. "Curcumin, the King of Spices: Epigenetic Regulatory Mechanisms in the Prevention of Cancer, Neurological, and Inflammatory Diseases." *Current Pharmacology Reports* 1: 129–139.

Branigan, Amelia, Kenneth McCallum, and Jeremy Freese. 2013. "Variation in the Heritability of Educational Attainment: An International Meta-Analysis." *Social Forces* 92: 109–140.

Bratsberg, Bernt, and Ole Rogeberg. 2018. "Flynn Effect and Its Reversal Are Both Environmentally Caused." *Proceedings of the National Academy of Sciences* 115: 6674–6678.

Braun, Bruce, and Sarah Whatmore. 2010. "The Stuff of Politics: An Introduction," in B. Braun and S. Whatmore, eds. *Political Matter: Technoscience, Democracy, and Public Life*. Minneapolis: University of Minnesota Press: ix–xl.

Bridges, Robert. 2016. "Long-term Alterations in Neural and Endocrine Processes Induced by Motherhood." *Hormones and Behavior* 77: 193–203.

Brinch, Christian, and Taryn Galloway. 2012. "Schooling in Adolescence Raises IQ Scores." *Proceedings of the National Academy of Sciences of the United States of America* 109: 425–430.

Brown, Donald. 1991. *Human Universals*. New York: McGraw-Hill.

Brown, Ivan, Roy Brown, and Alice Schippers. 2019. "A Quality of Life Perspective on the New Eugenics." *Journal of Policy and Practice in Intellectual Disabilities* 16: 121–126.

Buchanan, Allen, and Dan Brock. 1989. *Deciding for Others: The Ethics of Surrogate Decision Making*. Cambridge: Cambridge University Press.

Buchanan, Allen, Dan Brock, Norman Daniels, and Daniel Wikler. 2000. *From Chance to Choice: Genetics and Justice*. New York: Cambridge University Press.

Buller, David. 2005. *Adapting Minds: Evolutionary Psychology and the Persistent Quest for Human Nature*. Cambridge, MA: MIT Press.

Burall, Simon. 2018. "Rethink Public Engagement for Gene Editing." *Nature* 555: 438–439.

Burden, B., J. Fletcher, P. Herd, B. Jones, and D. Moynihan. 2017. "How Different Forms of Health Matter to Political Participation." *Journal of Politics* 79: 166–178.

Buzatu, D., K. Taylor, D. Peret, J. Darsey, and N. Lang. 2001. "The Determination of Cardiac Surgical Risk Using Artificial Neural Networks." *Journal of Surgical Research* 95: 61–66.

Cabrera, Laura. 2017. "Reframing Human Enhancement: A Population Health Perspective." *Frontiers in Sociology* 2: 1–5.

Calarco, Jessica. 2014. "Coached for the Classroom: Parents' Cultural Transmission and Children's Reproduction of Educational Inequalities." *American Sociological Review* 79: 1015–1037.

Calkins, Kara, and Sherin Devaskar. 2011. "Fetal Origins of Adult Disease." *Current Problems in Pediatric and Adolescent Health Care* 41: 158–176.

Calo, Ryan. 2015. "Robotics and the Lessons of Cyberlaw." *California Law Review* 103: 513–563.

Campbell, Stephen, and Joseph Stramondo. 2017. "The Complicated Relationship of Disability and Well-Being." *Kennedy Institute of Ethics Journal* 27: 151–184.

Campos, Paul. 2004. *The Obesity Myth: Why America's Obsession with Weight Is Hazardous to Your Health*. New York: Gotham Books.

Carey, Allison. 2015. "Citizenship," in R. Adams, B. Reiss, and D. Serlin, eds. *Keywords for Disability Studies*. New York: New York University Press: 37–39.

Carzis, B., T. Wainstein, L. Gobetz, and A. Krause. 2019. "Review of 10 Years of Preimplantation Genetic Diagnosis in South Africa: Implications for a Low-to-Middle-Income Country." *Journal of Assisted Reproduction and Genetics* 36: 1909–1916.

Cavaliere, Giulia. 2020. "The Problem with Reproductive Freedom: Procreation Beyond Procreators' Interests." *Medicine, Health Care and Philosophy* 23: 131–140.

Chakrabarty, Dipesh. 2009. "The Climate of History: Four Theses." *Critical Inquiry* 35: 197–222.

Chan, S., and M. Medina Arellano. 2016. "Genome Editing and International Regulatory Challenges: Lessons from Mexico." *Ethics, Medicine and Public Health* 2: 426–434.

Ching, Boby, and Jason Xu. 2018. "The Effects of Gender Neuroessentialism on Transprejudice: An Experimental Study." *Sex Roles* 78: 228–241.

Chiao, Joan, and Bobby Cheon. 2012. "Cultural Neuroscience as Critical Neuroscience in Practice," in S. Choudhury and J. Slaby, eds. *Critical Neuroscience: A Handbook of the Social and Cultural Contexts of Neuroscience*. Hoboken, NJ: Willey Blackwell: 287–303.

Childress, James. 2003. "*Principles of Biomedical Ethics*: Reflections on a Work in Progress," in J. Walter and E. Klein, eds. *The Story of Bioethics: From Seminal Works to Contemporary Explorations*. Washington, DC: Georgetown University Press: 47–66.

Chneiweiss, H., F. Hirsch, L. Montoliu, A. Müller, S. Fenet, M. Abecassis, et al. 2017. "Fostering Responsible Research with Genome Editing Technologies: A European Perspective." *Transgenic Research* 26: 709–713.

Chomsky, Noam. 1987. "Language and Freedom," in J. Peck, ed. *The Chomsky Reader*. New York: Pantheon Books: 139–155.

Clocksin, William. 2003. "Artificial Intelligence and the Future." *Philosophical Transactions of the Royal Society of London A* 361: 1721–1748.

Cochrane, Alaisdair. 2012. "Evaluating 'Bioethical Approaches' to Human Rights." *Ethical Theory and Moral Practice* 15: 309–322.

Cohen, Joshua. 1994. "Pluralism and Proceduralism." *Chicago–Kent Law Review* 69: 589–618.

Comfort, Nathaniel. 2012. *The Science of Human Perfection: How Genes Became the Heart of American Medicine*. New Haven, CT: Yale University Press.

Conley, D., B. Domingue, D. Cesarini, C. Dawes, C. Rietveld, and J. Boardman. 2015. "Is the Effect of Parental Education on Offspring Biased or Moderated by Genotype?" *Sociological Science* 2: 82–105.

Conley, Dalton, and Jason Fletcher. 2017. *The Genome Factor: What the Social Genomics Revolution Reveals about Ourselves, Our History and the Future*. Princeton, NJ: Princeton University Press.

Convention for the Protection of and Dignity of the Human Being with Regard to the Application of Biology and Medicine (Oviedo Convention), 4 April 1997, www.coe.int/en/web/bioethics/oviedo-convention

Crutzen, Paul. 2002. "Geology of Mankind." *Nature* 415: 23.

Crutzen, Paul, and Eugene Stoermer. 2000. "The Anthropocene." *Global Change Newsletter* 41: 17–18.

Csibra, Gergely, and Gergely György. "Natural Pedagogy as Evolutionary Adaptation." 2011. *Philosophical Transactions of the Royal Society B* 366: 1149–1157.

Culver, Charles, and Bernard Gert. 1990. "The Inadequacy of Incompetence." *The Milbank Quarterly* 68: 619–643.

Cyranoski, David. 2019. "The CRISPR-Baby Scandal: What's Next for Human Gene-Editing." *Nature* 566: 440–442.

Daniels, Norman. 2008. *Just Health*. Cambridge: Cambridge University Press.

Darwin, Charles. 1854. *A Monograph on the Sub-Class Cirripedia*, vol. 2. London: Ray Society.

2004 [1859]. *The Origin of Species by Means of Natural Selection*. New York: Barnes & Noble Classics.

Davies, G., A. Tenesa, A. Payton, J. Yang, S. Harris, D. Liewald, et al. 2011. "Genome-Wide Association Studies Establish That Human Intelligence Is Highly Heritable and Polygenic." *Molecular Psychiatry* 16: 996–1005.

Davies, Jeremy. 2016. *The Birth of the Anthropocene*. Oakland: University of California Press. 2016.

de Miguel Beriain, Iñigo. 2018. "Human Dignity and Gene Editing: Using Human Dignity as an Argument against Modifying the Human Genome and Germline is a Logical Fallacy." *EMBO Reports* 19: 1–4.

Deary, Ian. 2012. "Intelligence." *Annual Review of Psychology* 63: 453–482.

Derex, Maxime, and Alex Mesoudi. 2020. "Cumulative Cultural Evolution within Evolving Population Structures." *Trends in Cognitive Science* 24: 654–667.

Des Portes, Vincent. 2020. "Intellectual Disability," in A. Gallagher, C. Bulteau, D. Cohen, and J. Michaud, eds. *Handbook of Clinical Neurology*, vol. 174. Amsterdam: Elsevier: 113–126.

Devitt, Michael. 2008. "Resurrecting Biological Essentialism." *Philosophy of Science* 75: 344–382.

Dewey, John. 1927. *The Public and Its Problems*. New York: Holt.

1981 [1925]. "Nature, Means and Knowledge," in J. A. Boydston, ed. *John Dewey: The Later Works, 1925–1953*, vol. 1. Carbondale: Southern Illinois University Press: 100–131.

Diderot, Denis. 1966 [1755]. *Encyclopédie ou Dictionnaire raisonné des sciences, des arts et des métiers par une société de gens de lettres*, vol. 5. Stuttgart: Frommann.

1966 [1755]. *Encyclopédie ou Dictionnaire raisonné des sciences, des arts et des métiers par une société de gens de lettres*, vol. 18. Stuttgart: Frommann.

1989 [1772]. *Supplément au Voyage de Bougainville*, in: Diderot, Œuvres Complètes, Tome XII. Paris: Hermann.

Doudna, Jennifer and Emmanuelle Charpentier. 2014. "The New Frontier of Genome Engineering with CRISPR-Cas9." *Science* 346: 1077–1087.

Downes, Stephen, and Edouard Machery. 2013. *Arguing about Human Nature: Contemporary Debates*. New York: Routledge.

Dryden, John. 1672. *The Conquest of Granada by the Spaniards: In Two Parts, Acted at the Theater-Royall*. London: Herringman.

Dryzek, J., D. Nicol, S. Niemeyer, S. Pemberton, N. Curato, A. Bächtiger, et al. 2020. "Global Citizen Deliberation on Genome Editing." *Science* 369: 1435–1437.

Dunbar, Robin. 2016. *Human Evolution: Our Brains and Behavior*. Oxford: Oxford University Press.

Dunbar, Robin, Clive Gamble, and John Gowlett. 2014. *Thinking Big: How the Evolution of Social Life Shaped the Human Mind*. London: Thames & Hudson.

Duncan, L., H. Shen, B. Gelaye, K. Ressler, M. Feldman, R. Peterson, et al. 2019. "Analysis of Polygenic Score Usage and Performance in Diverse Human Populations." *Nature Communications* 10: 1–9.

Dupras, Charles, and Vardit Ravitsky. 2016. "The Ambiguous Nature of Epigenetic Responsibility." *Journal of Medical Ethics* 42: 534–541.

Dupré, John. 1999. "On the Impossibility of a Monistic Account of Species," in R. Wilson, ed. *Species: New Interdisciplinary Essays*. Cambridge, MA: MIT Press: 3–22.

Dzau, Victor, Marcia McNutt, and Venki Ramakrishnan. 2019. "Academies' Action Plan for Germline Editing." *Nature* 567: 175.

Elliott, Carl. 1998. "The Tyranny of Happiness: Ethics and Cosmetic Psychopharmacology," in E. Parens, ed. *Enhancing Human Traits: Ethical and Social Implications*. Washington, DC: Georgetown University Press: 177–188.

2004. *Better than Well: American Medicine Meets the American Dream*. New York: Norton.

Estlund, David. 2008. *Democratic Authority: A Philosophical Framework*. Princeton, NJ: Princeton University Press.

European Convention on Human Rights, 14 March 2014, www.assembly.coe.int/nw/xml/XRef/Xref-XML2HTML-en.asp?fileid=20550&lang=en

Evans, James, and Wylie Burke. 2008. "Genetic Exceptionalism: Too Much of a Good Thing?" *Genetics in Medicine* 10: 500–501.

Farrelly, Colin. 2019. "Aging, Geroscience, and Freedom." *Rejuvenation Research* 22: 163–170.

Feil, Robert, and Mario Fraga. 2012. "Epigenetics and the Environment: Emerging Patterns and Implications." *Nature Review Genetics* 13: 97–109.

Feinberg, Joel. 1970. "The Nature and Value of Rights." *Journal of Value Inquiry* 4: 243–257.

1980. "The Child's Right to an Open Future," in W. Aiken and H. LaFollette, eds. *Whose Child? Children's Rights, Parental Authority, and State Power*. Totowa, NJ: Rowman and Littlefield: 124–153.

Ferguson, H., S. Bovaird, and M. Mueller. 2007. "The Impact of Poverty on Educational Outcomes for Children." *Paediatrics and Child Health* 12: 701.

Fernell, Elizabeth, and Christopher Gillberg. 2020. "Borderline Intellectual Functioning," in A. Gallagher, C. Bulteau, D. Cohen, and J. Michaud, eds. *Handbook of Clinical Neurology*, vol. 174. Amsterdam: Elsevier: 77–81.

Fisher, H., T. Murphy, L. Arseneault, A. Caspi, T. Moffitt, J. Viana, et al. 2015. "Methylomic Analysis of Monozygotic Twins Discordant for Childhood Psychotic Symptoms." *Epigenetics* 10: 1014–1023.

Fishkin, James. 1997. *The Voice of the People: Public Opinion and Democracy*. New Haven, CT: Yale University Press.

2011. *When the People Speak: Deliberative Democracy and Public Consultation*. New York: Oxford University Press.

Fitzgerald, Kevin. 2008. "Medical Enhancement: A Destination of Technological, Not Human, Betterment," in B. Gordijn and R. Chadwick, eds., *Medical Enhancement and Post-Modernity*. Dordrecht: Springer: 39–54.

Fletcher, Michael. 2015. "Google, Others Pave Way for Self-Driving Cars." *US Black Engineer and Information Technology* 39: 64–65.

Fowler, Tim. 2015. "In Defence of State Directed Enhancement." *Journal of Applied Philosophy* 32: 67–81.

Frati, P., V. Fineschi, M. Di Sanzo, R. La Russa, M. Scopetti, F. Serveri, et al. 2017. "Preimplantation and Prenatal Diagnosis, Wrongful Birth and Wrongful Life: A Global View of Bioethical and Legal Controversies." *Human Reproduction Update* 23: 338–357.

Frith, Chris. 2007. *Making Up the Mind: How the Brain Creates Our Mental World*. Malden, MA: Wiley-Blackwell.

Fuentes, Agustin. 2008. *Evolution of Human Behavior*. New York: Oxford University Press.

Fukuyama, Francis. 2000. *The Great Disruption: Human Nature and the Reconstitution of Social Order*. New York: Free Press.

2002. "How to Regulate Science." *The Public Interest* 146: 3–22.

Galton, Francis. 1869. *Hereditary Genius: An Inquiry into Its Laws and Consequences*. New York: Macmillan.

Garfinkel, Harold. 1967. *Studies in Ethnomethodology*. Englewoods Cliffs, NJ: Prentice Hall.

Garland-Thomson, Rosemarie. 2015. "Eugenics," in R. Adams, B. Reiss, and D. Serlin, eds. *Keywords for Disability Studies*. New York: New York University Press: 74–79.

2020. "How We Got To CRISPR: The Dilemma of Being Human." *Perspectives in Biology and Medicine* 63: 28–43.

Gastil, John, and Peter Levine, eds. 2005. *The Deliberative Democracy Handbook: Strategies for Effective Civic Engagement in the 21st Century*. San Francisco: Jossey-Bass.

Geertz, Clifford. 1973. *The Interpretation of Cultures*. New York: Basic Books.

Gehl, Robert. 2014. *Reverse Engineering Social Media: Software, Culture, and Political Economy in New Media Capitalism*. Philadelphia: Temple University Press.

Gehlen, Arnold. 1957. *Die Seele im technischen Zeitalter: Sozialpsychologische Probleme in der industriellen Gesellschaft*. Hamburg: Rowohlt.

Geuss, Raymond. 2008. *Philosophy and Real Politics*. Princeton, NJ: Princeton University Press.

Gewirth, Alan. 1982. *Human Rights: Essays on Justification and Applications*. Chicago: University of Chicago Press.

Gil-White, Francisco. 2001. "Are Ethnic Groups Biological 'Species' to the Human Brain? Essentialism in Our Cognition of Some Social Categories." *Current Anthropology* 42: 515–554.

Gillborn, David. 2016. "Softly, Softly: Genetics, Intelligence and the Hidden Racism of the New Geneism." *Journal of Education Policy* 31: 365–388.

Giubilini, Alberto, and Neil Levy. 2018. "What in the World Is Collective Responsibility?" *Dialectica* 72: 191–217.

Glackin, Shane. 2019. "Grounded Disease: Constructing the Social from the Biological in Medicine." *Philosophical Quarterly* 69: 258–276.

Godfrey, K., K. Lillycrop, G. Burdge, P. Gluckman, and M. Hanson. 2007. "Epigenetic Mechanisms and the Mismatch Concept of the Developmental Origins of Health and Disease." *Pediatric Research* 61: 5–10.

Goold, S., M. Neblo, S. Kim, R. de Vries, G. Rowe, and P. Muhlberger. 2012. "What Is Good Quality Public Deliberation?" *Hasting Center Report* 42: 24–26.

Gould, Carol. 2004. *Globalizing Democracy and Human Rights*. New York: Cambridge University Press.

Gould, James. 2020. "The Complicated but Plain Relationship of Intellectual Disability and Well Being." *Revue Canadienne de bioéthique* 3: 37–51.

Gould, Stephen Jay. 1986. "Evolution and the Triumph of Homology, or Why History Matters." *American Scientist* 74: 60–69.

Gregg, Benjamin. 2002. "Proceduralism Reconceived: Political Conflict Resolution under Conditions of Moral Pluralism." *Theory and Society* 31: 741–776.

2003a. *Coping in Politics with Indeterminate Norms*. Albany, NY: SUNY Press.

2003b. *Thick Norms, Thin Politics: Social Integration across Communities of Belief*. Durham, NC: Duke University Press.

2012a. *Human Rights as Social Construction*. New York: Cambridge University Press.

2012b. "Genetic Enhancement: A New Dialectic of Enlightenment?," in D. Wetzel, ed. *Perspektiven der Aufklärung: Zwischen Mythos und Realität*. Paderborn, Germany: Verlag Wilhelm Fink: 133–146.

2013. "Might the Noble Savage Have Joined the Earliest Cults of Rousseau?," in J. Reiling and D. Tröhler, eds. *Entre hétérogénéité et imagination. Pratiques de la réception de Jean-Jacques Rousseau*. Genève, Switzerland: Éditions Slatkine: 347–366.

2016a. *The Human Rights State: Justice within and beyond Sovereign Nations*. Philadelphia: University of Pennsylvania Press.

2016b. "Human Rights as Metaphor for Political Community Beyond the Nation State." *Critical Sociology* 42: 897–917.

2018a. "Human Genetic Engineering: Biotic Justice in the Anthropocene?," in D. DellaSala and M. Goldstein, eds. *Encyclopedia of the Anthropocene*, vol. 4. Amsterdam: Elsevier: 351–359.

2018b. "How to Read for Current Developments in Human Genetics Relevant to Justice." *Politics and the Life Sciences* 37: 262–277.

2020a. "Vom Nutzen und Nachteil der Biotechnik: Zur normativen Einschätzung der Humangenmanipulation," in B. Keplinger and F. Schwanniger, eds. *Optimierung des Menschen*. Innsbruck, Austria: Studienverlag: 49–63.

2020b. "Beyond Due Diligence: The Human Rights Corporation." *Human Rights Review* 22: 65–89.

2020c. "The Human Rights State: Advancing Justice through Political Imagination," in K. Schmidt, ed. *The State of Human Rights: Historical Genealogies, Political Controversies, and Cultural Imaginaries*. Heidelberg, Germany: Winter Verlag: 47–69.

2020d. "A Socialism beyond Human Rights yet in Partnership with Them," review essay on *Not Enough: Human Rights in an Unequal World* by Samuel Moyn. *Kritikon Litterarum* 47: 376–381.

2020e. "Construção Social de uma Natureza Humana Voltada para os Direitos Humanos." *Boletim Goiano de Geografia [Brazil]* 40: 1–24. https://doi.org/10.5216/bgg.v40i01.63868

2021a. "Il contenimento di Covid-19: diritto alla privacy contro diritto alla salute pubblica." *Lessico di etica pubblica [Italy]* 2021: 125–163.

2021b. "Human Rights Require yet Contest National Sovereignty: How a Human Rights Corporation Might Help," in A. Santos Campos and S. Cadilha, eds. *Sovereignty as Value*. Lanham, MD: Rowman and Littlefield: 215–232.

Griffin, James. 2008. *On Human Rights*. Oxford: Oxford University Press.

Griffiths, Paul. 2002. "What Is Innateness?" *Monist* 85: 70–85.

Griffiths, Paul, Edouard Machery, and Stefan Linquist. 2009. "The Vernacular Concept of Innateness." *Mind & Language* 24: 605–630.

Grönlund, Kimmo, André Bächtiger, and Maija Setälä, eds. 2014. *Deliberative Mini-Publics: Involving Citizens in the Democratic Process*. Colchester: ECPR Press.

Gupta, Aarti. 2004. "When Global Is Local: Negotiating Safe Use of Biotechnology," in S. Jasanoff and M. Martello, eds. *Earthly Politics: Local and Global in Environmental Governance*. Cambridge, MA: MIT Press: 127–148.

Gutmann, Amy, and Dennis Thompson. 1996. *Democracy and Disagreement*. Cambridge, MA: Harvard University Press.

1997. "Deliberating about Bioethics." *Hastings Center Report* 27: 38–41.

Gutmann, Amy, and James Wagner. 2017. "Reflections on Democratic Deliberation in Bioethics." *Hastings Center Report* 47: S35-S38.

Gyngell, C., T. Douglas, and J. Savulescu. 2017. "The Ethics of Germline Gene Editing." *Journal of Applied Philosophy* 34: 498–513.

Habermas, Jürgen. 1981. *Theorie des kommunikativen Handelns*. Frankfurt: Suhrkamp.

1990. "Discourse Ethics: Notes on a Program of Philosophical Justification." In *Moral Consciousness and Communicative Action*. Cambridge, MA: MIT Press: 43–115.

1993. *Justification and Application*. Cambridge, MA: MIT Press.

1996. *Between Facts and Norms: Contributions to a Discourse Theory of Law and Democracy*. Cambridge, MA: MIT Press.

2001. *Die Zukunft der menschlichen Natur: Auf dem Weg zu einer liberalan Eugenik?* Frankfurt am Main: Suhrkamp.

2004. "Freiheit und Determinismus." *Deutsche Zeitschrift für Philosophie* 26: 871–890.

Haddock, Adrian, Alan Millar, and Duncan Pritchard, eds. 2009. *Epistemic Value*. New York: Oxford University Press.

Haff, Peter. 2014. "Humans and Technology in the Anthropocene: Six Rules." *The Anthropocene Review* 1: 126–136.

Hansen, Mark, and Ruth Müller. 2017. "Epigenetic Inheritance and the Responsibility for Health in Society." *The Lancet* 5: 11–12.

Harris, John. 2011. "Taking the 'Human' Out of Human Rights." *Cambridge Quarterly of Healthcare Ethics* 20: 9–20.

Harris, John. 2015. "Germline Manipulation and Our Future Worlds." *American Journal of Bioethics* 12: 30–34.

Harris, J. 2016. "Germline Modification and the Burden of Human Existence." *Cambridge Quarterly of Healthcare Ethics* 25: 6–18.

Haslam, Nick, and Sheri Levy. 2006. "Essentialist Beliefs about Homosexuality: Structure and Implications for Prejudice." *Personality and Social Psychology Bulletin*, 32: 471–485.

Hasson, U., A. Ghazanfar, B. Galantucci, S. Garrod, and C. Keysers. 2012. "Brain-to-Brain Coupling: A Mechanism for Creating and Sharing a Social World." *Trends in Cognitive Sciences* 16: 114–121.

Hayes, Brian. 2011. "Computing Science: Leave the Driving to It." *American Scientist* 99: 362–366.

Hedlund, Maria. 2012. "Epigenetic Responsibility." *Medicine Studies* 3: 171–183.

Heidegger, Martin. 1927. *Sein und Zeit*. Tübingen: Max Niemeyer Verlag.

Heijmans, B., E. Tobi, A. Stein, H. Putter, G. Blauw, E. Susser, et al. 2008. "Persistent Epigenetic Differences Associated with Prenatal Exposure to Famine in Humans." *Proceedings of the National Academy of Sciences of the USA* 105: 17046–17049.

Heine, Steven. 2017. *DNA Is Not Destiny: The Remarkable, Completely Misunderstood Relationship between You and Your Genes*. New York: W. W. Norton.

Heine, Steven, Benjamin Cheung, and Anita Schmalor. 2019. "Making Sense of Genetics: The Problem of Essentialism." *Hastings Center Report* 49: S19–S26.

Herrick, Charles and Daniel Sarewitz. 2000. "Ex post Evaluation: A More Effective Role for Scientific Assessments in Environmental Policy." *Science, Technology & Human Values* 25: 309–331.

Herrick, Clare. 2009. "Shifting Blame/Selling Health: Corporate Social Responsibility in the Age of Obesity." *Sociology of Health and Illness* 31: 51–65.

Heyes, Cecilia. 2018. "Human Nature, Natural Pedagogy, and Evolutionary Causal Essentialism," in E. Hannon and T. Lewens, eds. *Why We Disagree about Human Nature*. Oxford: Oxford University Press: 76–91.

Hickson, Linda, and Ishita Khemka. 2013. "Problem Solving and Decision Making," in M. Wehmeyer, ed. *Oxford Handbook of Positive Psychology and Disability*. Oxford University Press: Oxford Handbooks Online: 1–44.

Hill, W., R. Arslan, C. Xia, M. Luciano, C. Amador, P. Navarro, et al. 2018. "Genomic Analysis of Family Data Reveals Additional Genetic Effects on Intelligence and Personality." *Molecular Psychiatry* 23: 2347–2362.

Ho, Patrick, and Yvonne Chen. 2017. "Mammalian Synthetic Biology in the Age of Genome Editing and Personalized Medicine." *Current Opinions in Chemical Biology* 40: 57–64.

Honneth, Axel. 1998. "Democracy as Reflexive Cooperation: John Dewey and the Theory of Democracy Today." *Political Theory* 26: 763–783.

2017. "Is There an Emancipatory Interest? An Attempt to Answer Critical Theory's Most Fundamental Question." *European Journal of Philosophy* 25: 908–920.

Honneth, Axel, and John Farrell. 1998. "Democracy as Reflexive Cooperation." *Political Theory* 26: 763–783.

Horkheimer, Max, and Theodor Adorno. 1981 [1944]. *Dialektik der Aufklärung*. Frankfurt am Main: Suhrkamp.

Huang, Jiaojiao, Yanfang Wang, and Jianguo Zhao. 2017. "CRISPR Editing in Biological and Biomedical Investigation." *Journal of Cell Physiology* 233: 3875–3891.

Huang, Jonathan, and Nicholas King. 2018. "Epigenetics Changes Nothing: What a New Scientific Field Does and Does Not Mean for Ethics and Social Justice." *Public Health Ethics* 11: 69–81.

Hull David. 1986. On Human Nature. *Proceedings of the Biennial Meeting of the Philosophy of Science Association* 2: 3–13.

Hull, D. 1992. "A Matter of Individuality," in M. Ereshefsky, ed. *The Units of Evolution: Essays on the Nature of Species*. Cambridge, MA: MIT Press: 293–316.

Hunt, James. 1864. *The Negro's Place in Nature: A Paper Read before the London Anthropological Society*. New York: Van Evrie, Horton & Co.

Hurlbut, J. B. 2015. "Limits of Responsibility: Genome Editing, Asilomar, and the Politics of Deliberation." *Hastings Center Report* 45: 11–14.

Husserl, Edmund. 1936. "Die Krisis der Europäischen Wissenschaften und die transzendale Philosophie." *Philosophia (Beograd)* 1: 77–176.

Hwang, Tim, Ian Pearce, Max Nanis. 2012. "Socialbots: Voices from the Fronts." *Interactions* 19: 38–45.

International Bioethics Committee, 2 October 2015, *Report of the IBC on Updating Its Reflection on the Human Genome and Human Rights*. https://unesdoc.unesco.org/ark:/48223/pf0000233258

International Covenant on Economic, Social and Cultural Rights, January 3, 1976, www.ohchr.org/en/professionalinterest/pages/cescr.aspx

Isaacs, Tracy. 2006. "Collective Moral Responsibility and Collective Intention." *Midwest Studies in Philosophy* 30: 59–73.

Isasi R., E. Kleiderman, and B. Knoppers. 2016. "Editing Policy to Fit the Genome?" *Science* 351: 337–339.

Ishii, Tetsuya. 2017. "The Ethics of Creating Genetically Modified Children Using Genome Editing." *Current Opinion in Endocrinology, Diabetes and Obesity* 24: 418–423.

Ismaili M'hamdi, H., I. de Beaufort, B. Jack, and E. Steegers. 2018. "Responsibility in the Age of Developmental Origins of Health and Disease (DOHaD) and Epigenetics." *Journal of Developmental Origins of Health and Disease* 9: 58–62.

Istvan, Zoltan. 2015. "Programming Hate into AI Will Be Controversial, but Possibly Necessary." *TechCrunch*, October 18.

Jablonka, Eva, and Marion Lamb. 1995. *Epigenetic Inheritance and Evolution: The Lamarckian Dimension*. Oxford: Oxford University Press.

2005. *Evolution in Four Dimensions: Genetic, Epigenetic, Behavioral, and Symbolic Variation in the History of Life*. Cambridge, MA: MIT Press.

Jablonka, Eva, and Marion Lamb. 2014. *Evolution in Four Dimensions: Genetic, Epigenetic, Behavioral, and Symbolic Variation in the History of Life*. Revised ed. Cambridge, MA: MIT Press.

Jackson, John, and David Depew. 2017. *Darwinism, Democracy, and Race: American Anthropology and Evolutionary Biology in the Twentieth Century*. Milton Park, UK: Routledge.

Jackson, Nate. 2019. "'Deaf Spectators' and Democratic Elitism: Participation, Democracy, and Disability." *The Pluralist* 14: 30–52.

Jasanoff, Sheila. 1987. "Contested Boundaries in Policy-Relevant Science." *Social Studies of Science* 17: 195–230.

Jasanoff, S. 1998. "Contingent Knowledge: Implications for Implementation and Compliance," in E. Weiss and H. Jacobson, eds. *Engaging Countries: Strengthening Compliance with International Environmental Accords*. Cambridge, MA: MIT Press: 63–87.

Jasanoff, Sheila, and J. Benjamin Hurlbut. 2018. "A Global Observatory for Gene Editing." *Nature* 555: 435–437.

Jasanoff, Sheila, J. Benjamin Hurlbut, and Krishanu Saha. 2015. "CRISPR Democracy: Gene Editing and the Need for Inclusive Deliberation." *Issues in Science and Technology* 32: 25–32.

Jennings, Bruce. 1990. "Bioethics and Democracy." *The Centennial Review* 34: 207–225.

Jirtle, Randy, and Michael Skinner. 2007. "Environmental Epigenomics and Disease Susceptibility." *Nature Reviews Genetics* 8: 253–262.

Jubb, Robert. 2014. "Participation in and Responsibility for State Injustices." *Social Theory and Practice* 40: 51–72.

Juengst, Eric. 2009. "What's Taxonomy Got to Do with It? 'Species Integrity,' Human Rights, and Science Policy," in J. Savulescu and N. Bostrom, eds. *Human Enhancement*. Oxford: Oxford University Press: 43–58.

Kahane, Guy, and Julian Savulescu. 2012. "The Concept of Harm and the Significance of Normality." *Journal of Applied Philosophy* 29: 318–332.

2016. "Disability and Mere Difference." *Ethics* 126: 774–788.

Kang, X., W. He, Y. Huang, Q. Yu, Y. Chen, X. Gao, et al. 2016. "Introducing Precise Genetic Modifications into Human 3PN Embryos by CRISPR/Cas-mediated Genome Editing." *Journal of Assisted Reproduction and Genetics* 33: 581–588.

Kant, Immanuel. 1784. "Was ist Aufklärung?" *Berlinische Monatsschrift* Dezember-Heft: 481–494.

1923 [1804]. *Physische Geographie, in Kants Gesammelten Schriften. Akademieausgabe*, vol. 9. Berlin: DeGruyter.

1963 [1785]. *Grundlegung zur Metaphysik der Sitten in Kants Gesammelten Schriften. Akademieausgabe*, vol. 4. Berlin: DeGruyter.

1968 [1797]. *Metaphysik der Sitten in: Kants Werke. Akademie Textausgabe*, vol. 6. Berlin: DeGruyter.

Kaplan, David, and Robert Manners. 1972. *Culture Theory*. Englewood Cliffs, NJ: Prentice-Hall.

Keenan, J. F. 1999. "'Whose Perfection Is It Anyway?' A Virtuous Consideration of Enhancement." *Christian Bioethics* 5: 104–120.

Kersten, Jens. 2013. "The Enjoyment of Complexity: A New Political Anthropology for the Anthropocene?" *Rachel Carson Center Perspectives* 3: 39–55.

Kettering, K. 2020. "'Is Down Always Out?': The Right of Icelandic Parents to Use Preimplantation Genetic Diagnosis to Select for a Disability." *George Washington International Law Review* 51: 1–29.

Kim, Scott. 2016. "Theory and Practice of Democratic Deliberation in Bioethics Research," in J. Ives, M. Dunn, and A. Cribb, eds. *Empirical Bioethics: Theoretical and Practical Perspectives*. Cambridge: Cambridge University Press: 177–194.

Knoppers, Bartha, and Erika Kleiderman. 2019. "Heritable Genome Editing: Who Speaks for 'Future' Children?" *The CRISPR Journal* 2: 285–292.

Kofler, N., J. Collins, J. Kuzma, E. Marris, K. Esvelt, M. Nelson, et al. 2018. "Editing Nature: Local Roots of Global Governance." *Science* 362: 527–529.

Kong, Camilla. 2017. *Mental Capacity in Relationship: Decision-Making, Dialogue, and Autonomy*. Cambridge: Cambridge University Press.

Kovas Y., T. Tikhomirova, F. Selita, M. Tosto, and S. Malykh. 2016. "How Genetics Can Help Education," in Y. Kovas, S. Malykh, and D. Gaysina, eds. *Behavioural Genetics for Education*. London: Palgrave Macmillan: 1–23.

Kramer, M. 1998. "Rights without Trimmings," in M. Kramer, N. Simmonds, and H. Steiner, eds. *A Debate over Rights*. Oxford: Oxford University Press: 7–111.

Kriebel, David, and Joel Tickner. 2001. "The Precautionary Principle and Public Health." *American Journal of Public Health* 91: 1351–1361.

Kumar, P., J. Radhakrishnan, M. Chowdhary, and P. Giampietro. 2001. "Prevalence and Patterns of Presentation of Genetic Disorders in a Pediatric Emergency Department." *Mayo Clinic Proceedings* 76: 777–783.

Kuzawa, Christopher. 2005. "Fetal Origins of Developmental Plasticity: Are Fetal Cues Reliable Predictors of Future Nutritional Environments?" *American Journal of Human Biology* 17: 5–21.

Laland, K., T. Uller, M. Feldman, K. Sterelny, G. Müller, A. Moczek, et al. 2014. "Does Evolutionary Theory Need a Rethink?" *Nature* 514: 161–164.

Lander, E., F. Baylis, F. Zhang, E. Charpentier, P. Berg, C. Bourgain, et al. 2019. "Adopt a Moratorium on Heritable Genome Editing." *Nature* 567: 165–168.

Lanphier, E., F. Urnov, S. Haecker, M. Werner, and J. Smolenski. 2015. "Don't Edit the Human Germ Line." *Nature* 519: 410–411.

Latour, Bruno. 2004. *Politics of Nature: How to Bring the Sciences into Democracy*. Cambridge, MA: Harvard University Press.

Lévi-Strauss, Claude. 1983. *Structural Anthropology*, vol. 2. New York: Basic Books.
Levy, Neil. 2012. "Ecological Engineering: Reshaping Our Environments to Achieve Our Goals." *Philosophy and Technology* 25: 589–604.
Lewens, Tim. 2018. "Introduction: The Faces of Human Nature," in E. Hannon and T. Lewens, eds. *Why We Disagree about Human Nature*. Oxford: Oxford University Press 2018: 1–17.
Lewontin, Richard. 1972. "The Apportionment of Human Diversity," in T. Dobzhansky, M. Hecht, and W. Steert, eds. *Evolutionary Biology*. New York: Springer: 381–398.
1992. *Biology as Ideology: The Doctrine of DNA*. New York: HarperCollins.
Li, Y., Y. Song, B. Liu, and X. Yu. 2016. "The Potential Application and Challenge of Powerful CRISPR/Cas9 System in Cardiovascular Research." *International Journal of Cardiology* 227: 191–193.
Liao, S. Matthew. 2006. "The Idea of a Duty to Love." *Journal of Value Inquiry* 40: 1–22.
2019. "Designing Humans: A Human Rights Approach." *Bioethics* 33: 98–104.
Link, B., M. Northridge, J. Phelan, and M. Ganz. 1998. "Social Epidemiology and the Fundamental Cause Concept: On the Structuring of Effective Cancer Screens by Socioeconomic Status." *Milbank Quarterly* 76: 375–402.
Linquist, S., E. Machery, P. Griffiths, and K. Stotz. 2011. "Exploring the Folkbiological Conception of Innateness." *Philosophical Transactions of the Royal Society B*, 366: 444–454.
Litfin, Karen. 1994. *Ozone Discourses: Science and Politics in Global Environmental Cooperation*. New York: Columbia University Press.
Littoz-Monnet, Annabelle. *Governing through Expertise: The Politics of Bioethics*. 2020. Cambridge: Cambridge University Press.
Liu, Hexuan. 2018. "Social and Genetic Pathways in Multigenerational Transmission of Educational Attainment." *American Sociological Review* 83: 278–304.
Lock, Margaret. 2013. "The Epigenome and Nature/Nurture Reunification: A Challenge for Anthropology." *Medical Anthropology* 32: 291–308.
Loi, Michele. 2013. "You Cannot Have Your Normal Functioning Cake and Eat It Too." *Journal of Medical Ethics* 39: 748–751.
Lucas, George. 2014. "Automated Warfare." *Stanford Law and Policy Review* 25: 317–339.
Luhmann, Niklas. 2012. *Theory of Society*, vol. 1. Stanford, CA: Stanford University Press.
Ma, H., N. Marti-Gutierrez, S. Park, J. Wu, Y. Lee, K. Suzuki, et al. 2017. "Correction of a Pathogenic Gene Mutation in Human Embryos." *Nature* 548: 413–419.
MacGillivray, Anna, and Hilary Livesey. 2018. "Report to the Royal Society: Evaluation of Genetic Technologies Public Dialogue and Opinion Survey." London: Royal Society (Genetic Technologies). https://royalsociety.org/~/media/policy/projects/gene-tech/genetic-technologies-public-dialogue-ursus-evaluation.pdf.
MacIntyre, Alasdair. 1999. *Dependent Rational Animals: Why Human Beings Need the Virtues*. Chicago: Open Court.
Macklin, Ruth. 2003. "Dignity Is a Useless Concept." *British Medical Journal* 327: 1419–1420.

Marmot, Michael. 2015. *The Health Gap: The Challenge of an Unequal World*. New York: Bloomsbury.
Martiny, Kristian. 2015. "How to Develop a Phenomenological Model of Disability." *Medicine, Health Care and Philosophy* 18: 553–565.
Martschenko, Daphne, Sam Trejo, and Benjamin Domingue. 2019. "Genetics and Education: Recent Developments in the Context of an Ugly History and an Uncertain Future." *AERA Open* 5: 1–15.
Marx, Karl. 1968 [1867]. *Das Kapital, Band 1, in Karl Marx – Friedrich Engels – Werke*, vol. 23. Berlin: Dietz Verlag.
1998 [1844]. "Thesen über Feuerbach," in Karl Marx and Friedrich Engels, *Gesamtausgabe*, vol. 3. Berlin: Dietz Verlag: 19–21.
Maslen, Hannah, Jonathan Pugh, and Julian Savulescu. 2015. "The Ethics of Deep Brain Stimulation for the Treatment of Anorexia Nervosa." *Neuroethics* 8: 215–230.
Matthen, Mohan. 1998. "Biological Universals and the Nature of Fear." *Journal of Philosophy*, 95: 105–132.
Mayr, Ernst. 2001. *What Evolution Is*. New York: Basic Books.
McCulloch, Warren, and Walter Pitts. 1943. "A Logical Calculus of the Ideas Immanent in Nervous Activity." *Bulletin of Mathematical Biophysics* 5: 115–133.
Mehlman, Maxwell, Jessica Berg, and Soumya Ray. 2017. *"Robot Law." Case Research Paper Series in Legal Studies, Working Paper 2017-1*. Case Western Reserve University.
Meloni, Maurizio. 2015. "Epigenetics for the Social Sciences: Justice, Embodiment, and Inheritance in the Postgenomic Age." *New Genetics and Society* 34: 125–151.
Meloni, Maurizio. 2016. *Political Biology: Science and Social Values in Human Heredity from Eugenics to Epigenetics*. London: Palgrave Macmillan.
Meloni, Maurizio, and Giuseppe Testa. 2014. "Scrutinizing the Epigenetics Revolution." *BioSocieties* 9: 431–456.
Mianné, J., G. Codner, A. Caulder, R. Fell, M. Hutchison, R. King, et al. 2017. "Analysing the Outcome of CRISPR-Aided Genome Editing in Embryos: Screening, Genotyping and Quality Control." *Methods* 121–122: 68–76.
Migliano, A., F. Battiston, S. Viguier, E. Page, M. Dyble, R. Schlaepfer, et al. 2020. "Hunter-Gatherer Multilevel Sociality Accelerates Cumulative Cultural Evolution." *Science Advances* 6: 1–7.
Mill, J. S. 1975 [1858]. *On Liberty*. New York: W.W. Norton.
1998 [1863]. *Utilitarianism*. Oxford: Oxford University Press.
Minsky, Marvin. 1952. *A Neural-Analogue Calculator Based Upon a Probability Model of Reinforcement*. Harvard University Psychological Laboratories Internal Report.
Miyamoto, Tatsuo, Silvia Akutsu, and Shinya Matsuura. 2018. "Updated Summary of Genome Editing Technology in Human Cultured Cells Linked to Human Genetics Studies." *Journal of Human Genetics* 63: 133–143.
Monast, Jonas. 2018. "Editing Nature: Reconceptualizing Biotechnology Governance." *Boston College Law Review* 59: 2377–2436.
Morgan, Daniel, and Emma Whitelaw. 2008. "The Case for Transgenerational Epigenetic Inheritance in Humans." *Mammalian Genome* 19: 394–397.
Morton, Thomas, Matthew Hornsey, and Tom Postmes. 2009. "Shifting Ground: The Variable Use of Essentialism in Contexts of Inclusion and Exclusion." *British Journal of Social Psychology* 48: 35–59.

Nagel, Thomas. 1986. *The View from Nowhere*. New York: Oxford University Press.

National Academies of Sciences, Engineering, and Medicine. 2015. *International Summit on Human Gene Editing: A Global Discussion*. Washington, DC: National Academies Press.

National Academies of Sciences, Engineering, and Medicine. 2017. *Human Genome Editing: Science, Ethics, and Governance*. Washington, DC: National Academies Press.

Nielsen, François, and J. Micah Roos. 2015. "Genetics of Educational Attainment and the Persistence of Privilege at the Turn of the 21st Century." *Social Forces* 94: 535–561.

Neimanis, A., C. Åsberg, and J. Hedrén. 2015. "Four Problems, Four Directions for Environmental Humanities: Toward Critical Posthumanities for the Anthropocene." *Ethics and the Environment* 20: 67–97.

Noble, D., E. Jablonka, M. Joyner, G. Müller, S. Omholt. 2014. "Evolution Evolves: Physiology Returns to Centre Stage." *Journal of Physiology* 592: 2237–2244.

Noë, Alva. 2009. *Out of Our Heads: Why You Are Not Your Brain, and Other Lessons from the Biology of Consciousness*. New York: Hill and Wang.

Nuffield Council on Bioethics. 2018. *Genome Editing and Human Reproduction: Social and Ethical Issues*. London: Nuffield Council on Bioethics.

Nussbaum, Martha. 1997. "Capabilities and Human Rights." *Fordham Law Review* 66: 273–300.

O'Doherty, Kieran, and Michael Burgess. 2013. "Public Deliberation to Develop Ethical Norms and Inform Policy for Biobanks: Lessons Learnt and Challenges Remaining." *Research Ethics Review* 9: 55–77.

Okasha, Samir. 2002. "Darwinian Metaphysics: Species and the Question Of Essentialism." *Synthese* 131: 191–213.

Oreskes, Naomi. 2007. "The Scientific Consensus on Climate Change: How Do We Know We're Not Wrong?," in J. Dimento and P. Doughman, eds. *Climate Change: What It Means for Us, Our Children, and Our Grandchildren*. Cambridge, MA: MIT Press: 65–99.

Painter, Rebecca, Tessa Roseboom, and Otto Bleker. 2005. "Prenatal Exposure to the Dutch Famine and Disease in Later Life: An Overview." *Reproductive Toxicology* 20: 345–352.

Panofsky, Aaron. 2015. "What Does Behavioral Genetics Offer for Improving Education?" *Hastings Center Report* 45: S43–S49.

Parekh, Sarena. 2007. "Resisting 'Dull and Torpid' Assent: Returning to the Debate over the Foundations of Human Rights." *Human Rights Quarterly* 29: 754–778.

Parens, Erik, and Paul Appelbaum. 2015. "An Introduction to Thinking about Trustworthy Research into the Genetics of Intelligence." *Hastings Center Report* 45: S2-S8.

Patel, Dilip, Maria Cabral, Arlene Ho, Joav Merrick. 2020. "A Clinical Primer on Intellectual Disability." *Translational Pediatrics* 9: S23–S35.

Peirce, Charles. 1986. "Toward a Logic Book, 1872–73," in C. Kloesel, ed. *Writings of Charles S. Peirce: A Chronological Edition*, vol. 3. Bloomington: Indiana University Press: 14–108.

Pembrey, M., L. Bygren, G. Kaati, S. Edvinsson, K. Northstone, M. Sjöström, et al. 2006. "Sex-Specific, Male-Line Transgenerational Responses in Humans." *European Journal of Human Genetics* 14: 159–166.

Persson, Ingmar, and Julian Savulescu. 2012. *Unfit for the Future: The Need for Moral Enhancement*. Oxford: Oxford University Press.

Peter, C., L. Fischer, M. Kundakovic, P. Garg, M. Jakovcevski, A. Dincer, et al. 2016. "DNA Methylation Signatures of Early Childhood Malnutrition Associated with Impairments in Attention and Cognition." *Biological Psychiatry* 80: 765–774.

Petit, Philip. 2007. "Responsibility Incorporated." *Ethics* 117: 171–201.

Pickering, John. 1993. "The New Artificial Intelligence and Biological Plausibility," in S. Valenti and J. Pittenger, eds. *Studies in Perception and Action II*. London: Psychology Press: 126–129.

Pinker, Steven. 2002. *The Blank Slate: The Modern Denial of Human Nature*. New York: Viking.

Plessner, Helmut. 1981 [1928]. "Die Stufen des Organischen und der Mensch. Einleitung in die philosophische Anthropologie," in *Gesammelte Schriften*, vol. 4. Frankfurt am Maim: Suhrkamp Verlag.

Plomin, Robert, and Sophie von Stumm. 2018. "The New Genetics of Intelligence." *Nature Reviews: Genetics* 19: 148–159.

Powell, Russell. 2015. "In Genes We Trust: Germline Engineering, Eugenics, and the Future of the Human Genome." *Journal of Medicine and Philosophy* 40: 669–695.

Powell, Russell, and Allen Buchanan. 2011. "Breaking Evolution's Chains: The Prospect of Deliberate Genetic Modification in Humans." *Journal of Medicine and Philosophy* 36: 6–27.

Powers, Madison. 2005. "Bioethics as Politics: The Limits of Moral Expertise." *Kennedy Institute of Ethics Journal* 15: 305–322.

Pratt, Gill. 2015. "Is a Cambrian Explosion Coming for Robotics?" *Journal of Economic Perspectives* 29: 51–60.

President's Council on Bioethics, July 2002, *Human Cloning and Human Dignity: An Ethical Inquiry*. https://bioethicsarchive.georgetown.edu/pcbe/reports/cloningreport/

Protzko, John. 2016. "Does the Raising IQ–Raising G Distinction Explain the Fadeout Effect?" *Intelligence* 56: 65–71.

Pulvermüller, F., M. Huss, F. Kherif, F. Martin, O. Hauk, and Y. Shtyrov. 2006. "Motor Cortex Maps Articulatory Features of Speech Sounds." *PNAS* 103: 7865–7870.

Rath, Johannes. 2018. "Safety and Security Risks of CRISPR/Cas9," in D. Schroeder, J. Cook, F. Hirsch, S. Fenet, and V. Muthuswamy, eds. *Ethics Dumping: Case Studies from North–South Research Collaborations*. Cham, Switzerland: Springer: 107–113.

Rawls, John. 1993. *Political Liberalism*. New York: Columbia University Press.

1997. "The Idea of Public Reason Revisited." *University of Chicago Law Review* 64: 765–807.

1999. *Collected Papers*. S. Freeman, ed. Cambridge, MA: Harvard University Press.

Reardon, Sara. 2019. "World Health Organization Panel Enters CRISPR-Baby Debate." *Nature* 567: 444–445.

Richardson, Ken. 2017. *Genes, Brains, and Human Potential: The Science and Ideology of Intelligence*. New York: Columbia University Press.

Richardson, Sarah. 2015. "Maternal Bodies in the Postgenomic Order: Gender and the Explanatory Landscape of Epigenetics," in S. Richardson and H. Stevens, eds. *Postgenomics: Perspectives on Biology after the Genome*. Durham, NC: Duke University Press: 210–231.

Richerson, Peter, and Robert Boyd. 2008. *Not by Genes Alone: How Culture Transformed Human Evolution*. Chicago: University of Chicago Press.

Rissanen, A., P. Hakala, L. Lissner, C-E. Mattlar, M. Koskenvuo, and T. Rönnemaa. 2002. "Acquired Preference Especially for Dietary Fat and Obesity: A Study of Weight-Discordant Monozygotic Twin Pairs." *International Journal of Obesity* 26: 973–977.

Rosenberg, Alexander. 1985. *The Structure of Biological Science*. Cambridge: Cambridge University Press.

Rosenberg, Noah. 2011. "A Population-Genetic Perspective on the Similarities and Differences among Worldwide Human Populations." *Human Biology* 83: 659–684.

Rothstein, Mark, Heather Harrell, and Gary Marchant. 2017. "Transgenerational Epigenetics and Environmental Justice." *Environmental Epigenetics* 3: 1–12.

Ruse, Michael, and Edward Wilson. 1986. "Moral Philosophy as Applied Science." *Philosophy* 61: 173–192.

Russell, Stuart. 2015. "Take a Stand on AI Weapons." *Nature* 521: 415–416.

Sadler, Brook. 2006. "Shared Intentions and Shared Responsibility." *Midwest Studies in Philosophy* 30: 115–144.

Sagoff, Mark. 2005. "Nature and Human Nature," in H. Baillie and T. Casey, eds. *Is Human Nature Obsolete? Genetics, Bioengineering, and the Future of the Human Condition*. Cambridge, MA: MIT Press: 67–98.

Sanchis-Gomar, F., J. Garcia-Gimenez, C. Perez-Quilis, M. Gomez-Cabrera, F. Pallardo, and G. Lippi. 2012. "Physical Exercise as an Epigenetic Modulator: Eustress, the 'Positive Stress' as an Effector of Gene Expression." *Journal of Strength and Conditioning Research* 26: 3469–3472.

Sandberg, Anders, and Julian Savulescu. 2011. "The Social and Economic Impacts of Cognitive Enhancement," in J. Savulescu, R. ter Meulen, and G. Kahane, eds. *Enhancing Human Capacities*. Chichester: Blackwell: 92–112.

Sandini, Giulio, Giorgio Metta, and David Vernon 2007. "The *iCub* Cognitive Humanoid Robot: An Open-System Research Platform for Enactive Cognition," in M. Lungarella, F. Iida, J. Bongard, and R. Pfeifer, eds. *Fifty Years of Artificial Intelligence*. Berlin: Springer: 358–369.

Santos, M., J. Figueredo, L. Bezerra, and Francisco Magalhães. 2016. "Neuronal Plasticity Mechanisms Induced by Brain–Machine Interfaces: Connecting Brain to Artificial Neural Network." *Revista de Medicina e Saúde de Brasília* 5: 264–269.

Saran, Ashrita, Howard White, and Hannah Kuper. 2020. "Evidence and Gap Map of Studies Assessing the Effectiveness of Interventions for People with Disabilities in Low- and Middle-Income Countries." *Campbell Systematic Reviews* 16: 1–34.

Savage, J., P. Jansen, S. Stringer, K. Watanabe, J. Bryois, C. de Leeuw, et al. 2018. "Genome-Wide Association Meta-Analysis in 269,867 Individuals Identifies New Genetic and Functional Links to Intelligence." *Nature Genetics* 50: 912–919.

Savulescu, Julian, and Guy Kahane. 2009. "The Moral Obligation to Create Children with the Best Chance of the Best Life." *Bioethics* 23: 274–290.

Savulescu, Julian, Anders Sandberg, and Guy Kahane. 2011. "Well-Being and Enhancement," in J. Savulescu, R. ter Meulen, and G. Kahane, eds. *Enhancing Human Capacities*. Hoboken, NJ: Wiley-Blackwell: 3–18.

Scarr, Sandra. 1992. "Developmental Theories for the 1990s: Development and Individual Differences." *Child Development* 63: 1–19.

Scorza, P., C. Duarte, A. Hipwell, J. Posner, A. Ortin, G. Canino, et al. 2019. "Intergenerational Transmission of Disadvantage: Epigenetics and Parents' Childhoods as the First Exposure." *Journal of Child Psychology and Psychiatry* 60: 119-132.

Schalock, Robert, and Ruth Luckasson. 2004. "American Association on Mental Retardation's *Definition, Classification, and System of Supports* and Its Relation to International Trends and Issues in the Field of Intellectual Disabilities." *Journal of Policy and Practice in Intellectual Disabilities* 1: 136–146.

Schalock, Robert, Ruth Luckasson, and Marc Tassé. 2019. "The Contemporary View of Intellectual and Developmental Disabilities: Implications for Psychologists." *Psicothema* 31: 223–228.

Schmidhuber, Jürgen. 2015. "Deep Learning in Neural Networks: An Overview." *Neural Networks* 61: 85–117.

Schroeder, D., J. Cook, F. Hirsch, S. Fenet, and V. Muthuswamy, eds. 2018. *Ethics Dumping: Studies from North–South Research Collaboration.* Heidelberg: Springer.

Searle, John. 1995. The Construction of Social Reality. New York: Free Press.

Segerstrale, Ullica. 2001. *Defenders of the Truth: The Sociobiology Debate.* Oxford: Oxford University Press.

Selzam, S., E. Krapohl, S. von Stumm, P. O'Reilly, K. Rimfeld, Y. Kovas, et al. 2017. "Predicting Educational Achievement from DNA." *Molecular Psychiatry* 22: 267–272.

Shakeshaft, N., M. Trzaskowski, A. McMillan, K. Rimfeld, E. Krapohl, C. Haworth, et al. 2013. "Strong Genetic Influence on a UK Nationwide Test of Educational Achievement at the End of Compulsory Education at Age 16." *PLOS ONE* 8(12): e80341. doi: 10.1371/journal.pone.0080341.

Sheehan, Mark, Michael Dunn, and Kate Sahan. 2017. "In Defence of Governance: Ethics Review and Social Research." *Journal of Medical Ethics* 44: 710–716.

Shockley, William. 1971. "Negro IQ Deficit: Failure of a 'Malicious Coincidence' Model Warrants New Research Proposals." *Review of Educational Research* 4: 227–248.

Shogren, Karrie. 2013. "Cognitive and Developmental Disabilities," in M. Wehmeyer, ed. *Oxford Handbook of Positive Psychology and Disability.* Oxford Handbooks Online: 442–451.

Sikela, James. 2006. "The Jewels of Our Genome: The Search for the Genomic Changes Underlying the Evolutionarily Unique Capacities of the Human Brain." *PLoS Genetics* 2(5): e80. http://dx.doi.org/10.1371/journal.pgen.0020080

Silvers, Anita, and Leslie Francis. 2009. "Thinking about the Good: Reconfiguring Liberal Metaphysics (or Not) for People with Cognitive Disabilities." *Metaphilosophy* 40: 475–498.

Sinclair, K., R. Lea, W. Rees, and L. Young. 2007. "The Developmental Origins of Health and Disease: Current Theories and Epigenetic Mechanisms." *Society of Reproduction and Fertility Supplement* 64: 425–443.

Singer, Beth. 1999. *Pragmatism, Rights, and Democracy.* New York: Fordham University Press.

Singer, Peter. 1972. "Moral Experts." *Analysis* 32: 115–117.

Smail, Daniel. 2008. *On Deep History and the Brain*. Berkeley: University of California Press.

Small, Mario, David Jarding, and Michèle Lamont. 2010. "Reconsidering Culture and Poverty." *Annals of the American Academy of Political & Social Science* 29: 6–27.

Smoyer-Tomic, Karen, John Spence, and Carl Amrhein. 2006. "Food Deserts in the Prairies? Supermarket Accessibility and Neighbourhood Need in Edmonton, Canada." *Professional Geographer* 58: 307–326.

Sober, Elliott. 1992. "Evolution, Population Thinking, and Essentialism," in M. Ereshefsky, ed., *The Units of Evolution: Essays on the Nature of Species*. Cambridge, MA: MIT Press: 247–278.

1993. *Philosophy of Biology*. Boulder, CO: Westview.

Solomon, Scott. 2016. *Future Humans: Inside the Science of Our Continuing Evolution*. New Haven, CT: Yale University Press.

Sparrow, Robert. 2012. "Can Machines Be People? Reflections on the Turing Triage Test," in P. Lin, K. Abney, and G. Bekey, eds. *Robot Ethics: The Ethical and Social Implications of Robotics*. Cambridge, MA: MIT Press: 301–315.

Stengers, Isabelle. 2003. "Including Nonhumans in Political Theory: Opening Pandora's Box?," in B. Braun and S. Whatmore, eds. *Political Matter: Technoscience, Democracy, and Public Life*. Minneapolis: University of Minnesota Press: 3–34.

Sterelny, Kim. 2018. "Skeptical Reflections on Human Nature," in E. Hannon and T. Lewens, eds. *Why We Disagree about Human Nature*. Oxford: Oxford University Press: 108–126.

Sterelny, Kim, and Paul Griffiths. 1999. *Sex and Death*. University of Chicago Press.

Sunstein, Cass. 2007. *Republic.com 2.0*. Princeton, NJ: Princeton University Press.

Szyf, Moshe. 2015. "Nongenetic Inheritance and Transgenerational Epigenetics." *Trends in Molecular Medicine* 21: 134–144.

Tabery, James. 2015. "Why Is Studying the Genetics of Intelligence So Controversial?" *Hastings Center Report* 45: S9–S14.

Tallis, Raymond. 2016. *Aping Mankind*. New York: Routledge.

Tamir, Sivan. 2016. "Postnatal Human Genetic Enhancement: A Consideration of Children's Right to Be Genetically Enhanced." *Frontiers in Sociology*: 1–15. https://doi.org/10.3389/fsoc.2016.00015

Tang, Huibin, and Joseph Schrager. 2016. "CRISPR/Cas-Mediated Genome Editing to Treat EGFR-Mutant Lung Cancer: A Personalized Molecular Surgical Therapy." *EMBO Molecular Medicine* 8: 83–85.

Tasioulas, John. 2010. "Taking Rights Out of Human Rights." *Ethics* 120: 647–678.

Taylor, Charles. 1991. *The Ethics of Authenticity*. Cambridge, MA: Harvard University Press.

Taylor, Maria. 2014. "Influences on a Changed Story and the New Normal: Scientists' Beliefs and Public Skepticism," in M. Taylor, ed. *Global Warming and Climate Change*. Canberra, Australia: ANU Press: 133–146.

Tergesen, Anne, and Miho Inada. 2010. "It's Not a Stuffed Animal, It's a $6,000 Medical Device: Paro the Robo-Seal Aims to Comfort Elderly, but Is It Ethical?" *Wall Street Journal*, June 21.

Terzi, Lorella. 2015. "Cognitive Disability, Capability Equality, and Citizenship," in N. Hirschmann and B. Linker, eds. *Civil Disabilities: Citizenship, Membership, and Belonging*. Philadelphia: University of Pennsylvania Press: 186–203.

Theofilopoulou, Areti. 2021. "Political Liberalism and Cognitive Disability: An Inclusive Account." *Critical Review of International Social and Political Philosophy*: 1–20. https://doi.org/10.1080/13698230.2021.1913888

Thrun, Sebastian, and Gideon Rose. 2013. "Google's X-Man: A Conversation with Sebastian Thrun." *Foreign Affairs* 92: 2–8.

Tocqueville, Alexis de. 1981 [1835]. *De la démocratie en Amérique*, vol. 2. Paris: Garnier-Flammarion.

Tolleneer, Jan, Sigrid Sterckx, and Pieter Bonte. 2013. *Athletic Enhancement, Human Nature and Ethics: Threats and Opportunities of Doping Technologies*. New York: Springer.

Tomasello, Michael. 2009. *The Cultural Origins of Human Cognition*. Cambridge, MA: Harvard University Press.

2019. *Becoming Human: A Theory of Ontogeny*. Cambridge, MA: Harvard University Press.

Tooby, John, and Leda Cosmides. 1992. "The Psychological Foundations of Culture," in J. Barkow, L. Cosmides, and J. Tooby, eds. *The Adapted Mind: Evolutionary Psychology and the Generation of Culture*. New York: Oxford University Press: 19–136.

Torrance, Steve. 2012. "Artificial Agents and the Expanding Ethical Circle." *AI & Society* 28: 399–414.

Trejo, S., D. Belsky, J. Boardman, J. Freese, K. Harris, P. Herd, et al. 2018. "Schools as Moderators of Genetic Associations with Life Course Attainments: Evidence from the WLS and Add Health." *Sociological Science* 5: 513–540.

Trischler, Helmuth, and Fabienne Will. 2017. "Technosphere, Technocene, and the History of Technology." *ICON: Journal of the International Committee for the History of Technology* 23: 1–17.

Turkheimer, Eric, and Irving Gottesman. 1991. "Individual Differences and the Canalization of Human Behavior." *Developmental Psychology* 27: 18–22.

Turkheimer, E., A. Haley, M. Waldron, B. D'Onofrio, and I. Gottesman. 2003. "Socioeconomic Status Modifies Heritability of IQ in Young Children." *Psychological Science* 14: 623–628.

Turner, Bryan. 1993. "Outline of a Theory of Human Rights." *Sociology* 27: 489–512.

Union of the Physically Impaired against Segregation. 1976. *Fundamental Principles of Disability*. London.

Universal Declaration of Human Rights, December 10, 1948, www.un.org/sites/un2.un.org/files/udhr.pdf

Universal Declaration on Bioethics and Human Rights, October 19, 2005, https://en.unesco.org/themes/ethics-science-and-technology/bioethics-and-human-rights

Universal Declaration on the Human Genome and Human Rights, December 9, 1998, www.ohchr.org/en/professionalinterest/pages/humangenomeandhumanrights.aspx

van Beers, Britta. 2020. "Rewriting the Human Genome, Rewriting Human Rights Law? Human Rights, Human Dignity, and Human Germline Modification in the CRISPR Era." *Journal of Law and the Biosciences* 7: 1–36.

van den Bergh, B., M. van den Heuvel, M. Lahti, M. Braeken, S. de Rooij, S. Entringer, D. Hoyer, et al. 2017. "Prenatal Developmental Origins of Behavior and Mental Health: The Influence of Maternal Stress in Pregnancy." *Neuroscience and Biobehavioral Reviews* 117: 26–64.

Varela, F., A. Coutinho, B. Dupire, and N. Vaz 1988. "Cognitive Networks: Immune, Neural, and Otherwise," in A. Perelson, ed. *Theoretical Immunology, Part II. SFI Series on the Science of Complexity*. Boston: Addison-Wesley: 359–375.

Vears, Danya, and Flavio D'Abramo. 2018. "Health, Wealth and Behavioural Change: An Exploration of Role Responsibilities in the Wake of Epigenetics." *Journal of Community Genetics* 9: 153–167.

Vico, Giambattista. 2008 [1710]. *L'antichissima sapienza degli italici*. In *Metafisica e Metodo*. Milano: Bompiani.

Vincent, Nicole. 2011. "The Challenges Posed to Private Law by Emerging Cognitive Enhancement Technologies," in N. Vincent, S. Muller, S. Zouridis, M. Frishman, and L. Kistemaker, eds. *The Law of the Future and the Future of the Law*. Oslo: Torkel Opsahl Academic EPublisher: 511–521.

Vladeck, David. 2014. "Machines without Principals: Liability Rules and Artificial Intelligence." *Washington Law Review* 89: 117–150.

Voltaire [François Marie Arouet]. 1878 [1756]. *Essai sur les mœurs et l'esprit des nations*, in *Œuvres Complètes de Voltaire, Tome XI*. Paris: Garnier Frères.

[François Marie Arouet]. 1878 [1756]. *Essai sur les mœurs et l'esprit des nations*, in *Œuvres Complètes de Voltaire, Tome XII*. Paris: Garnier Frères.

Wade, Nicholas. 2014. *A Troublesome Inheritance: Genes, Race and Human History*. New York: Penguin Press.

Waggoner, Miranda, and Tobias Uller. 2015. "Epigenetic Determinism in Science and Society." *New Genetics and Society* 34: 177–195.

Wakefield, Jerome. 2015. "Psychological Justice: DSM-5, False Positive Diagnosis, and Fair Equality of Opportunity." *Public Affairs Quarterly* 29: 32–75.

Waldschmidt, Anne, and Marie Sépulchre. 2019. "Citizenship: Reflections on a Relevant but Ambivalent Concept for Persons with Disabilities." *Disability & Society* 34: 421–448.

Wallach, Wendell, and Colin Allen. 2009. *Moral Machines: Teaching Robots Right from Wrong*. Oxford: Oxford University Press.

Warren, Mark, and John Gastil. 2015. "Can Deliberative Minipublics Address the Cognitive Challenges of Democratic Citizenship?" *Journal of Politics* 77: 562–574.

Weber, Max. 2002 [1922]. *Wirtschaft und Gesellschaft: Grundriß der verstehenden Soziologie*. Tübingen: Mohr Siebeck.

Weber, Wendell. 2007. "Epigenetics," in J. Taylor and D. Triggle, eds. *Comprehensive Medicinal Chemistry II*, vol. 1. Amsterdam: Elsevier Science: 251–278.

Wehmeyer, Michael. 2005. "Self-determination and Individuals with Severe Disabilities: Re-Examining Meanings and Misinterpretations." *Research and Practice for Persons with Severe Disabilities* 30: 113–120.

Weizenbaum, Joseph. 1976. *Computer Power and Human Reason: From Judgment to Calculation*. New York: W.H. Freeman.

Wells, Jonathan. 2007. "The Thrifty Phenotype as an Adaptive Maternal Effect." *Biological Reviews* 82: 143–172.

West-Eberhard, Mary. 2003. *Developmental Plasticity and Evolution*. New York: Oxford University Press.

Wichansawakun, Sanit, and Harpal Buttar. 2019. "Antioxidant Diets and Functional Foods Promote Healthy Aging and Longevity through Diverse Mechanisms of

Action," in R. Singh, R. Watson, and T. Takahashi, eds. *The Role of Functional Food Security in Global Health*. London: Academic Press: 541–563.

Wilson Edward. 1975. *Sociobiology: The New Synthesis*. Cambridge, MA: Harvard University Press.

Wilson, Edward. 2012. *On Human Nature*. Cambridge, MA: Harvard University Press.

World Economic Forum. 2015. *Global Risks*, 10th ed. Geneva. http://go.nature.com/20Re03f

2017. "Global Risks 2015." Tenth edition. http://go.nature.com/20Re03f

World Health Organization. 2001. *International Classification of Functioning, Disability and Health*. Geneva. www.cdc.gov/nchs/data/icd/icfoverview_finalforwho10sept.pdf

2020. *ICD-11 for Mortality and Morbidity Statistics: Disorders of Intellectual Development*. https://icd.who.int/browse11/l-m/en#/http%3a%2f%2fid.who.int%2ficd%2fentity%2f605267007

World Wide Web Foundation. 2017. *Algorithmic Accountability: Applying the Concept to Different Country Contexts*. https://webfoundation.org/docs/2017/07/Algorithms_Report_WF.pdf

Yao, Xin. 1999. "Evolving Artificial Neural Networks." *Proceedings of the IEEE* 87: 1423–1447.

Yong, Ed. 2013. "Chinese Project Probes the Genetics of Genius." *Nature* 497: 297–299.

Yu, C-C., M. Furukawa, K. Kobayashi, C. Shikishima, P. Cha, J. Sese, et al. 2012. "Genome-Wide DNA Methylation and Gene Expression Analyses of Monozygotic Twins Discordant for Intelligence Levels." *PLoS ONE* 7(10): e47081. https://doi.org/10.1371/journal.pone.0047081

Zhou, T., H. Zhu, Z. Fan, F. Wang, et al. 2017. "History of Winning Remodels Thalamo–PFC Circuit to Reinforce Social Dominance." *Science* 357: 162–168.

Zinn, Jens. 2016. "Living in the Anthropocene: Towards a Risk-Taking Society." *Environmental Sociology* 2: 385–394.

Index

Made in the USA
Coppell, TX
10 January 2024

27529837R00159